THE BEST PRACTICAL

FOLK

REMEDIES

From Around the World

THE BEST PRACTICAL FOLK REMEDIES

From Around the World

Compiled by the Editors of
Bookman Health Library

BOOKMAN

Published by Bookman Press
325 Flinders Lane
Melbourne Victoria 3000
Australia

FOLK REMEDIES
From Around The World

National Library of Australia
Cataloguing-in-publication entry

FOLK REMEDIES
From Around The World

Includes Index
ISBN 1 86395 042 7
1. Homoeopathy, 2. Medicine, popular

Printed by Griffin Paperbacks, Adelaide SA.
FIRST EDITION

Foreword

How would your great grandmother advise you to cure your cold or arthritis or other common ailments?

This is the question that provided the spark for this book of natural healing wisdom. The idea then spread from not only researching the healing wisdom from one country but from all countries and throughout history.

There is so much more to healing than a visit to the doctor! The aim of this book is to draw on the wisdom of the ages to help give you back the power of healing.

Bookman Health Books gratefully acknowledges the efforts of its hard working staff in producing this book as well as the research conducted by Percy Mason and the special editorial work of Carol Bagdanov.

Contents

Contents

Contents

Introduction
If you want to try one of the Folk Remedies in this book...

Be sensible when using folk remedies. If you are under a doctor's care for any ailment use the remedies only as a complement to you conventional medication, and only after consulting with your doctor. Do not exceed the recommended dose.

Be as careful using folk remedies during pregnancy and while breast feeding as you would be with any conventional medication. If you have any doubts, do not use the remedy.

If you experience any discomfort, skin rash or indigestion while using a folk remedy you should discontinue its use.

Ingredients in Folk Remedies

Herbs and spices

Many ingredients in this book are common cooking herbs and spices. They are available at markets, greengrocers and health food stores.

Other herbs and medicinal plants will only be available from health food stores, chemist shops (pharmacies) and herbalists.

Growing your own

You may decide that you want to grow your own herbs and spices. With some ingredients this may be your only option. There are specialist herb gardens that sell herb plants and seeds. Herb gardening can be a fascinating hobby. You will find that a large number of books are devoted to this subject. What ever you do, if you are growing your own, use organic methods.

Drying and other preserving methods

If you are growing your own herbs you will eventually want to try drying your own herbs. This is an easy and straight forward process, simply hang the herbs to dry in a warm dry spot, out of direct sunlight until the plant is completely dry.

Another way to preserve herbs and spices is to freeze them. While it is not truly in the spirit of folk remedies, you may want to experiment with drying your herbs in the microwave, it is fast and efficient.

Remember though that whether you are using fresh or dried medicinal plants they are delicate and need to be treated with tender loving care. Do not store them in direct sunlight or in warm conditions.

Fresh or dried

Some recipes call for fresh herbs others call for dried product. Unless noted you can substitute one for the other, but remember that drying concentrates the herbs and spices. So if you are using fresh instead of dried, use 2 to 3 times the amount, while if you are substituting dried for fresh, use ⅓ to ½ as much.

If a recipe calls for powdered or crushed herbs it is best to do the grinding or crushing with a mortar and pestle. A mechanical grinder generates heat that can destroy the active principle in the medicinal plant. Always do the preparation just before you use the plant to minimise deterioration.

Standard instructions for making your own herbal remedies

When you make your folk remedies use only non-metallic pots and pans, utensils, cups, storage containers, etc. (i.e. glass, earthenware, fabric, or if necessary plastic) unless otherwise noted.

In Australia we are lucky to have good quality water in most parts of the country. If you live in an area that does not have good quality water use purified, distilled or bottled spring water for your remedies.

There are a few standard methods for preparing folk remedies used in this book. The two most common are **infusions** and **decoctions.** Both of these methods are usually used to extract the active ingredient from the herb and release it into the liquid (usually water). Sometimes the process is used to soften the herb or remove a bitter or otherwise unpleasant component. In these cases the softened plant material is used and the liquid may be discarded.

Infusions

Making an infusion is like making tea. You pour boiling water over the medicinal plant and allow the mixture to steep (brew or soak) for a specified time, usually covered. After that time you will usually strain the mixture so that you can use the liquid or the solid material.

In this book most remedies will be accompanied by a graphic representation of the standard procedure for making the remedy. Detailed instructions for the standard methods of preparation follow. Unless otherwise noted, it is assumed that the standard procedure is used. Use either the metric or the imperial measurements, do not mix the two as conversions between these systems may not be exact.

Any variation from the standard procedure will be noted in the text accompanying the remedy.

Making an infusion:

Amounts
About 30 grams (1 ounce) dried or 60 grams (2 ounces) fresh material
500 millilitres (2 cups) water

Procedure:
1. Put herb into a teapot or other non-metallic pot with a tight fitting lid
2. Bring water to the boil
3. Pour the boiling water over herb
4. Steep 10 to 15 minutes

For remedies that are traditionally used as drinks:
Strain, discarding solids and drink one third of the liquid, about 150 millilitres three times a day. Store the remaining liquid in a cool location, out of direct sunlight, but do not store for more than 24 hours. If the liquid is to be taken warm, you can reheat each portion before drinking.

For remedies that are traditionally used as washes or applied as a compress:
Strain, discarding solids and use as needed. For a wash use the liquid to bathe the affected area. For a compress soak a piece of cotton towelling in the liquid, wring the cloth to remove excess liquid and apply the damp cloth to the affected area. Store the remaining liquid in a cool location, out of direct sunlight, but do not store for more than 24 hours. If the liquid is to be used warm, you can reheat the remaining liquid before each use.

For remedies that are traditionally used as a poultice or plaster:
Strain, discarding the liquid. Squeeze excess liquid from the warm solid material. You may have to mash the softened solids. Cover affected area with a thin layer of petroleum jelly or good quality, cold pressed oil. Apply the softened plant material to the affected area. Hold in place with a piece of clean cotton cloth or gauze. Store excess material in a cool location, out of direct sunlight. If the plaster is to be used warm, reheat for subsequent use throughout the day. Store any unused material in a cool location, out of direct sunlight. Do not store for more than 24 hours

For remedies that are used as both a drink (or wash/ compress) and a poultice (or plaster) you strain and save both the liquid and the solid material and use as described above.

Decoctions

Making a decoction is like making soup. This process is usually used for the tougher parts of a plant—like roots, bark and twigs—parts that require more vigorous treatment to extract the active principles. To make a decoction you either put the plant ingredients into cold water, bring to the boil and simmer, or add the plant ingredients to boiling water and simmer

In this book most remedies will be accompanied by a graphic representation of the standard procedure for making the remedy. Detailed instructions for the standard method of preparation follow. Unless otherwise noted, it is assumed that the standard procedure is used. Use either the metric or the imperial measurements, do not mix the two, as conversions between these systems may not be exact.

Any variation from the standard procedure will be noted in the text accompanying the remedy.

Making an decoction:

Amounts
About 30 grams (1 ounce) dried or 60 grams (2 ounces) fresh plant material
750 millilitres (3 cups) water

Procedure
1. Place plant material in a non-metallic saucepan
2. Pour cold water over plant material
3. Bring to the boil
4. Simmer gently until the liquid is reduced by 1/3 (up-to 1 hour)

For remedies that are traditionally used as drinks:
Strain, discarding solids and drink one third of the liquid, about 150 millilitres, three times a day. Store the remaining liquid in a cool location out of direct sunlight, but do not store for more than 24 hours. If the liquid is to be taken warm, you can reheat each portion before drinking.

For remedies that are traditionally used as washes or applied as a compress:
Strain, discarding solids. Use as needed. For a wash use the liquid to bathe the affected area. For a compress, soak a piece of cotton towelling in the liquid, wring the cloth to remove excess liquid and apply the damp cloth to the affected area. Store the remaining liquid in a cool location, out of direct sunlight. If the liquid is to be used warm, you can reheat each portion before use.

For remedies that are traditionally used as a poultice or plaster:
Strain, discarding the liquid. Squeeze excess liquid from the warm solid material. You may have to mash the softened solids. Cover affected area with a thin layer of petroleum jelly or good quality, cold pressed oil. Apply the softened plant material to the affected area. Hold in place with a piece of clean cotton cloth or gauze. Store excess material in a cool location. If the poultice or plaster is to be used warm, reheat gently for subsequent use throughout the day. Store any unused material in a cool location, out of direct sunlight. Do not store for more than 24 hours.

For remedies that are used as both a drink (or wash/ compress) and a poultice (or plaster) you strain and save both the liquid and the solid material and use as described above.

Steam Inhalation

Steam inhalation is another common way of using plants medicinally. The standard procedure for making a steam inhalation is as follows:

1. Put 60 grams (2 ounces) of plant material in a bowl or basin.
2. Pour 1 litre (1 quart) of boiling water over the plant material
3. Cover your head with a towel and hang your head over the bowl or basin, trapping the steam under the towel. Inhale deeply for 20 to 30 minutes.

Two less common recipe types in this book are tinctures and syrups.

Tincture

A tincture is made by steeping the medicinal plant in an alcohol and water mixture (1 part alcohol, three parts water). This extracts the active components and preserves the remedy.

Unlike infusions and decoctions, which should be used within 24 hours, tinctures can be stored for up to one month. Commercial remedies usually use plain ethyl alcohol, but you can use diluted spirits when making your own remedies.

Never use wood alcohol, methylated spirits, or rubbing alcohol in your herbal remedies, they are poisonous.

Syrup

A syrup is usually made with honey and is another way of preserving herbal remedies. Syrups are good for strong or bitter remedies, for remedies that children will be taking, and for people who have a religious or other objection to using alcohol in any form.

Details for making syrups accompany the text for those recipes. But in general you just add an equal amount of honey (golden syrup will also do) to your warm decoction or infusion. You may need to heat the mixture to get the honey to mix, so stir constantly so that the mixture doesn't get too hot.

Essential oils

You will have to buy essential oils. Virtually all essential oils mentioned in this book are readily available in health food stores and from herbalists.

● Essential oils are highly concentrated—a single drop of an essential oil may contain the active, volatile components from thousands of plants—they must be used with care.

● Never use essential oils full strength. Always dilute the oil either in another, neutral vegetable or nut oil or as described in the specific recipe in this book. Unless otherwise noted in the text the general rule for diluting essential oils is 1 - 2 drops essential oil in 10 millilitres of nut or vegetables.

● Never use essential oils on broken or irritated skin.

● Never use essential oils on mucus membranes (mouth, nose, genital region).

● Never use essential oils near or in the eyes.

● Essential oils can cause photosensitivity and other skin reactions. This can happen when the oils are used internally or externally. So be especially careful in the sun when you are using essential oils. Of course you *always* wear sun screen! If you experience any skin irritation while using a folk remedy discontinue its use.

For most massage and aromatherapy treatments the instructions are as follows.
Dilute the 1-2 drops of the essential oil with 10 millilitres (2 tablespoons) of carrier oil. The carrier oil should be cold pressed almond, olive, wheatgerm or sunflower oil. This will make enough for one or two uses. Always make small amounts of the essential oil mixtures as the essential oil will deteriorate with exposure to the carrier oil and the air.

Acne

It never fails, the big day arrives and you wake-up with a big red spot, right on the tip of your nose or the middle of your forehead. Whether you call them white heads, pimples, zits, spots, or %$#/!! they ruin a perfect day.

Even though it might feel like it, acne is not the end of the world. You will probably out-grow it, though admittedly that's not very comforting today. If you are a not-so-young adult and you are still troubled by acne, you probably didn't out grow it and should probably reconcile yourself to periodic outbreaks throughout your life.

The inside story on acne

Acne starts with the oil secreting glands responsible for normal lubrication of your skin. When these glands' access to the outside world get blocked the oil that should have moisturised your skin builds up inside the pores. The build-up irritates surrounding skin, which gets red. Eventually the pressure is great enough to break through the surface.

Remedies with 🫖 *are made using an infusion. Those with* 🍲 *are made using a decoction. Instructions for both methods are on pages 4 - 7. Variations and other procedures are contained in the text following the description of that remedy.*

Either way, once a spot starts there is not much you can do besides let nature take its course. There are some folk remedies that may hurry mother nature on her way though, and you can control some of the factors that cause acne. So control what you can, then when a spot starts try one of the following folk remedies, it just may hasten that nasty spot's departure.

Why do some people get acne while others lead an acne free life? Contrary to many teenager's belief, popular kids get acne too, it just looks cool on them, so you don't notice it as much. There are two main triggers for acne, one you have control over the other you do not.

Hormones

Yes, Hormones

Those same hormones that make you crazy and get puberty off to a flying start are responsible for many acne outbreaks, especially in adolescence and, unfortunately, during the menopause.

One thing you better get used to whether you have acne or not: hormones can make you loopy, taking control of your body and sometimes your mind throughout your life. When you look at it that way, acne is probably the least of your worries.

Diet

While you can't do much to control your hormones you can control your diet, especially the kind and quality of fats and carbohydrates you eat. This is an area where you can do something to help control the severity and frequency of your acne outbreaks.

Eat More of these Foods:

- Vegetables, (cooked and raw) • Vegetable juice
- Seaweed soup • Dried skim milk • Herbal tea
- Salads • Whole grain cereal and breads
- Unsaturated Vegetable oils • Non-citrus fruit
- Poached Eggs • Cashew Nuts • Almonds
- Cold water ocean fish

Stay Away from these Foods:
All fried and refined foods including:

- Carbonated Drinks • Alcohol • Tea and Coffee
- Dairy Products • Ice-Cream • Yogurt • Sugar
- Commercial Bread • Margarine • Peanut butter

Finally, don't make it worse!

Don't scrub your skin with rough materials. This only irritates your skin and encourages your glands to produce more oil, which is the last thing you want.

Don't use harsh soap, for the same reasons you shouldn't scrub. No matter what your mother says, your acne is not caused by dirty skin.

Avoid antibiotics, they can destroy friendly bacteria that contribute to your overall health.

Treat the problem now. It's never too early to develop good healthy habits.

Aloe [1] *(Aloe vera)*
also known as *A. barbadensis*

The gel that oozes out of a broken aloe leaf has been used to soothe skin and promote healing for more than a thousand years. In fact aloe was one of Cleopatra's favourite beauty secrets (and we all know the effect she had on men). If you have the slightest hint of green in your thumb you can grow your own aloe treatment.

1. Collect the gel from a freshly broken aloe leaf

2. Apply the fresh gel to clean, just-washed skin

3. Use sparingly at first, if any irritation occurs discontinue use

Basil [2] *(Ocimum basilicum)*

Basil oil has been used as an external remedy in India for more than two thousand years.

1. Dilute 1 - 2 drops of basil oil with 10 millilitres of good quality nut or vegetable oil and apply to freshly washed skin

2. Use sparingly at first. If any irritation occurs, discontinue use

---

[1] *consuming large quantities can cause vomiting, avoid in pregnancy*

[2] *do not use essential oil in any form during pregnancy*

Cucumber *(Cucumis sativa)*

Clever women with a busy social life already know about the soothing, refreshing effect thin slices of cucumber have when placed over tired eyes. Extracted cucumber juice may also be useful when diet is a factor in your acne. To make this remedy you will need a juice extractor, and a cucumber of course!

1. Peel the cucumber then use a juice extractor to make cucumber juice

2. Apply cucumber juice on and around the affected pores

Asparagus *(Asparagus officinalis)*

To make this cleansing treatment you'll need fresh, spring asparagus.

1. Trim 12 large spears of fresh asparagus

2. Stand the spears in 1 litre (1 quart) water

3. Bring to the boil

4. Simmer 30 minutes

5. Discard the asparagus (it will be all soft and mushy and all the vitamins, minerals and nutrients will have been extracted by the water)

6. Use the asparagus water as a wash for your skin at least twice a day

Birch *(Betula verrucosa)*

If you have access to a birch tree you can make a decoction of birch bark to use in a compress for acne affected skin. Apply as often as needed.

Pot Marigold [1] *(Calendula officinalis)*

This traditional Indian remedy uses calendula oil, which is collected from pot marigold. Dilute 1-2 drops of calendula oil with 10 millilitres of good quality nut or vegetable oil. Apply to acne and acne prone skin.

Bergamot *(Monarda didyma, M. fistulosa, M. citriodora and M. punctata)*

In Spain bergamot oil is used as an acne and pimple treatment. Spanish explorers brought bergamot to Europe from the Canary Islands during the seventeenth and eighteenth centuries. Dilute 1 - 2 drops of bergamot oil with 10 millilitres of good quality nut or vegetable oil and apply to affected skin.

Lovage *(Levisticum officinale)*

Scandinavians use this lovage decoction as a general complexion aid. They drink the strained liquid and save a little to daub directly on acne affected skin.

Physic Nut *(Jatropha curcas)*

This treatment comes from the West Indies and it couldn't be simpler, all you need is access to a physic nut tree. Then you can make a paste from ground physic nut seeds and apply the paste to your pimples.

Juniper *(Juniperus communis)*

In the Middle Ages juniper oil was a favourite acne treatment. Dilute 1-2 drops of juniper oil with 10 millilitres of good quality vegetable or nut oil and apply directly to the affected skin.

---

[1] *do not confuse with French Marigold, Tagetes patula*

Burdock *(Arctium lappa)*

The Native American Potawatomi tribe drank an infusion of burdock root as a tonic and purifier. They also recommend acne sufferers switch to a dairy free diet rich in raw fruits and vegetables.

Teasel *(Dipsacus fullonum)* and Yarrow [1] *(Achillea millefolium)*

The Romany people, who are also called Gypsies, have been using this drink to treat acne since the fourteenth century. It's a mixture of a decoction of wild teasel and an infusion of yarrow blossoms. The Romany believe that this drink, along with a diet rich in fresh vegetables, particularly nettle leaves, to be an effective acne treatment. But you will need to collect your wild teasel roots after the first full moon in autumn and clean, cut and air dry the roots in a shady location if you want to make this the traditional Romany way.

Wild teasel with Yarrow blossoms

Mix the infusion of wild teasel with the defusion of Yarrow blossoms and drink 250 millilitres (1 cup) morning and night.

Lady's Mantle [2] *(Alchemilla vulgaris)*

In the 1650s Nicholas Culpeper, a famous English physician and herbalist, recommended drinking an infusion of lady's mantle to treat acne.

---

[1] avoid during pregnancy
[2] avoid during pregnancy

Lavender [1] *(Lavandula angustifolia)*

Almost 2000 years ago the Egyptians taught the Romans about the medicinal values of lavender. This remedy relies on lavender oil applied directly on problem spots. Before applying, dilute 1-2 drops of lavender oil with 10 millilitres of good quality vegetable or nut oil.

Garlic [2] *(Allium sativum)*

If you don't get relief from any of the other treatments you may want to try garlic oil, which the ancient Greeks used as a topical treatment for acne. An added benefit of this treatment, you'll have plenty of room to yourself on the bus!

---

[1] *avoid high doses during pregnancy*
[2] *avoid during pregnancy and if breast feeding*

Allergies

For some it starts out with a telltale tickle at the back of the throat; some break out in a rash or double up with cramps; for others it is weepy eyes; some are treated to a runny nose; while others sneeze, and sneeze and sneeze.

All these miserable people have something in common, they are suffering from allergies and despite their wide range of symptoms they would all agree that allergies are down right irritating.

Whatever type of allergy you have your reaction is caused when your body over-reacts to a substance that most people take in their stride. That means that whatever makes you go all twitchy may not have any effect on your neighbour, allergies are a very personal thing, a case of one man's (or woman's) meat really being another's poison.

Speaking of food, foods and food preservatives are common culprits, as are chemicals, pollens, vaccines and drugs. Even stress can cause an allergic reaction. If you are looking for something to blame your parents for, allergies may fit the bill. If they suffer from allergies you probably will too.

Remedies with 🫖 *are made using an infusion. Those with* 🍲 *are made using a decoction. Instructions for both methods are on pages 4 - 7. Variations and other procedures are contained in the text following the description of that remedy.*

Because you can be allergic to something you eat, smell or touch and you can react immediately, in minutes, hours or days and symptoms range from a cough, runny nose or sneeze; to stomach cramps, hives or swelling mucus membranes (including those in the lungs) it is difficult and time consuming to determine the exact cause of an allergic reaction.

This lack of predictability adds to the frustration of an allergy attack and is one of the reasons that herbal remedies concentrate on relieving the symptoms rather than identifying the causes.

So, the next time you're overcome with a coughing fit, runny nose, watery eyes, skin rash, indigestion, cramps or heart palpitations try one of these folk remedies, you may find one that's just right for you.

Cough

Coltsfoot [1] *(Tussilago farfara)*

If you are troubled by an allergic cough take a tip from the Greek physician Dioscorides. Almost 2000 years ago he described the medicinal qualities of coltsfoot, though he recommended smoking the leaves. Apparently you were supposed to inhale the smoke through a reed to cure your cough. Customs have changed over the intervening 2000 years. Today drinking a decoction of coltsfoot is a popular cough remedy with French folk healers, and smoking anything is seen as a health hazard.

---

[1] restricted herb in Australia and New Zealand, due to presence of alkaloid pyrrolizidine, which has been shown to cause liver damage in rats

White Horehound *(Marrubium vulgare)*

If coltsfoot is not to your liking try white horehound, a slightly less ancient herbal remedy. We can thank Gerard, a famous nineteenth century herbalist, for this cough treatment. He made a syrupy cough tonic from fresh, white horehound leaves, extracting the juice from the leaves with a sugar and water mixture. You can try drinking an infusion of white horehound, it's easier to make and lower in kilojoules as well!

Cramps

Fennel [1] *(Foeniculum officinale)*
Periwinkle *(Vinca major)*
Prickly Ash *(Zanthhoxylum americanum)*
Self-heal *(Prunella vulgaris)*
Woundwort *(Stachys palustris)*
or Yarrow [2] *(Achillea millefolium)*

If you prefer a soothing warm drink when you have cramps try drinking an infusion made with any of these herbs.

Biochemic Tissue Salt, Mag Phos

Mag Phos is the Biochemic recommendation for cramps. Buy Mag Phos at a health food store or from a natural pharmacist. Mag Phos is usually sold as 6x potency, but consult a natural practitioner for guidance on the appropriate dose for you.

---

[1]   *avoid during pregnancy,*
[2]   *avoid during pregnancy*

Biochemic tissue salts

The system known as Biochemics, and the cornerstone of that system the so-called 'Biochemic Tissue Salts', was developed by Dr Wilhelm H. Schuessler, a German doctor who identified twelve inorganic salts that he believed to be essential for health. Dr Schuessler also believed that many common ailments were caused by an imbalance in one or more of these salts. In fact, according to Dr Schuessler the imbalance in any one of these salts was in itself a disease state.

Tissue salts are given in the homoeopathy potency 6x, which refers to a dilution of 1 part of the salt in 1 000 000 total parts (1 part salt combined with 999 999 parts of water).

The twelve, inorganic, Biochemic Tissue Salts are usually referred to by the following abbreviations:

Calcium fluoride – Calc. Fluor.	Potassium sulphate - Kali. Sulph.
Calcium phosphate - Calc. Phos.	Magnesium phosphate - Mag. Phos.
Calcium sulfate - Calc. Sulph.	Sodium chloride - Nat. Mur.
Iron phosphate - Fer. Phos.	Sodium phosphate -Nat. Phos.
Potassium chloride - Kali. Mur.	Sodium sulfate - Nat. Sulph.
Potassium phosphate - Kali. Phos.	Silicon oxide - Silica

While the abbreviations may seem strange at first, Kali for potassium Nat for sodium, and Mur for chloride, they make sense when you realise that kalium is German for potassium, muriaticum is chloride and natrum is sodium.

Dizziness

Lemon *(Citrus limon or C. medica, var. limonum)*
and honey

These two, together and separately, are perennial favourites with folk healers. This particular remedy comes from England. It should be taken as soon as a dizzy spell begins.

1. Squeeze enough fresh lemons to make 250 millilitres (1 cup) lemon juice and sweeten with a little honey
2. Drink whenever you feel dizzy

Feverfew [1] *(Tanacetum parthenium)*
Rose *(Rosa canina)*
or Rosemary *(Rosmarinus officinalis)*

If the pucker power of the lemon juice remedy above is too much for you to handle try drinking a warm herbal infusion of feverfew, rose or rosemary.

Or try aromatherapy, a New Age favourite with an ancient pedigree. While no one knows exactly how ancient, we do know that more than 2000 years ago the Egyptians were teaching the Romans about the healing properties of herbal oils.

Lavender [2] *(Lavandula angustifolia)*
or Peppermint [3] *(Mentha piperita)*

Gently massage a small amount of lavender or peppermint oil into your forehead and the back of your head and neck.

---

[1]   avoid if taking blood thinning drugs
[2]   avoid high doses during pregnancy
[3]   avoid during pregnancy and if breast feeding. Do not give in any form to very young babies

Dilute 1 - 2 drops of the essential oil with 10 millilitres of good quality vegetable or nut oil. Keep essential oils well away from your mouth, eyes and all mucous membranes. Do not use essential oils internally.

Allergic indigestion or dyspepsia

Papaya *(Carica papaya)*
or Pineapple *(Ananas comosus)*

This delicious treatment is a favourite with East and West Indians.

Drink about 500 millilitres (two cups) of either juice each day until you feel better

Peppermint [1] *(Mentha piperita)*
Ginger [2] *(Zingiber officinalis)*
Mallow *(Althaea officinalis)*
or Thyme *(Thymus vulgaris)*

Drinking an infusion of any of these herbs can also soothe an upset tummy.

Biochemic Tissue Salt, Nat Phos

According to Biochemic theory taking the appropriate tissue salt can help maintain or restore your body's natural balance and good health. Nat Phos (sodium phosphate) is the Biochemic recommendation for stomach upsets.

---

[1] *avoid during pregnancy and if breast feeding. Do not give in any form to very young babies*

[2] *use sparingly during pregnancy*

Palpitation

Cypress *(Cupressur sempervirens)*
or Frankincense *(Boswelia carterii)*

If you know that your speeding heart beat is caused by allergies and not by any underlying heart condition you may want to try aromatherapy to soothe your psyche and slow your racing heart. Gently massage a small amount of either of these oils (diluted 1 -2 drops of essential oil to 10 millilitres of good quality vegetable or nut oil) into your temples, forehead and the back of your head and neck.

Runny Nose

Allium Cepa

Allium Cepa is a homoeopathic remedy that has been used for more than 200 years. It is available from homoeopaths and health food and herbal stores. Take one 30c-pill every two hours until your runny nose has run its course. In case you're wondering, allium cepa is made from onions, that's why it takes the scientific name   for onions.

Butterbur *(Petasites hybridus)*

If you're driving, give this remedy a miss. If you are staying home this decoction, with a kick, just might do the trick.

30 grams (1 ounce) butterbur
750 millilitres (3 cups) water
1. Bring to the boil

2. Simmer until volume of liquid has been reduced by about one-third
3. Strain, discarding solids
4. Mix the decoction with an equal volume of white wine
5. Drink 150 millilitres (5 ounces) every two hours

Skin Rash

Chamomile [1] *(Chamaemelum nobile, Roman, or C. recutita, German)*

Chamomile is well known for its soothing properties so it is no surprise that it crops up in folk remedies—in lotions, soothing herbal teas and as an essential oil in aromatherapy. This time it's chamomile oil's turn, in an aromatherapy technique that takes advantage of chamomile's anti-inflammatory properties. Dilute 1 - 2 drops of chamomile oil with 10 millilitres of good quality vegetable or nut oil. Gently massage the diluted oil into irritated skin.

Chickweed *(Stellaria media)*

This treatment goes back to the Middle Ages.

1. Pre-heat your oven to 80 degrees Celsius (160 degrees fahrenheit)
2. Warm 500 millilitres (2 cups) cold-pressed virgin olive oil in a non-metallic pan
3. Add 180 grams (6 tablespoons) beeswax to the warm olive oil and heat gently until beeswax is liquefied and blended with the olive oil
4. Place 375 grams (1 1/2 cups) coarsely-chopped, fresh chickweed in an oven-safe ceramic pan

---

[1]   *avoid excessive doses and the oil in any amount during pregnancy*

5. Pour the oil/beeswax mixture over the chickweed and place the pan in the oven for 2 hours

6. Remove mixture from oven and strain immediately into a jar

7. Cool before closing the lid

8. Use ointment on irritated skin as needed

Gooseberry *(Ribes grossularia)*

If your allergic rash appears during gooseberry season try this soothing wash made from decocted gooseberries.

Banana [1] *(Musa)*

This remedy turns a packed lunch into a first aid kit. It's so simple even a child can do it! Just place the inside of the banana peel against your irritated skin. Hold the banana peel in place with a bandage.

Strap Wattle *(Acacia holosericea)*

If you are allergic to wattle give this treatment a miss. But if you're not, take advantage of ancient Australian Aboriginal wisdom and give this remedy a go.

1. Collect a handful of ripe acacia pods and seeds

2. Rub the pods and seeds with a little water until you produce a lather

3. Apply the acacia lather to irritated skin

---

[1]   *because all cultivated bananas are sterile hybrids, they do not have exact species names.*

Sneezing

Chamomile [1] *(Chamaemelum nobile, Roman, or C. recutita, German)*

According to old-time German folk healers a sneeze was a sign of anxiety and a soothing drink of infused chamomile was just what the doctor ordered.

Light

Yes light, if you are tormented by an itchy nose and a sneeze that never seems to develop try this old-fashioned trick from European folk healers. Glance at the sun for just a second. If it's night time, or the day is overcast stare at a bright light, the brighter the better. It works!

Honey

This sweet remedy for stubborn sneezing comes from native Columbian healers. They recommend a finger's worth (you can use 5 grams or 1 teaspoon) of honey every couple of hours to put a halt to non-stop sneezing.

Golden Rod *(Solidago virga aurea)*

In North America, Native American healers used an infusion of golden rod to bring an end to sneezing fits.

Eyebright *(Euphrasia officinalis)*

This old stand-by wasn't just used for eye complaints, it was also recommended to banish bouts of chronic sneezing. If you

---

[1]   avoid excessive doses and the oil in any amount during pregnancy

want to try it you'll have to have a fresh plant, as the remedy calls for eyebright juice, extracted from a whole plant. Mix the juice with an equal part of alcohol and drink a 20 millilitre (1 tablespoon) dose as needed.

Watery Eyes

Eyebright *(Euphrasia officinalis)*

Scottish Highlanders used to make an eyebright solution in milk, which they applied to irritated eyes with, of all things, a feather. In Europe they drink an infusion of eyebright to soothe irritated eyes.

Wallflower *(Cheiranthus cheiri)*

Back in 130 AD the famous Greek physician Galen was born. He didn't fritter away the days, instead he got right down to business. During his lifetime he compiled eleven books on medicine, invented cold cream and eventually became a physician to the Roman gladiators.

For a gladiator going into battle with watery, runny-eyes could have been the kiss of death — literally. So the gladiators probably shouted Galen a few beers when he told them that drinking this infusion of wallflower could clear their runny eyes.

Angina

Angina pain is your heart's way of telling you that it is not getting enough blood. When your heart talks you better listen — or else! During an angina attack you may find that your blood pressure has gone up, your body feels cold, and you may have difficulty breathing. Other symptoms can include blurred vision, drowsiness and dizziness or a feeling of light-headedness.

Don't ignore chest pains, especially those that start near the heart, or run up your shoulder and down your arm. Seek medical attention immediately.

If your doctor has diagnosed angina you have probably already worked together to identify the kind of things that trigger your attacks and a plan of action for those times when angina strikes. Remember to be alert for any change in your normal pattern and report it to your doctor at once.

Some common angina triggers are stress, over exertion, fatigue, emotional strain, over eating and smoking. As with all heart and circulatory problems, diet and exercise can be important in preventing and controlling angina.

Remedies with 🫖 *are made using an infusion. Those with* ☕ *are made using a decoction. Instructions for both methods are on pages 4 -7. Variations and other procedures are contained in the text following the description of that remedy.*

Diet

Avoid excessive saturated fats, carbohydrates, salt, sugar, coffee and alcohol;

Eat Most

Whole grain cereals and breads
Raw and cooked vegetables and mixed salads
Fresh fruit
Vegetable and fruit juices (unsweetened)
 Legumes and pulses

Eat Moderately

Cold water fish
Low-fat milk and yoghurt
Chicken or turkey without skin
Very lean red meat
Eggs (not fried)
Nuts (unsalted and dry roasted)
Eggs

Eat Least

Fats and oils
Cheese
Sugar
Refined flours

Exercise

Many people first experience angina after exercising and are reluctant to exercise after they have been diagnosed. But taking up a sedentary lifestyle always does more harm than good, so you are only hurting yourself if you let angina keep you from exercising.

A sensible exercise program will not only relieve stress and strengthen your heart, it will help lower your blood pressure and slow your resting heart rate all of which spell good news for your heart. For angina sufferers the 2 Ms are the keys to a sensible exercise program Moderate exercise and Monitor your angina.

Obesity

Being overweight is never good for your heart, or any other part of you for that matter. If you are overweight a sensible exercise program is even more important because it helps you lose weight.

Recent research has shown exercise to be at least as significant a factor as counting calories in a successful weight loss or maintenance program.

Smoking

Let's not beat around the bush, cigarettes earned their nick name 'coffin nails', and it isn't because they are popular with carpenters, it's because they are business boosters for funeral parlours. Cigarettes do no good and much harm, especially to your heart, lungs and circulatory system, the very organs responsible for getting oxygen around to the parts of your body that need it.

If you have angina, you already have a problem, cigarettes only make it worse so STOP SMOKING NOW. NO IFS, NO ANDS, AND CERTAINLY NO BUTS!

Cholesterol

That pain in your chest should be excellent motivation for you to adopt a healthy diet. A healthy diet will probably lower your cholesterol. Reduce the amount of meat in your diet, increase the amount of vegetables and avoid saturated fats and vegetable oils.

Alcohol

If you are partial to the odd cleansing ale, refreshing glass of wine or medicinal gin you are in luck. The latest research indicates that a tipple with your tucker is good for your ticker. It seems that alcohol in the bloodstream influences substances involved with blood clotting and dissolving blood clots and may reduce the risk of heart attacks and other ailments caused by blood clots, like stroke. But don't go overboard, a little is good a lot is not.

In addition to your doctor's recommended treatment you may want to try one of these folk remedies. Some target the causes of angina pain while others are designed to soothe the pain of an attack. However do not substitute any of these treatments for your doctor's recommendations.

Bach Remedies

Try:

Elm - if overwhelmed by responsibility

Hornbeam - if mentally exhausted

Impatiens - if suffering from general tension

Olive - if overworked

White Chestnut - if suffering from insomnia

Rescue Remedy - if suffering from shock or fear

Flower What?

In 1915 Dr Edward Bach, an English physician and bacteriologist, developed a system of natural healing based on his theory that dew on flowers had medicinal properties. According to Dr Bach dew from 38 different flower varieties can be used to cure every ailment.

Bach Flower Remedies are primarily aimed at the emotional or psychological cause of an illness, though they are sometimes used to treat specific, physical complaints. Bach Flower Remedies are popular and are available from most health food shops and shops specialising in natural medicines.

If you haven't tried Dr Bach's remedies because you're uncertain about how to pronounce his name, it rhymes with latch not lock.

Osteopathy

In cases of angina, osteopathy can help relieve tension in the neck, shoulders and back which can aggravate the chest pains angina sufferers experience.

Osteopathy

In the 1870s, an American, Andrew Taylor Still, developed the practice of osteopathy. Still believed that many illnesses are caused by the miss-alignment of the body and he developed a system of manipulation to restore the structural balance and thus restore the patient to health.

According to osteopathic principles adjustment can be used to treat structural, functional or organic illnesses.

Fruit Vinegars

For centuries the Romany people (sometimes called Gypsies) have sipped fruit vinegars to soothe angina pain.

1. Mix 30 millilitres (1 ounce) of fruit vinegar (like apple vinegar) with 30 millilitres (1 ounce) honey
2. Add to 250 millilitres (1 cup) water
3. Sip every morning

Romany folk healers also believe that diet is important in controlling angina pain and they recommend eliminating pork and all oils (except olive oil) from your diet. As well they will tell you to eat six almonds along with 37 grams (1 3/4 ounces) of fresh yeast, with some coarse, whole-wheat or rye bread every day and to supplement your diet with onions, spinach, nettle salad, wild garlic, dandelion, sorrel and fresh watercress.

Cayenne Pepper *(Capsicum frutescens)* and Hawthorn Berries

(Crataegus oxycantha, C. monogyna, C. pinnatifida)
also called shan zha in China

This remedy, an infusion of cayenne and hawthorn berries, is another hot favourite with Romany folk healers.

2.5 grams (½ teaspoon) cayenne pepper and a couple of hawthorn berries
250 millilitres (1 cup) boiling water
1. Steep covered 10 - 15 minutes
2. Drink as needed

Fermented Cider

This old fashioned remedy, a hot compress of fermented cider, has been used for centuries. It uses the fruit acids in the warmed cider to open your circulation and soothe your blood vessels and nervous system.

1. Bring fermented cider, the older the better, to the boil
2. Remove from heat
3. Soak towels in the hot liquid and place them, as hot as you can bear, on your arms, covering each arm completely
4. Leave in place until the towels cool then remove and repeat if necessary

Linseed [1] *(Linum ustatissimum)*

If you don't have any fermented cider, get some linseed oil from your local pharmacy. Like the fermented cider remedy, this treatment is soothing and is believed to open up your circulation.

Gently warm linseed oil (do not over heat, test it against your skin, the oil should be hot, but not uncomfortably so)

Soak a small towel in the warmed oil and place the towel on your chest, over your heart

Walnut *(Juglans regia)*

While the warm linseed compress (described above) is in place drink an infusion, made from the woody lining of English walnut shells.

40 grams (2 tablespoons) of the woody lining of walnut shells
250 millilitres (1 cup) boiling water
1. Steep covered 30 minutes
2. Strain, discarding solids
3. Drink 250 millilitres (1 cup), 3 times a day

Saki

Saki is an acquired taste but if you like Japanese rice wine you may want to try this remedy. It's a favourite of Japan's traditional Kampo doctors who claim the rice wine tonic helps relieve the pain of angina.

---

[1]   use sparingly as linseed oil contains prussic acid, don't use artists' or craft linseed oil

Mix a raw egg with 750 millilitres (3 cups) each saki and apple juice (you can use a sweet wine if you do not have, or do not like, saki)

1. Bring to the boil
2. Cool to lukewarm
3. Drink 250 millilitres (1 cup), 3 times a day for three or four days

Hawthorn Berries *(Crataegus oxycantha,*
C. monogyna, C. pinnatifida called shan zha in China)

This old Irish remedy, an infusion of hawthorn berries, requires ripe hawthorn berries which you'll need to collect in autumn.

10 grams (2 teaspoons) ripe hawthorn berries
250 millilitres (1 cup) boiling water

1. Steep covered 20 minutes
2. Strain, discarding solids
3. Drink 250 millilitres (1 cup), 3 times a day

Garlic [1] *(Allium sativum)*

Garlic is an ancient and versatile ingredient in folk remedies. In the Mediterranean folk healers recommend drinking a little garlic juice every day. You can make your own in a juice extractor or you can buy garlic juice (some brands come deodorised) from your health food store or natural pharmacy.

---

[1]   *avoid during pregnancy and if breast feeding*

Ylang-Ylang *(Cananga odorata)*
also called Canangium odoratum

A body massage using ylang-ylang oil is a very popular anti-anxiety remedy with Indonesian and Philippine folk healers. Since anxiety can trigger angina a soothing massage can't hurt. Remember to dilute 1 - 2 drops of the ylang-ylang oil with 10 millilitres of good quality vegetable or nut oil before applying to the skin.

Anorexia Nervosa

This is a life threatening condition that affects more and more young women and men each year. The outward signs of anorexia give it its common name, "the slimmers disease". But sufferers' obsessive desire to lose weight, often to the point of starving themselves to death, is a symptom of a complex psychological condition. Because anorexia is such a complex condition it can be very difficult to treat.

If you suspect that you or anyone in your family is suffering from anorexia or the other common eating disorder, bulimia nervosa, consult a medical practitioner immediately. However, you may want to try these remedies as a complement to your doctor's treatment.

Gentian (Gentiana marcrophylla)

Colonial Americans in the Appalachian Mountain region of Pennsylvania learned about gentian from the Native Americans of the Susquehanna tribe. Tribal healers used a drink of decocted gentian root, as tonic, which they believed would stimulate digestive juices. Drink warm, 250 millilitres (1 cup) 15 - 30 minutes before each meal.

Remedies with ☕ are made using an infusion. Those with 🍲 are made using a decoction. Instructions for both methods are on pages 4 - 7. Variations and other procedures are contained in the text following the description of that remedy.

Alfalfa *(Medicago sativa also called lucerne)*

It's funny, even though we call this plant lucerne, when we dish up its young sprouts onto our own plates we follow the American custom and call it alfalfa. But whatever it's called you can't deny that cattle do well eating it. It may be its ability to fatten-up livestock that made folk healers think of using alfalfa medicinally. Whatever the reason it is a long-standing folk belief that drinking fresh alfalfa-sprout juice will help people gain weight.

You'll need a juice extractor to make alfalfa-sprout juice, and be warned it has a very grassy flavour, so you will probably want to mix it with carrot or fruit juice.

Extract the juice from a handful of alfalfa sprouts and drink once a day.

Rose *(Rosa canina)*

In England folk healers treat anorexia with a drink of infused, fresh rose petals.

Sweeten with a touch of maple syrup if you like.

Clematis *(Clematis hexasepala)*

Across the Tasman, drinking a decoction of clematis bark and stems is the traditional Kiwi way to improve the appetite.

Bach Flower Remedies

These popular remedies are believed to address the psycho-logical cause of illness.

Try:

>   **Heather** - if the refusal to eat food is seen as a plea
>   for attention
>
>   **Beech** - if there is an emotional inability to accept food
>
>   **Wild Rose** - if the patient collapses
>
>   **Wild Oat or Walnut** - if the sufferer is an adolescent

Bergamot *(Monarda didyma,*
M. fistulosa, M. citriodora and M. punctata)
or Cardamom *(Elettaria cardamomum)*

These fragrant essential oils are believed to balance the
appetite and the psyche. They bring the power of aromatherapy to therapeutic massage (dilute 1 - 2 drops of the
essential oil with 10 millilitres of good quality nut or vegetable
oil). The massage should concentrate on the abdomen, neck
and temples. Either oil can also be added to the bath.

Hypnotherapy

The treatment of eating disorders like anorexia often includes
psychological counselling. Many traditional physicians and
psychologists now use hypnosis in their practices to treat
illnesses that have a psychological basis. Your general practitioner can recommend a qualified hypnotherapist if he or
she believes that hypnosis would be helpful in your condition.

Hypnosis

Nothing more exotic than a mental state in which people
are open to suggestions, hypnosis has come a long
way from the days when it was seen as a dangerous
parlour trick.

(continued next page)

Hypnosis (continued)

Now hypnosis is used in almost equal measure by traditional and alternative medical practitioners. It is most commonly used in conditions that have some psychological component, including many eating disorders. Hypnosis is also very useful in stop smoking and stress reduction programs. Hypnosis was used by the ancient Greeks, although it wasn't until the late eighteenth century when Austrian doctor Franz Anton Mesmer began studying what he called animal magnetism that the practice of hypnotism became known in the west. The modern study of hypnosis was so closely associated with Mesmer's work that hypnosis was called Mesmerism until the nineteenth century when the term hypnosis began to be used.

An element of mystery still surrounds the practice of hypnotism, thanks in no small part to the work of stage hypnotists. Contrary to the stage image of a person with a glazed expression, walking stiff-armed, in a 'trance', a slave to the hypnotist's every suggestion, there is nothing mysterious or bizarre about a hypnotic trance. You have probably hypnotised yourself without even knowing it. If you have ever gotten lost, in a book, movie, television program or while watching a sporting event and suddenly realised that a great deal of time has past, you have been hypnotised.

While these episodes of intense concentration are true hypnotic states, they don't qualify as therapeutic hypnosis. To have a therapeutic effect your state of hypnosis

(continued next page)

Hypnosis *(continued)*

must be accompanied by hypnotic suggestions. This is just a fancy way of saying that while you are hypnotised someone talks about your condition and if the suggestions include action that you will undertake after the hypnosis session, it is called a post-hypnotic suggestion. That someone making the suggestions can even be yourself, in the case of self-hypnosis.

Hypnosis, used properly, can be a powerful addition to treatment for any medical condition, whether of physical or psychological origin. Consult your physician for a referral to a qualified hypnotist if you feel that this type of treatment may be of use.

Arthritis

When you wake-up in the morning do your joints ache? Does it take you a few minutes to get your stiff joints moving again after you have been sitting for awhile? Do you blame arthritis for all this and anything else you can think of including why you lost your last tennis match? Of course you do. Who doesn't? And when your joints are aching you don't care what kind of arthritis you have. You just want the pain to stop.

Arthritis is one of the oldest known medical conditions. Think about how your joints feel when you wake up in your nice warm bed. Now imagine how much worse you would feel after spending the night in a cold cave. We know that our cave dwelling ancestors suffered from arthritis. So it wouldn't be hard to imagine that arthritis pain was one of the first problems early healers tried to solve. Since healers were often the elder members of a clan, they had a personal interest in easing their own stiff and painful joints. After all, regaining the ability to move easily, would have been a great inspiration. In a nomadic life, if you couldn't keep up with the clan you usually faced an early death. Your only choice, jump or be pushed.

Remedies with 🍵 *are made using an infusion. Those with* ☕ *are made using a decoction. Instructions for both methods are on pages 4 - 7. Variations and other procedures are contained in the text following the description of that remedy.*

So take heart, while folk medicine can't do anything for your cross-court volley, there are several folk remedies from around the world that may help soothe your pain.

What are you complaining about?

Archaeologists have found signs of arthritis in the joints of Egyptian mummies and in cavemen and women. But it doesn't end there.

Arthritis is older than human history. The dinosaurs had arthritis too. Imagine how tyrannosaurus felt lumbering around with stiff, aching joints. At 15 m (50 ft) long and 6.5 m (20 ft) tall, weighing in at 10 tonnes (21,978 pounds), that's a lot of arthritis pain!

Manipulative therapies

Many people find that manipulative therapies help relieve arthritis pain. You may want to try therapeutic massage or hydrotherapy. Chiropractors, osteopaths and reflexologists as well as partitioners of acupuncture and acupressure are other options. Always consult a registered practitioner for any of these treatments.

Celery (Apium graveolens)

Not quite as old as arthritis itself, but still ancient is India's Ayurvedic practitioners' traditional recommendation to drink an infusion of celery seed to soothe arthritis pain.

Fenugreek [1] *(Trigonella foenum-graecum)*

Ayurvedic physicians also recommended drinking a decoction of fenugreek seeds to treat arthritis.

Boneset *(Eupatorium perfoliatum)*

We get many arthritis remedies from Native Americans, including this one a drink of infused boneset leaves and flowers.

Chaparral *(Larrea tridentata)*

Native Americans in the south-west of what is now the USA drank an infusion of this native shrub to soothe arthritis pain.

Blue Cohosh *(Caulophyllum thalictrodes)*

Drinking a decoction of blue cohosh root is another Native American traditional remedy for soothing arthritis pain.

 Don't keep any unused portion of this drink, it turns very bitter on standing.

Purple Coneflower [2] *(Echinacea augustifolia)*

Native Americans from the plains of what is now the USA recommended drinking a decoction of purple coneflower root.

Bay *(Laurus nobilis)*

Colonial American's learned a lot from Native Americans. They paid special attention to the types of medicinal and food plants the locals favoured and this double duty recipe using

---

[1]   *avoid during pregnancy*

[2]   *restricted herb in Australia and New Zealand due to presence of alkaloid, shown to cause liver damage in rats*

bay leaves to soothe arthritis pain is one of the uses the colonials took to heart. You drink the liquid from the infusion and use the leaves to make a poultice to soothe the arthritic joint.

Surprisingly this method is almost identical to that recommended by the Roman Physician, Galen, 1800 years before!

Blackcurrant Leaves *(Rubes nigrum)*

During the seventeenth and eighteenth centuries European folk healers used a poultice of blackcurrant leaves to treat arthritis.

To make the poultice

A handful of leaves

A little hot water

1. Use the hot water to soften the leaves, then mash the leaves into a paste
2. Apply directly to the affected areas

Buchu *(Barosma betulina)*

About 300 years ago Dutch settlers took up the indigenous South African practice of drinking an infusion of buchu leaves to soothe arthritis pain.

Burdock *(Arctium lappa)*

Nineteenth century American physicians treated arthritis with a drink of decocted burdock.

Cabbage *(Brassica oleracea)*

This is a common folk remedy that your Grandmother may remember.

To prepare the leaves:

1. Remove tough mid-ribs from several large green cabbage leaves
2. Iron the leaves with a steam iron (Grandma had to use a dry iron and a spritz of water)
3. Rub a little olive oil on one side of the warm leaves and apply, (oiled side against your skin) to the sore joints.
4. Cover the leaves with a cloth or towel and leave on for one hour, then repeat

Alfalfa *(Medicago sativa, also called Lucerne)*

In Spain folk healers tell arthritis sufferers to eat a salad of young alfalfa sprouts, but you can just ask for double-sprouts on your salad sandwich at the delicatessen.

Angelica *(Angelica sinesis also known as dang gui)*

Angelica is a common healing herb in Chinese folk medicine. You can use the leaves or seeds to make an infusion or use the roots to make an decoction to make a soothing drink to ease arthritis pain. 🫖 leaves or seeds   or 🍲 root

Devil's Claw *(Harpagophytum procumbens)*

This Nabmibian arthritis drink requires a particular part of the stem of the herb called devil's claw. You must use the underground portion of the stem, that which is between the above ground stem and the roots, to make your decoction.

Feverfew *(Tanacetum parthenium)*

During the Middle Ages in England drinking an infusion of feverfew was a popular arthritis remedy.

Coconut oil *(Cocos nucifera)*
or Peanut Oil *(Arachis hypogaea)*
also known as Groundnut

Hawaiian folk healers massage arthritic joints with coconut oil or cold pressed peanut oil to relieve pain.

Wheatgrass *(Agropyron spicatum,*
A. cristatum, A. intermedium, A. trachycaulum, A. smithii)

Sangomas, South African healers, advise chewing wheatgrass sprouts. Be warned though, if you take to this remedy you'll have to buy a spittoon. You'll have to spit the residue out!

Birch *(Betula verrucosa)*

A soothing warm bath makes everything feel better. It's a great way to ease mental and physical aches and pains. Folk healers in the former Soviet Union get extra value from their recommendation to take a warm bath, by telling their patients to add the leaves from a decoction of birch leaves to the bath water.

1 kilogram (2 pounds) of fresh leaves
2 litres (2 quarts) water
1. Bring to the boil
2. Simmer 30 minutes
3. Add the leaves to bath water as warm as you can stand it
4. Relax in the bath water 'til the water cools.

Comfrey [1] *(Symphytum officinale)*
also known as Knitbone

Herbalists in the Philippines use a comfrey leaf poultice to treat painful arthritic joints. Mash a handful of comfrey leaves in enough water to make a paste, apply the paste to the painful joint. Cover with plastic then wrap with a towel. Leave on over night.

Gentian Root *(Gentiana marcrophylla)*
also known as gin jiao

This herb is such a world traveller it's no wonder it keeps popping up in folk remedies all around the world. The Greeks taught sixth century Arab physicians about gentian root. The Arabs took it on their travels and eventually introduced it to the Chinese. Since then, Chinese traditional physicians have recommended drinking a decoction of gentian root to treat arthritis pain.

Drink 5 ml (1 teaspoon) 3 - 4 times per day (before every meal)

Note: gentian is bitter, so you may want to add a bit of sugar or honey to make it palatable

Cayenne Pepper *(Capsicum frutescens)*

When Samuel Thomson, early nineteenth century American doctor and founder of the Vermont Botanic Medical School, wrote about capsicum he said it was "one of the safest and best [plants] ever discovered to remove disease". And, he said, "Every family should keep on hand 2 ounces (60 grams) of cayenne for a year's supply". He recommended drinking an

---

[1]   restricted herb in Australia and New Zealand due to presence of alkaloid, shown to cause liver damage in rats

infusion of dried cayenne powder whenever the pain of arthritis flared.

2.5 - 5 grams (one-half to one teaspoon) dried cayenne powder
250 millilitres (1 cup) hot water
Drink as needed

Juniper Berries *(Juniperus communis)*

Juniper grows wild throughout Europe, which is probably why it is such a common flavouring. You'll find it in traditional alcoholic drinks like gin, brandy, schnapps, even Scandinavian beers. Goodness knows how many gin and tonics have been drunk around the world in the quest to dull the ache of arthritis. Unfortunately a nice stiff G & T is not what the natural doctor ordered. An infusion of dried juniper berries is what you'll need.

5 grams (1 teaspoon) crushed, dried, juniper berries
250 millilitres (1 cup) boiling water
1. Steep covered 20 minutes
2. Strain, discarding solids
3. Drink 1 cup in the morning and at night

Green Lipped Mussels

The Maori recommendation for arthritis sufferers is to eat some of New Zealand's world famous green lipped mussels, which the Maori call 'perna'. Guess what? Research on extracts from the green lipped mussels, looking at the claimed ability to reduce arthritis pain, has shown some encouraging results. So don't feel guilty when you order a half-dozen green lipped mussels. You're eating them for purely medicinal purposes. Well, that's your story and you're sticking to it.

If you think eating delicious green lipped mussels to soothe arthritis pain sounds a little fishy, wait until you hear about the salmon and sardine connection.

Fish oils

Fish produce omega-3 fatty acids and according to some recent research omega-3 fatty acids have anti-inflammatory properties. If you have arthritis, reducing inflammation is just what the doctor ordered. Whether or not eating fish like salmon and sardines (which produce more omega-3 fatty acids than other types of fish) is enough to make a difference in your arthritis is open to debate, but it couldn't hurt. Omega-3 fatty acids are also being studied for their ability to help reduce cholesterol and triglyceride levels in blood.

If you're wondering whether you have to break the bank to get these benefits, the answer is no! Canned salmon and sardines work just as well (as long as they aren't packed in oil).

Some folk remedies are really wild!

When arthritis pain is at its worst you'll try anything. You'll even be game to give this Polish folk remedy a go.

According to Polish folk healers, carrying a wild chestnut in your pocket will miraculously banish arthritis pain!

Go ahead, try it, what have you got to lose. Even if it doesn't work, it can't hurt!

Only for the bold!

Black ants

In Senegal, where they call their folk healers 'Marabout', they use black ants to treat arthritis. If you're game take a handful of live ants, mash them in 5 millilitres (1 teaspoon) water and apply the mashed ant paste to the sore joint. The ants release formic acid which heats the skin and is claimed to provide relief. By the way, it's the formic acid in an ant's bite (and the hairs on nettle leaves for that matter) that makes a bite itch and burn. So if you have a strong reaction to ant bites or exposure to nettles give this remedy a wide berth.

Asthma

Everyone is touched by asthma. According to recent estimates 25% of Australian children and about 10% of adults suffer from asthma. That adds up to about 1.4 million Australians! So it's not surprising that everyone seems to know someone with asthma.

Being an adult with asthma is bad enough, but many asthma sufferers are children. Asthma is the most common cause of admission to Australian paediatric hospitals. About 30 percent of all asthma admissions are for children under 5 years of age.

Because it is so common it's tempting to think that asthma is not a serious condition, but you couldn't be more wrong. Asthma is responsible for five deaths per week in Victoria alone, and almost 800 deaths nationally each year. Accurate, up-to-date information is the key to understanding and controlling asthma. Most people with asthma can lead a perfectly normal life, if their asthma is managed properly.

Let's go through four common beliefs about asthma, knowing the right answers should help you to breath easier.

Remedies with ⬤ are made using an infusion. Those with ⬤ are made using a decoction. Instructions for both methods are on pages 4 - 7. Variations and other procedures are contained in the text following the description of that remedy.

1. *"Exercise is bad for people with asthma."*

Wrong! Exercise is good for almost everyone, including people with asthma. While some people do experience an asthma attack after exercising this can often be controlled by taking asthma medication prior to exercising. And exercise improves your overall health as well as the health of your lungs.

2. *"Food allergies are a common cause of asthma."*

Wrong! While food allergies are common in children, food allergies are rarely the cause of asthma. Food allergies most often cause stomach and skin problems.

3. *"Nerves cause asthma."*

Wrong! Asthma is not a psychological problem, it is a physical condition. Asthma can cause stress and stress can aggravate any chronic illness including asthma. But stress or nerves cannot cause asthma. And while we're on the subject, if you are the parent of a child with asthma, your nerves won't cause their asthma either, so don't let people make you feel guilty.

4. *"You can always tell when your asthma is getting worse."*

Wrong! Sometimes dead wrong! Without a quantitative measurement of your lungs' performance it is very difficult for you or your doctor to judge the severity of an asthma attack. This is one reason people die from asthma. They believe that they 'know their condition'. Unfortunately they don't realise how severe their attack is until it is too late. That is why peak flow metres are so valuable. *(see box over page, Smile and say "Peak Flow Metre").*

Smile, and say "Peak Flow Metre"

Peak flow metres are putting smiles on the faces of many people with asthma, because these inexpensive, easy-to-use devices are revolutionising the way many sufferers monitor and control their asthma.

Peak Flow Meters measure your lungs' performance. You use the meter to collect information about your normal breathing patten over several days and nights. This gives you a base-line record of your breathing pattern.

Once you have this information you use it to monitor your breathing and spot decreased lung function, often the first sign that you are going to have an asthma attack. As well, peak flow metres can be used to record your response to different treatments and exercise programs.

Once you have worked with your doctor and developed a program to monitor and control your asthma you may want to discuss adding some of these folk remedies to your regular therapy.

Yerba Santa *(Eriodictyon glutinosum)*
also called Mountain Balm, Bearsweed

In Mexico, drinking a decoction of yerba santa has been a popular remedy for breathing difficulties for 200 years. In Spanish yerba santa means holy or saintly herb.

Cashew Nut *(Anacardium semecarpus)*

A thousand years ago the physicians and natives of Telinga, an Arabian province close to Babylon, used the inside of the cashew nut shell to make a decoction to treat breathing difficulties. They boiled the seeds in whey[1] for 20 to 30 minutes before having their patients drink the liquid.

Even if you happen to have a cashew tree in your backyard don't go trying to make this remedy. The delicious cashew nut has one very unsavoury characteristic and it's why you'll never see cashew nuts in-the-shell for sale. Between the shell and the nut is a bitter juice that burns the skin, like strong carbolic acid would. The irritating liquid is removed during the roasting process.

Lungwort *(Pulmonaria officinalis)*
also called Jerusalem Cowslip
Mallow *(Althaea officinalis)*
Lavender *(Lavandula angustifolia)*
and Coltsfoot [2] *(Tussilago farfara)*

Drinking a decoction of these herbs after a good upper-body massage is a traditional Romany treatment for breathing difficulties. Use 30 grams (1 ounce) of a mixture of equal parts lungwort and coltsfoot leaves, mallow and lavender blossoms to make the decoction. Drink sweetened with honey after a good upper body massage.

---

[1]   *watery liquid left after separation of curd from milk*
[2]   *restricted herb in Australia and New Zealand, due to presence of alkaloid pyrrolizidine,which has been shown to cause liver damage in rats*

Cocoa *(Theobroma cacao)*

America's nineteenth century herbalists recommended drinking a nice cup of hot cocoa to ease breathing difficulties.

20 grams (1 tablespoon) cocoa
Add to 250 millilitres (1 cup) boiling water
Drink, warm as required

Milkweed *(Asclepias syriaca)*

This milkweed infusion was used by Native American healers as a drink to ease breathing difficulties.

Elecampane *(Inula helenium)*
also called Scabwort, Horseheal

For over 2000 years India's traditional Ayurvedic physicians have recommended drinking a cold decoction of elecampane to ease breathing difficulties. To make a cold decoction do not simmer the herb, instead soak overnight (8 - 10 hours) in 3 cups cold water.

Ma Huang [1] *(Ephedra simca)*

Since 3000 BC, Chinese folk healers have recommended drinking a decoction of ma huang to treat breathing difficulties

Cypress oil *(Cupressur sempervirens)*

Use 1 - 2 drops of this essential oil diluted with 10 millilitres of good quality vegetable or nut oil to massage the chest (up to the neck) of asthma sufferers.

---

[1]   *this is a restricted herb in Australia and New Zealand, and can only be sold by registered practitioners in the US*

Coltsfoot [1] *(Tussilago farfara)*

This Chinese remedy for coughs, drinking an infusion of coltsfoot is sometimes recommended to people suffering from asthma induced coughs. This is one of the oldest recorded cough remedies.

Ginkgo *(Ginkgo bilobe) also known as Maidenhair Tree*

Traditional Chinese physicians use ginkgo to treat asthma. You'll need to buy ginkgo pills from a health food store or pharmacy, it takes a huge number of leaves to make a single dose.

Honeysuckle *(Lonicera periclymenum)*

This is an ancient herb that is still used in many remedies today. As you can imagine the infusion smells divine, you be the judge whether the drink smells better than it tastes.

A handful of honeysuckle flowers
250 millilitres (1 cup) boiling water

1. Steep covered 10 - 15 minutes
2. Strain, discarding solids
3. Drink 150 millilitres (5 ounces) several times a day

---

[1] restricted herb in Australia and New Zealand, due to presence of alkaloid pyrrolizidine, which has been shown to cause liver damage in rats

How things have changed!

The ancient Greek physician Dioscorides, along with the Romans, Pliny and Galen recommended coltsfoot as a treatment for breathing complaints. But their recommendations wouldn't receive much credence today. They dried coltsfoot leaves and flowers, ground them to a powder, and smoked it!

They weren't the last to prescribe smoking as a remedy for breathing complaints either. Medicine men of the Native American Cherokee tribe recommended smoking jimson weed *(Datura stramonium)* followed with a chaser - apple brandy on the rocks (poured over rock candy that is).

Add some music and party hats and you've got something that sounds more like a party left over from the sixties than an asthma treatment. Of course jimson weed is a toxic hallucinogen. So a fair few braves and squaws didn't have to worry about breathing difficulties, or anything else for that matter, after partaking in this remedy.

On a more serious note, we now know that inhaling particulate matter—in smoke, photochemical smog, in virtually any form—can damage your lungs. This is never more true than for people with asthma.

As Yul Brynner said in his famous public service announcement, made just before he died of lung cancer, "Don't smoke, whatever you do, just don't smoke".

Massage

Have the asthma sufferer sit—back to front—on a chair. Use both hands to massage their spine, working upwards. This relieves stress and any aches in the back and shoulders. Also, according to some folk healers, there is a small area in the hollow of the throat which, if massaged with the little finger in a gentle circular motion without pressure, can bring almost magical relief

Eucalyptus *(Eucalyptus globus)*

European settlers learned how to use eucalyptus from Australia's original inhabitants, the Australian Aborigine. Use the fragrant steam rising from an infusion of eucalyptus leaves to soothe breathing difficulties.

Clary Sage *(Salvia sclarea)*

Use this essential oil as part of massage therapy in asthma treatment, dilute 1 - 2 drops of clary sage oil with 10 millilitres of good quality vegetable or nut oil before using.

Frankincense *(Boswelia carterii)*

Olibanum or Olium Libanum, meaning oil of Lebanon, has been used by Egyptians for over 5000 years. You can use this essential oil in massage treatment for people with asthma. Dilute 1 - 2 drops of frankincense oil with 10 millilitres of good quality vegetable or nut oil.

Peach (Prunus persica)

Some Native American tribes use this syrup prepared from a decoction of peach kernels and bark to treat breathing difficulties.

1. Pound 170 grams (⅔ cup) peach bark
2. Split 170 grams (⅔ cup) peach kernels
3. Add 2 cups each apple cider vinegar and water to the peach bark and kernels
4. Steep covered for 5 days, store the container in a warm place, but out of the direct sunlight
5. Shake the container several times each day
6. After five days bring the liquid to the boil
7. Simmer gently for 30 minutes
8. Add 125 millilitres (½ cup) brandy or whisky as a preservative
9. Use 20 millilitres (1 tablespoon) every 3-4 hours
10. Store in a well-sealed bottle or jar discard any unused liquid after 1 month

Would madam like a little red wine with her asthma medication?

We don't recommend trying this remedy, the only fox livers to be found in Australia will come from a feral fox, and who knows what kind of diseases and parasites are lurking in its liver.

Nevertheless, folk healers in the former Soviet Union prescribe fox liver in red wine for asthma sufferers.

Athlete's Foot

What did one toe say to the other toe on the athlete's foot?

Don't look now, but there's a fungus among us.

It's not a very funny joke, but then if you've ever had athlete's foot you know that it's not a very funny experience. And if you think that being a card-carrying certified Norm or Norma protects you from athlete's foot, think again. All you need to do is let your feet swelter in sweaty socks, no exercise required.

Athlete's foot is caused by a fungus that finds the dark, damp environment of your sweaty feet ideal. So ideal that these interlopers set-up housekeeping and dig in. Their living quarters are the raw, itchy cracks in the skin between your toes. These squatters are not easy to evict either, so prevention is always preferable to cure.

To keep your feet a fungus-free zone make sure that you completely dry them after you bathe or shower. Change your socks after exercising or any time that they get sweaty, and always wear natural fibre socks (wool, cotton, or if you like silk). Natural fibres allow your feet to breathe and draw

Remedies with ☕ are made using an infusion. Those with ☕ are made using a decoction. Instructions for both methods are on pages 4 - 7. Variations and other procedures are contained in the text following the description of that remedy.

moisture away from your skin. While you are at it, give your toes room to wiggle and stay away from tight fitting shoes. Whenever possible go barefoot, let your toes breathe in the fresh, dry air.

Finally always wear thongs or shower slippers when you use communal showers at the gym or pool. After taking such good care of your feet you don't want a stray fungus hitchhiking home on your feet.

If you do get athlete's foot get down to business quickly with an antifungal cream. Once the open skin has started to mend, try one of these folk remedies to hasten the healing process and soothe the itchy, burning sensation of athlete's foot.

Natural Healing

Wash your feet and between your toes with dilute vinegar 3 or 4 times a day. Soak your feet for 10 to 20 minutes three times a day in a bucket with 20 grams (1 tablespoon) boric acid per litre (quart) of water.

Lavender *(Lavandula angustifolia)*,
Tea Tree *(Melaleuca alternifolia)*
and Sweet Marigold *(Tagetes lucida)*

Add 2 drops of each oil to a bucket of warm water. Soak your feet for ten minutes each night. Or use the same oils to make a compress to use on your feet, dilute 1 - 2 drops of the essential oils with 10 millilitres of good quality vegetable or nut oil. Place the compress on the affected areas. Hold the compress in place with a cotton bandage or a sock. Each morning add a drop of two of calendula oil to the same mixture and massage into affected areas.

Clove *(Syzgium aromaticum)*

Traditional Chinese physicians treat athlete's foot with a poultice made from dried cloves.

1. Make a paste from powdered cloves and a few drops of water
2. Apply directly to the affected skin
3. Leave the paste in place overnight or at least until your next shower

Salt *(sodium chloride)*
and Cornstarch *(also called cornflower)*

Greek healers recommend soaking your feet in salt water – about 20 grams (1 tablespoon) in a bucket of water. After soaking, dry your feet thoroughly then dust between your toes with cornstarch.

Lemon *(Citrus limon or C. medica, var. limonum)*
Salt *(sodium chloride)*
and Bleach *(sodium hypochlorite)*

Haitian folk healers are called 'Houngans' and they'll tell you to rub salt and lemon between your toes then soak them in dilute household bleach, 5 millilitres (1 teaspoon) bleach in a bucket of water.

Yoghurt

Yoghurt is a favourite, old-time folk remedy, massage natural yoghurt (the kind sold with 'live' culture) between your toes. Leave the yoghurt in place overnight and wash thoroughly in the morning. Dry thoroughly and dust between the toes with an anti-fungal powder.

Is it food or is it medicine?

You may be surprised to find many herbs and spices used medicinally by folk healers are familiar cooking ingredients. What's really surprising is that we see cooking and healing as separate activities. Separating the two functions is a relatively recent phenomenon (historically speaking, that is).

It wasn't until the seventeenth century that people started to think of healing and flavouring properties of herbs and spices as separate uses. Prior to this these functions were seen as one.

In the nineties we are learning that our ancestors' way of thinking about food and health may have been closer to the truth than our modern, separatist way of thinking. Their philosophy is being proven almost every day. From "you are what you eat" to medical research linking diet with health, and disease, it seems that we were fooling ourselves when we began to think that eating and healing didn't have anything to do with each other.

Thyme (Thymus vulgaris)
or Rosemary (Rosmarinus officinalis)

Add a few drops of either thyme or rosemary oil to 10 millilitres olive oil and rub vigorously into the affected areas.

Coconut (Cocos nucifera)

This old Ayurvedic remedy for athletes foot uses an empty coconut shell that has been dried in the sun for a week. You break the shell into tiny pieces (use a sledge hammer) and soak the shell fragments in 1 litre 1 (quart) vodka or Scotch. If you want to be very traditional use thurrah. Soak the shell fragments in the alcohol for 11 days, shaking the solution twice each day. Strain, then bottle. Soak your feet in a pan of the solution every day until your athlete's foot is long-gone.

Backache

If you think a couple of days laid up in bed with a bad back sounds like a pretty good lurk, you've never had a backache. When a backache strikes, it's no holiday. You can't ignore the pain. You can't get comfortable no matter what you do. It doesn't matter if it's a throbbing dull ache, a sharp stabbing pain, muscle cramping or a general debilitating soreness. A backache robs you of your mobility, good humour and ability to concentrate.

Though backaches are common they are rarely a symptom of serious disease. They can however be a sign that the discs that act as shock absorbers for your spine have been damaged.

Backaches are like in-laws, it is easier to get them than to get rid of them, so watch out for these common causes (of backaches not in-laws). Poor posture, obesity, improper lifting technique, and pregnancy. Yes, sad but true, one of the joys of pregnancy is the strain it can put on your back. Be especially conscious of what you do, and don't do, during your pregnancy.

Backaches are becoming more common, perhaps because of our increasingly sedentary western lifestyle, But take heart, the number and variety of folk remedies for backache pain

Remedies with ☕ are made using an infusion. Those with ☕ are made using a decoction. Instructions for both methods are on pages 4 - 7. Variations and other procedures are contained in the text following the description of that remedy.

shows that even our more vigorous ancestors also suffered from backaches.

Massage

A gentle massage is one of the best all around treatments for a backache. Massage works in a number of ways, it helps to relax muscles, soothe muscle fatigue and overcome postural problems. A massage can also help you recover from stress and tension, both of which can be the cause and the effect of a backache. That means that sometimes a massage works as a prevention and cure!

A massage is always improved by the use of an oil of some sort. When you choose a fragrant oil, with a reputation for specific healing properties, you add the benefit of aromatherapy.

Chamomile *(Chamaemelum nobile, Roman chamomile and C. recutita, German chamomile)*

You can make your own chamomile massage oil, but you need chamomile flowers, not leaves to make this cold oil infusion.

1. Collect enough chamomile flowers to loosely fill a small bottle
2. Add enough good quality olive oil to cover the flowers
3. Put a tight lid on the bottle
4. Allow the infusion to develop, setting the bottle in the sun for two weeks
5. Store in the refrigerator
6. Gently warm the oil before use (test a small amount of the oil on the inside of your forearm to make sure that it is not too warm).

Ask your grandmother about these two remedies, she probably still swears by them.

Cabbage *(Brassica oleracea)*

This old-timer's remedy, a plaster made from cabbage leaves, is still very popular with folk healers in the hills of the US state of Kentucky.

1. Choose several large green cabbage leaves, midribs removed
2. Iron leaves with a steam iron until they are soft (of course way back then, before steam irons were invented they had to improvise)
3. Rub a little olive oil on one side of the leaves
4. Place the cabbage leaves, oil side against your skin, on the affected area
5. Cover the leaves with a heavy towel
6. Leave it in place overnight

Mustard *(Brassica hirta)*
also known as Sinapsis alba

If you haven't heard about this one from your grandmother you probably have heard about it in old Western movies. In the 'olden days,' this was a common remedy. It was used for a variety of ailments, including backaches.

1. Grind mustard seeds with a little water
2. Coat the skin of the affected area with petroleum jelly (this prevents the mustard from blistering or irritating the skin)
3. Apply pulped mustard seeds, holding the plaster in place with gauze and adhesive tape. This plaster can be kept on for several hours, for best results leave on overnight

Hold the mustard!

Mustard plasters and poultices are examples of a type of treatment called a rubefacient.

Rubefacients stimulate blood flow and cause local reddening of the skin. Be careful with rubefacients, do not allow the skin to blister, or you will be left with the proverbial cure that turns out worse than the disease.

It's useful to know that the ingredient that gives mustard it's characteristic hotness, in flavour and heating ability, isn't found in the mustard plant or seeds. The heating ingredient is formed when certain constituents found only in the seeds of black and brown mustard come into contact with water. White mustard seeds contribute flavour but none of the characteristic hotness associated with mustard and none of the characteristic warming produced by mustard plasters and poultices.

Willow *(Salix alba)*
Birch *(Betula verrucosa)*
and Nettle *(Laminum album)*

Follow the lead of the Romany people, sometimes called Gypsies. They know that at the end of a day's travel the last thing you want is a backache.

Romany folk healers have used this double duty recipe for 500 years. They make an infusion to drink and save a little of the liquid for a compress to soothe the sore area. Make your infusion from equal parts willow, birch and blind nettle bark, if it is too bitter sweeten with a little honey. Save a little of the infusion to use in your compress. Rest while the compress is in place, 2 - 3 hours.

Elecampane *(Inula helenium, in China I. japonica is used)*

Galen, Greek physician and founder of experimental physiology, recommended drinking an infusion of elecampane for backaches. Make the infusion with fresh elecampane, use dried elecampane roots to make a soothing poultice to apply to the sore area.

Gentian *(Gentiana lutea)*

Native Americans used a decoction of gentian root to make a wash for sore backs.

Manipulative therapies

Physiotherapists often recommend hydrotherapy for backaches. Manipulative therapists, like chiropractors, osteopaths, reflexologists and practitioners of acupuncture and acupressure can sometime relieve the pain of backaches. Consult a registered practitioner for any of these treatments.

If you don't mind the stink give this old-fashioned remedy a go.

An embrocation is a strong smelling remedy, usually used like liniment. This one qualifies on both counts, if you can't pronounce embrocation, just hold your nose and say pong.

1. Shake 250 millilitres (1 cup) each vinegar and turpentine with 20 grams (1 tablespoon) powdered camphor and 1 egg

2. Gently rub the mixture into the sore area of the back

A strange remedy, just right for navel gazers

You'll have to have faith to try this remedy. Find a child who was born feet first (you'll have to ask their Mum since most children don't remember which direction they were pointing when they came into the world) and have them stand on your back. Remember to use a child (and a small one at that) otherwise your backache may get worse instead of better.

Bad Breath

If you think you have bad breath you probably do, and getting rid of it is more important than figuring out why you have it! So if you are reading this section because you are looking for a fast fix for foul breath go directly to the remedy section below and try one of the many folk remedies collected from around the world. Your friends, work mates and your family will thank you for it.

But read on even if you are just curious, looking for ways to avoid getting bad breath, want to suggest a remedy to a friend or like the Scouts, you want to 'be prepared'.

The computer industry has an expression, garbage in, garbage out. In the breath business the saying is odour in, odour out. If it smells when you put it in your mouth it will still smell long after you have finished the meal. This means that onions, garlic, highly spiced foods and strong cheeses are off limits whenever you are going to be working in close quarters. The only exception to this rule is when everyone eats the double peperoni pizza with goat's cheese, garlic, onions, anchovies and chilli peppers. Go ahead and enjoy. For some

Remedies with 🫖 are made using an infusion. Those with ☕ are made using a decoction. Instructions for both methods are on pages 4 - 7. Variations and other procedures are contained in the text following the description of that remedy.

reason, if everyone's breath smells it doesn't seem to worry anyone.

The effect of these strong flavoured foods on your breath will most likely last for 24 hours or so. So, check today's and tomorrow's appointments before you order garlic bread for lunch.

Alcohol also lingers on the breath. Why do you think the instrument used by police to check if you have been drinking is called a 'breathalyser'? Though in this case they are actually measuring the presence of alcohol molecules on your breath not how your breath smells.

The other big no-no if you are worried about your breath is smoking. No matter what you do if you smoke you are never going to have sweet smelling breath. At best your breath will resemble a toothpaste scented ashtray.

If your bad breath hangs around (like a bad smell)

Poor dental health and some diseases and medications can also cause foul smelling breath.

If you have bad breath that wont budge no matter what you eat (or don't eat) see your dentist or your general practitioner, there may be another cause.

Seeds can stop seedy breath. In the same way that some foods can spoil your breath, sweet smelling seeds and herbs can counteract the effect of that garlic, onion and limburger cheese sandwich you ate for lunch. The flavour of many popular toothpastes comes from the plants, herbs, spices and seeds commonly used in folk remedies for bad breath, including spearmint, peppermint, anise, caraway and eucalyptus.

Anise, fenugreek, cloves, dill, cardamom, fennel and caraway seeds are all used in folk remedies for bad breath. Most of these natural breath fresheners do double duty and settle the upset tummy that can sometime accompany over indulging in rich, spicy foods. Before toothbrushes were invented most people used these naturally fragrant plants, seeds etc to sweeten their breath.

The pleasant flavour and scent of many varieties of anise has made the anise seeds a favourite folk remedy for bad breath and indigestion. Pop some anise seeds into an attractive container and you'll have a rapid remedy on hand when ever bad breath strikes.

Anise (Pimpinella anisum)

Gaius Pliny, the great Roman naturalist recommended chewing fresh anise seeds as a breath freshener in 60 AD.

Chinese Star Anise (Illicium verum)

Ancient Chinese physicians also recommended chewing fresh anise seeds as a breath freshener. In today's China anise is still used as an after-dinner mouth freshener.

Japanese Star Anise (Illicium antsatum)

This variety of anise has been used in India for over a thousand years and remains popular today as both an ingredient in curries and a remedy for bad breath. After meal a small amount of star anise is chewed to sweeten the breath.

Fenugreek [1] *(Trigonella foenum- graecum)*

Dried, ground fenugreek seeds are used in many curry powders and in Pakistan, where chewing betelnut is a common pastime, they chew fenugreek seed to get rid of the flavour of betel nut.

Clove *(Syzgium aromaticum)*

If you've ever sat in a confined space with someone and their bad breath, you may have decided that bad breath should be against the law. Well in China, during the Han Dynasty—207 BC to 220 AD—bad breath was against the law! Whenever anyone came to the emperor with their grievances they were required by law to hold cloves in their mouth to avoid bad breath.

Dill *(Anethum graveolens)*

Chewing tiny dill seeds is a popular Hungarian folk remedy for bad breath. But don't use the dill seeds from a jar of dill cucumbers! The garlic used in these popular pickles will negate the breath freshening ability of dill seeds many times over.

Cardamom *(Elettaria cardamomum)*

In Italy folk healers recommend chewing cardamom seeds and going on a special diet, which includes meat, fish, milk, whole grains, vegetables, alfalfa, parsley, tea and black coffee. Avoid garlic, onions, beer and bourbon.

---

[1]   *avoid during pregnancy*

Coffee *(Coffea arabica, C. liberica, C. robusta)*
and Cardamom *(Elettaria cardamomum)*

Try a cup of black coffee made from freshly ground beans to which you have added a couple of cardamom seeds. Drunk first thing in the morning it's a pleasant change from your usual cappuccino and the cardamom freshens your breath.

Fennel [1] *(Foeniculum officinale)*

Fennel seeds are popular for flavouring sweet and savoury foods in many Mediterranean countries. Fennel's flavour is similar to both anise and dill. And like anise and dill, fennel seeds can be chewed to freshen your breath and soothe an upset stomach.

Gargles

Gargles are another way to freshen your breath and these folk remedies make a nice alternative to commercial products.

Honey and oil of cloves
or honey and lemon

Either combination makes a refreshing gargle that also soothes the throat.

1. Mix 5 millilitres (1 teaspoon) honey with a few drops of clove oil or 150 millilitres (1/2 cup) lemon juice
2. Use either gargle morning and night

---

[1]   *avoid during pregnancy*

Coriander, orange peel, parsley, peppermint and a chopped date

All these ingredients go into this old Chinese remedy for bad breath.

70 grams (3 1/2 tablespoons) coriander seeds

2 litres (2 quarts) water

1. Bring to the boil
2. Simmer 90 minutes, or until water is reduced by one-half
3. Add 10 grams (2 teaspoons) finely grated orange peel and 1 pitted date, finely chopped
4. Simmer an additional 15 minutes
5. Remove from heat
6. Add 5 grams (1 teaspoon) dried coriander leaf, some finely chopped fresh parsley and a drop or two of peppermint oil
7. Steep 30 minutes, stirring occasionally
8. Strain through a fine sieve
9. Store in a jar or bottle with a tight fitting lid
10. Gargle and rinse your mouth with 150 millilitres (1/2 cup) of the liquid twice a day, morning and night.

Sage [1] *(Salvia officinalis)*

On the Adriatic coast they use sage to flavour strong meats and gargle with an infusion of sage to sweeten the breath.

Carrot *(Daucus carota)*

Earlier this century the French herbalist Maurice Messegne advised his patients to use carrot tops to sweeten their breath.

---

[1]   *avoid therapeutic doses in pregnancy, small amounts used in cooking are quite safe.*

According to Monsieur Messegne smart homemakers didn't throw away their carrot tops, they made a decoction of the tops and used it as a mouth wash.

The tops from one bunch of carrots

750 millilitres (3 cups) water

1. Bring to the boil
2. Simmer 20 minutes then let stand for an additional 20 minutes
3. Strain, discarding solids
4. Bottle the liquid and use, morning and night as a mouthwash or gargle
5. Discard unused portion after one week

Chewing fresh greens can also help freshen your breath. The chlorophyll that makes the leaves green is a natural breath freshener. Some of these greens are also naturally fragrant, which adds to their ability to counteract bad breath.

Mint *(Peppermint[1], Mentha piperita, or Spearmint[2] Mentha spicata)*

Chewing the leaves of either of these mints will disguise off odours on your breath and settle your tummy. A few drops of either oil added to a glass of water is a favourite mouthwash. What's more it's simple and inexpensive to make fresh each time you use it.

Parsley *(Petroselinum crispum)*

If you keep your eyes open you might find the antidote for bodgie breath sharing the plate with the odour producing

---

[1]   *avoid during pregnancy and if breast feeding, do not give in any form to very young babies,*

[2]   *avoid during pregnancy and if breast feeding, do not give in any form to very young babies,*

food. Parsley is used by the farmers in Belgium, Hungary and Germany, and smart diners everywhere, to counteract the food that spoils their breath. What could be simpler, just eat the garnish when you finish your meal.

Liquorice *(Glycyrrhiza glabra)*

In the Middle East a glass of liquorice water is a night-time breath sweetener. Dissolve a small piece of liquorice—5 grams (1 teaspoon) in 250 millilitres (1 cup) boiling water should do the trick. Sip this liquorice water at night before going to sleep. Buy real liquorice though. Commercial lollies some-times use artificial flavourings and add sugar.

I've tasted this before

While many people describe anise and fennel as tasting like liquorice, liquorice comes from another plant en-tirely.

True liquorice lollies are made from the root of *Glycyrrhiza glabra*. The root is pounded to extract the juice, which solidifies into the black, glossy liquorice stick sold as lollies around the world.

Liquorice is naturally sweet, because of glycyrrhizin, the main constituent of liquorice. Glycyrrhizin is 50 times sweeter than sucrose. Liquorice was originally sold as a natural sweet, but it is difficult to find it in this form today, except in health food stores and from some herbalists.

Bed-Wetting

Your little one is really growing up. You thought you'd never see the day, but finally he or she proudly proclaims "Cots and nappies are for babies", and you think to yourself, "Finally, parenthood is going to be fun".

Then one morning you're greeted with a little surprise. The bed is wet, your big boy or girl is embarrassed. If this happens often enough you'll feel like you are at your witts end. Nappies are bad enough, but washing sheets and airing out a mattress really puts a damper on your day.

Whatever you do, don't panic. That will only make the situation worse. No matter how bad it seems today, bed-wetting is something that time will correct. Put a plastic sheet under the regular sheets to keep the mattress dry. Buy an extra set (or two) of sheets. And add one of these folk remedies to your daily routine, they may help you get a good start.

Chinese Herbal Remedies

You buy these Chinese herbal remedies from a herbalist or a practitioner of traditional Chinese medicine. They will give you instructions for making your infusion or decoction. Be

---

Remedies with *are made using an infusion. Those with* *are made using a decoction. Instructions for both methods are on pages 4 - 7. Variations and other procedures are contained in the text following the description of that remedy.*

warned though, Chinese herbal preparations are usually much stronger than western style infusions and decoctions. So you may have a battle on your hands to try and get junior to drink the stuff.

Xiao Jian Zhong Tang
Symptoms
Fatigue
Frequent urination
Lack of appetite
Pale, white coated tongue
Cold hands and feet
Dry mouth and throat

Zhu Ye Shi Gao Tang
Symptoms
Thirst
Sweating
Red tongue
Rapid pulse
Hot, flushed skin

**Xiao Chai Hutang
and Gui Zhi Tang**
Symptoms
Frequent colds
Frequent upset stomach,
Indigestion
Low energy

Jin Gui Shen Qi Wan
Symptoms
Over weight
Fatigue
Frequent constipation
Sleepy

Ge Gen Tang
Symptoms
Stiff muscles in neck, shoulders, back
Poor appetite
Diarrhoea or loose stools
Frequent colds

Agrimony *(Agrimonia eupatoria, A. pilosa*
Chinese variety, called xian he cao)

In England they treat bed-wetting with a drink of infused agrimony.

Massage

Some folk healers recommend a gentle massage (using warm olive oil) just before bed time can end bed-wetting problems. Concentrate your massage on the lower back and abdomen.

Exercise

Other folk healers believe that light exercise before bedtime can relieve pressure on the bladder and minimise bed-wetting.

Hot milk, honey and cinnamon

While others say a drink of hot milk with a little honey and cinnamon is a simple and soothing treatment for bed-wetting.

Nettle [1] *(Urtrica dioica)*
and Rye *(Secale cereale)*

If you don't want to tempt your luck with a liquid remedy before bedtime try this one, nettle seed cakes.

15 grams (1/2 oz) nettle seeds,

50 grams (2 oz) rye flour

A little honey

1. Pound the mixture into a paste

2. Form the paste into about 30 small flat cakes (2 grams each)

3. Bake low heat 175°C (250°F) about 1 our or until firm.
   Eat one every evening until the problem stops.

---

[1]   stinging comes from formic acid and histamine which are found in the fine hairlike needles of the leaves.

Belching

Holding the 12 years and under record for continuous belching may have made you the hit of the party in primary school. Unfortunately that record is not going to win you a promotion or get you asked back to dinner. It also won't do you any good to explain to your boss or new flame that in many cultures belching is an acceptable sign that you appreciated a good meal, unless they happen to be from one of those cultures. All is not lost, one of these folk remedies may help you clear the air.

Wood Betony *(Stachys officinalis)*

The English physician and herbalist Nicholas Culpeper recommended drinking an infusion of wood betony to remedy sour belching, it probably works on sweet belching too, if their is any such thing. 🫖

Olive Oil

If you're the type who grits your teeth and rips the sticking plaster off in one go, try drinking 250 millilitres (1 cup) equal

---

Remedies with 🫖 are made using an infusion. Those with ☕ are made using a decoction. Instructions for both methods are on pages 4 - 7. Variations and other procedures are contained in the text following the description of that remedy.

parts cold-pressed, extra virgin olive oil and the citrus juice of your choice.

If you have to steel yourself to removing a sticking plaster bit by bit, and the thought of all that oil in one gulp sounds more like a folk torture than a folk remedy, try taking your medicine (equal parts oil and the citrus juice of your choice) in eight 30 millilitres (1 ounce) portions every 15 minutes.

If you don't like citrus juice you can take the olive oil on its own, sadly the juice on its own won't help your belching problem.

Oregon Grape Root *(Berberis aquifolium)*

Or try drinking an infusion of oregon grape root.

Yellow Dock *(Rumex crispus)*

Or maybe drinking an infusion of yellow dock is more to your liking.

Bites

You'd think being ugly, repulsive creatures would be enough, but no, bugs bite too. Some bugs' bites will only bug you. But others can be dangerous, even deadly.

Australia has a reputation for unusual creatures many of them dangerous. In fact, Australia has more dangerous creatures than any other continent. There are more of them and they are more dangerous than almost any where else in the world. Many of these dangerous Australians are insects, insects that bite. Creepy, crawly spiders, fleas, ticks, and mosquitos are lying in wait for the unaware. If that doesn't convince you, we can go on to discuss Australia's infamous snakes, but you get the picture now don't you.

Spiders

Know how to recognise Trap Door, Red Back, Funnel Web and Wolf spiders. Avoid them if you can, they can be deadly. While you're at it, learn how to recognise White Tail spiders too, they aren't deadly but their bites can pack a wallop just the same (see box below). If you are unlucky enough to be bitten by any

---

Remedies with 🫖 *are made using an infusion. Those with* 🍲 *are made using a decoction. Instructions for both methods are on pages 4 -7. Variations and other procedures are contained in the text following the description of that remedy.*

---

of these spiders, try to stay calm and capture the villain. This sounds like a joke but it really isn't. Take the spider to the doctor with you, it will help your doctor decide on the best course of treatment.

Going to pieces over a spider bite.

If deadly spider bites aren't enough to convince you to stay clear of these creatures and you need more convincing, how do you feel about decomposing skin?

Recently scientists identified the White Tailed spider as the culprit responsible for a mysterious, painful, cata-strophic decomposing skin condition. Many people who have been bitten by these spiders are still, years later, suffering continual, irreversible putrefaction and decay through all layers of the skin.

The decomposition can start slowly, but often starts almost immediately after the bite. If that isn't enough, you can also enjoy a bit of vomiting and diarrhoea as you watch your self dissolve before your very eyes.

One woman reported that within minutes of being bitten she felt an agonising burning pain and a piece of skin the size of a fifty-cent coin washed away under a stream of water leaving a deep hole in the under-layers of her flesh.

Now at least we know which spider is responsible for this formerly mysterious condition and researchers can start studying how the spider's bite cause such destruc-tion.

Ticks, fleas and mites

These promiscuous little devils like to travel. They think nothing of jumping from one vehicle to another. Unfortunately their preferred mode of transport is a warm blooded creature, and yes, you'll do nicely, thank you.

Some people mistakenly think that fleas are nothing more than a nuisance. When you become half-hearted in your attempts to control fleas on your pets you're not only being unfair to your pet. Fido and Fluffy don't enjoy itching any more than you do, that's why they scratch. You're also putting Fido, Fluffy and the assorted humans in your home at risk. Some insect born diseases only infect dogs and cats. Some infect other warm blooded animals like cows and sheep and people.

Tick paralysis, Q Fever, Lyme Disease, Scrub Typhus and Murine Typhus are some of the tick, flea and mite born diseases that infect humans. None of these diseases is fun to have and some are debilitating, even deadly.

Ticks also pose a problem all their own, they are tricky to remove. Do it wrong and a tick will leave you a little something for you to remember it by, its head! A tick's head embedded in your skin is disgusting and it's a perfect place for an infection to brew. Still not convinced? Some people develop severe, life threatening, allergic reactions to tick bites.

Wear socks, long sleeves and trousers when you're bushwalking. Learn the proper procedure for removing a tick. Always check for ticks when returning from a bushwalk or camping trip. And always have someone else check your scalp, the back of your neck and any other difficult to see parts of you body that have been exposed to the environment. You want to make sure you don't bring a stowaway home with you.

Bees and wasps

Even people who only suffer a temporary, unpleasant stinging sensation from a bee or wasp sting can be frightened of bees and wasps. People who are allergic to bee and wasp stings face a more serious situation. For them, a sting can be a real killer.

Everyone needs to be wary of large numbers of bees and wasps. A swarm can sting you hundreds, even thousands of times in a few minutes, injecting enough venom to overload your system and literally irritate you to death. European wasps are especially aggressive and don't need any excuse to attack. Stay well clear of them. Always call a professional if you spot a hive near your house. You're taking your life in your hands if you decide to get rid of it yourself.

Mosquitos

Last but not least there's Australia's national insect, the good old Aussie Mossie. The Aussie Mossie is another insect that we ignore at our peril. We forget that mosquitos carry disease (see box over page). Avoid mosquito bites if you can.

Aussie Mossies –
they're worse than you think

Mossie bites mean more than a little itch. Encephalitis, Dengue Haemorrhagic Fever and Ross River Fever are three serious, mosquito-born, diseases that worry Australian epidemiologists.

It wasn't that long ago, 1981 to be exact, that Australia was officially declared to have eradicated malaria. Prior to that malaria was endemic in all parts of northern Australia above an arc drawn between Townsville in the east, and Broome in the west. Just off our northern coast (in Timor, the Torres Strait and Solomon Islands, Vanuatu and Irian Jaya) malaria is still endemic.

And there's more. Some people develop a violent allergic reaction to mossies bites, like those some people experience from bee and wasp stings.

Get tough with Aussie mossies. Make sure they don't feel welcome in your garden. Don't let stagnant water accumulate. Dry or empty containers that fill with water. This will help to keep the mossie population in check.

These folk remedies concentrate on relieving the pain, burn or sting of a bite. A few popular practices for keeping the interlopers away are also included.

Bracken *(Pteridium esculentum)*

This is a double duty plant that's use can be traced back at least to the Middle Ages. Rub the fronds on an insect bite to minimise the itch, and stuff your pillow and mattress with the fronds to repel insects.

Never use fern pillows or mattresses for infants though, soft bedding has been implicated in Sudden Infant Death Syndrome (Cot Death).

Pot Marigold *(Calendula officinalis)*

For thousands of years Indian physicians have used a tincture of calendula oil to relieve the pain and itching of insect bites. You can buy the tincture ready-made or make your own with 1 drop of calendula oil to 10 drops of alcohol. Apply the tincture directly to the bite.

Lavender *(Lavandula angustifolia)*

This remedy, from the Egyptians this time, also uses an essential oil. The Egyptians and some modern day folk healers recommend rubbing a drop of lavender oil into a bite to stop the itch. It's one of the few cases where you can use an essential oil undiluted, but be careful if you do and stop immediately if your skin becomes irritated.

Purple Coneflower *(Echinacea augustifolia)*

Native American tribes from the Plains area of what is now the USA made a decoction of purple coneflower roots and used the softened roots as a poultice to soothe the pain and itch of insect bites. Drain and mash the softened root into a paste, apply to the bite.

If you have a pet you know how hard it is to get rid of fleas. It was even worse for our ancestors.

Salt and Vinegar

Not chips, but a paste made of equal parts salt and vinegar applied directly to the bite. This is one of those mouldy-oldies that many people have heard of but no-one knows where it originated.

Garlic [1] *(Allium sativum)*

If folk healers had to pick just one medicinal plant to use garlic would probably be their choice. It's one of the oldest and most commonly used medicinal plants, and you'll find it used in almost every culture. Cut a clove of garlic and rub the cut side on a bite to ease the pain and help prevent infection and unwanted attention at the supermarket.

Bicarbonate of Soda and Honey

Some healers recommend applying a paste of equal parts honey and baking soda to bites.

Lemon *(Citrus limon or C. medica, var. limonum)*

Others recommend applying a little lemon juice or lemon rind to the bite.

Essential oils

The essential oils of **lavender** *(Lavandula spica)*, **eucalyptus** *(Eucalyptus globus)*, **chamomile** *(Chamaemelum nobile,*

---

[1]   avoid during pregnancy and if breast feeding

Roman, *or C. recutita,* German), or **ylang-ylang** *(Cananga odorata* also called *Canangium odoratum)*—all have a reputation for keeping the little creeps away <u>and</u> soothing the bites received from those that don't get the message.

Dilute 1 - 2 drops of the essential oil with 10 drops of alcohol and rub into exposed skin for an insect repellent. Rub the same mixture into any bites you may get.

Thyme *(Thymus vulgaris)*

For centuries the Romany people (who are sometimes called Gypsies) have treated insect bites with this cold infusion of thyme, apple vinegar and garlic cloves. You'll have to think ahead, it takes four weeks to make.

A handful of thyme

600 millilitres (1 pint) apple vinegar

1. Combine in a clear bottle
2. Tightly seal the bottle and set in a warm spot, out of direct sunlight
3. Shake the bottle each morning and evening
4. After 2 weeks add 7 crushed garlic cloves
5. After 2 more weeks strain the mixture into a clean bottle with a tight fitting lid
6. Apply the liquid to the bites several times a day
7. Discard unused portion after 1 week

Onion *(Allium cepa)*

French folk healers recommend putting a slice of peeled onion against an insect sting or bite and leaving the onion in place for 3 hours. If there's a stinger involved, the onion is supposed to remove that too.

Lemon *(Citrus limon or C. medica, var. limonum)*

Another French folk remedy for insect bites. This time it's the pulp left after squeezing the juice from a lemon that you apply to the bite.

Tulip *(Tulipa gesneriana)*

This old Chinese remedy uses a crushed tulip bulb to soothe an insect bite. Apply the crushed bulb directly to the bite.

Papaya *(Carica papaya)*

Hawaiian healers place papaya leaves on an insect sting.

Sesame *(Sesamum indica or S. orientale)*

This eighth century Chinese treatment for insect bites uses sesame seeds. It's supposed to be especially effective against painful spider and centipede bites.

1. Coarsely grind 60 - 90 grams (2 - 3 tablespoons) sesame seeds
2. Add enough water to make a paste
3. Apply the paste to the bite
4. Leave in place until any swelling has gone down

Clary Sage *(Salvia sclarea)*

Rub a little clary sage oil, diluted with coconut oil into a scorpion sting, that's the traditional Jamaican way to soothe the pain.

Oregon Grape Root (Berberis aquifolium)

Native Americans of the Navajo tribe drank a decoction of oregon grape root to counteract the effects of scorpion stings. They also saved the softened root from the decoction and applied it, mashed as a poultice, to the sting.

Sand and Gin

Lifeguards in Mexico rub jellyfish stings with dry sand and apply gin to the stings.

Don't get stung by this foolish remedy!
Tobacco (Nicotiana tabacum)

In the past, Turkish and Portuguese healers have used wet tobacco to soothe stings but in the present, this foolish remedy is only suitable for very foolish people. You see tobacco isn't just a health hazard when smoked, it's deadly no matter how you use it. Nicotine is one of the most toxic pesticides known.

People who chew tobacco or use snuff may not have the same high incidence of smoking related diseases—like lung cancer and emphysema—as smokers do. But don't think that makes them lucky. They've just traded lung cancer and emphysema for cancer of the throat, lip and tongue.

Maybe one dose of this very foolish folk remedy wouldn't do that much harm, but why take the chance.

Most people would rather avoid a bite than soothe one, so try one of these folk recipes, they are supposed to send the insects packing before they get the chance to bite.

Epsom Salts

Make a wash using 30 grams (1 ounce) Epsom Salts in 1.5 litres (1 ½ quarts) water. Use it to wash all exposed skin before going outside.

Garlic *(Allium sativum)*

Put crushed garlic cloves or cut onions on your open window-sill, to keep mossies away (this is supposed to keep vampires away too).

or

Tansy *(Tanacetum vulgare),*
Feverfew *(Tanacetum parthenium)*
Eucalyptus *(Eucalyptus globus)*
Lemon Balm *(Melissa officinalis)*
also known as Sweet Balm and Bee Herb
or Elder *(Sambucus nigra)*

When you hang bouquets of tansy, feverfew, eucalyptus, lemon balm or elder in your windows and doorways you not only give your house a cosy, country look you also may side-track winged pests.

Snake Bites

There's no denying it, snakes can be dangerous to be around and if you are afraid of snakes it really isn't much comfort to know that if you don't bother them they won't bother you. But it's true nevertheless.

Give snakes a wide berth—that's the best way to deal with snakes. That way you won't have to treat a snake bite. There's probably more misinformation about treating a snake bite than almost any other first-aid emergency. The truth is first-aid recommendations for snake bite have changed dramatically in the past several years and if you are a bushwalker or live in the bush or any other area in which snakes are likely to be found, the only responsible thing for you to do is to take a first-aid course.

Just in case you think you already know it all, were you taught to cut and wash the bite, maybe to use a tourniquet? Wrong . . . Wrong . . . Wrong . . .!

In brief you should try to identify the snake. Capture it if you can without risking getting bitten yourself. Keep the person still and apply a firm (not tight!) elastic bandage along the length of the limb and use a splint to hold the limb immobile if you can. And get the person who has been bitten to the hospital, preferably by ambulance, as soon as possible.

Whatever you do, don't try any of these folk remedies for snake bite, they come from European folk traditions, and Australian snakes are bigger and badder than almost any others in the world. Australian Aboriginal traditions are more sensible, you see the Aborigines have always known which snakes are harmless and which are deadly. They stayed clear of the deadly kind or handled them very carefully. They knew that a person bitten by one of the poisonous snakes had little hope of surviving, no matter what the local healer did.

For interest and amusement only - do not use to treat snake bite of any sort!

Agrimony *(Agrimonia eupatoria, also known as Church Steeples)*

Early Saxons used an infusion of agrimony leaves and flowers. They drank the liquid and used the softened solids as a poultice. Australian snakes would just laugh at such treatment.

Centaury *(Centaurium erythraea) also known as Feverwort, European or Common Centaury*

The Saxon herbalists also believed that this plant could heal bites from the hydra a mythical water-serpent.

Lovage *(Levisticum officinale)*

The Romans brought this plant, a regular in monastery gardens, to Northern Europe. They used it as a vegetable and believed it useful to treat poisonous snake bites. It's a good thing they liked to eat it, since on a scale of 1-10 lovage's ability to heal a poisonous snake bite is zero.

Rosemary *(Rosmarinus officinalis)*

In ancient Greece, Rome, Spain and Arabia rosemary was believed to be a charm to guard against bites of all sorts, including snakebite. A bag of rosemary around your neck was supposed to give you magical protection.

Virginian Snakeroot *(Aristolachia serpentaria)*

An infusion of Virginian snakeroot was just one of the ways Native American healers tried to save people who had been bitten by a rattlesnake or other poisonous snake. The plant is a vine that resembles a snake, which is probably why it came to have a reputation as a snake bite remedy. An infusion of garden hose would probably be equally effective, and for the same reasons.

Black-Eye

A black-eye is just a bruise that happens to surround your eye. The major difference between a black-eye and any other bruise is that a black-eye is impossible to hide, unless you are a pop star and can get away with sun-glasses 24 hours a day. Don't worry about thinking up a plausible story to explain how you got your shiner. No matter what you say, no one will believe you.

What do vegetarians put on a black-eye? Ice, just like anyone else with any sense. The old fighter's trick of using a steak is a waste of a good steak. The only thing the meat ever did was cool the injured area, slowing the seepage of blood from damaged vessels and capillaries. It's this leaking blood that causes the technicolour display.

So use an icepack and save the steak for dinner. Don't forget to try some of these folk remedies to chase the blues (and yellows and greens) away.

Remedies with ☕ are made using an infusion. Those with 🍲 are made using a decoction. Instructions for both methods are on pages 4 - 7. Variations and other procedures are contained in the text following the description of that remedy.

Comfrey [1] *(Symphytum officinale) also called Knitbone*

Drinking an infusion of comfrey is an old American folk remedy for black-eyes. Save some of the liquid and apply to the black eye with a clean cotton towel or cotton wool.

Potato *(Solanum tuberosum)*

For centuries the Romany people (sometimes called Gypsies) have used a slice of potato on black-eyes. Slice a potato and rest, eyes closed with the potato slice on your black-eye.

Pot Marigold *(Calendula officinalis)*

Or make a decoction of dried marigold petals and use them in a poultice for your shiner. Mash the decocted petals and place them place between two layers of gauze. While the petals are still warm lie down, eyes closed and place the petal poultice on your black-eye.

The worst thing you have to worry about is explaining how you got your shiner unless . . .

You are dizzy, light headed, seeing double, nauseous or uncontrollably sleepy. Or if you have a headache that is out of proportion to the pain of the actual knock that gave you the shiner.

If you have any of these symptoms you may have been concussed in the process of getting that black eye, and you should see your doctor immediately.

---

[1] restricted her in Australia and New Zealand due to presence of alkaloid, shown to cause liver damage in rats

Bladder Infection

When you have a bladder infection (sometimes called cystitis, a urinary tract infection or UTI) you feel like you are caught in a never ending, painful circle. You have a constant, urgent need to urinate. Then, when you actually do, you are overcome with a painful, burning sensation. Then the cycle starts all over again.

If you're female, no one would blame you for thinking that bladder infections are a sexist plot, because men are rarely troubled with bladder infections, while most women will have at least one in their life. Some unlucky women will be plagued with recurrent infections,—the most unlucky suffering several infections each year. What causes bladder infections? Let's see, bacteria, childbirth, some sorts of physical activity—yes including sex, that rumour is true—and even according to some research, drinking excessively chlorinated water.

If you are plagued with recurrent attacks of cystitis you may want to try some of these preventative strategies. Wear only natural fabric underwear, avoid high acid or acid forming foods (like refined sugars and white flour, alcohol, tea and

---

Remedies with ☕ *are made using an infusion. Those with* ☕ *are made using a decoction. Instructions for both methods are on pages 4 - 7. Variations and other procedures are contained in the text following the description of that remedy.*

coffee and dairy products) and drink at least two litres (2 quarts) of water every day.

Don't fool around with a suspected bladder infection. See your doctor, and then try one of these folk remedies as a complement to any conventional medication he or she may give you.

Biochemic Tissue Salts

Try Nat Sulph *(sodium sulphate)* when it is difficult to retain urine, Calc Phos *(calcium phosphate)* for frequent urination and Mag Phos *(magnesium phosphate)* when the need to urinate is constant when waking or standing.

Chamomile *(Chamaemelum nobile,*
Roman chamomile, or C. recutita, German chamomile)

India's ancient traditional physicians recommend drinking an infusion of chamomile when you have a bladder infection.

Buchu *(Barosma betulina)*

Traditional Chinese medical practitioners recommend drinking an infusion of buchu if you are suffering from a bladder infection.

Kanono *(Coprosma australis)*

The Maori drank an infusion of kanono leaves or fresh young shoots to reduce the pain of urinary complaints, like kidney stones, bladder stoppages etc.

Blisters

Friction is the enemy of tender skin. When your skin goes one-on-one with a hard or rough object, like a new pair of shoes or the handle of your new tennis racket, your skin comes out the loser. You'll have a blister as a reminder of your foolishness.

The best way to treat a blister is leave it alone. The blister is the best protective cushion and covering you can give to the raw flesh beneath it. Keep it clean and dry and it will heal quickly. If you must burst the blister—if it's in a spot that will be under constant pressure, like the sole of your foot—use a sterile (not just clean, sterile) needle to make a small hole in the blister. Let the fluid drain then leave the skin over the raw flesh, this is the second best way to treat a blister quickly.

Don't use any of the following remedies for a blister caused by a burn. Burn blisters can be quite serious and require extra care.

Cabbage *(Brassica oleracea)*

Use grandma's favourite, cool cabbage leaves, to make this soothing poultice. Simmer cabbage leaves in milk for five

---

Remedies with 🫖 *are made using an infusion. Those with* 🍵 *are made using a decoction. Instructions for both methods are on pages 4 - 7. Variations and other procedures are contained in the text following the description of that remedy.*

minutes on low heat - do not boil. Allow the leaves to cool then apply to the blistered skin. Leave in place for ten minutes, repeat as required

Walnut (Juglans regia or J. cinerea)

Or try another of grandma's old stand-bys, an infusion of walnut leaves for this soothing compress.

5 grams (1 teaspoon) dried walnut leaves
250 millilitres (1 cup) boiling water
1. Steep, covered for 15 minutes
2. Strain, discarding solids
3. Apply to blister with a soft cotton cloth

Camphor (Cinnamomum camphora)

Persian healers use camphorated oil on blisters. Dilute 1 - 2 drops camphorated oil with 10 millilitres of good quality vegetable or nut oil and apply to the blister.

Garlic (Allium sativum)

This remedy uses the antiseptic properties of garlic to help the blister heal quickly. Apply a few drops of commercial garlic oil directly to the blister.

Cornflour and Honey

A paste made of equal parts cornflour and honey applied to a burst blister is supposed to help guard against infection.

Lavender *(Lavandula angustifolia)*
and *Myrrh* *(Commiphora molmol)*

Try lavender and myrrh oil on blisters. These oils are supposed to cool, ease pain and help a blister to dry. Dilute the essential oils with 10 millilitres of good quality vegetable or nut oil. Put a little of the mixture onto a piece of gauze and apply directly to the blister.

Biochemic Tissue Salts

To relieve blister pain try four tablets of Nat Mur (sodium chloride), half-hourly until the pain has gone.

Blood Nose

A blood nose is usually more dramatic than it is dangerous, and while a blood nose is common enough during childhood, as adults we usually have forgotten just how dramatic a little bright red blood flowing down your face and onto your white shirt can be. Anything from a bump on the bridge of your nose, to dry nasal membranes during winter, to high blood pressure can cause a blood nose.

If you are tempted to scream, "Who cares how I got it, how do I get rid of it?' remember your first-aid training, and the first rule of first-aid. . . Don't Panic!

Some people swear by an ice pack against the bridge of the nose. Others go for firm pressure against the nostrils at the bridge of the nose, while others plug their nostrils with a wad of clean, wet cotton wool or gauze. These simple, tried and true remedies will stop bleeding from 9 out of 10 noses with 10 - 15 minutes.

If you're over 60 years old and suffer from a cardiovascular disease—like high blood pressure—and your nose doesn't stop bleeding in 10 minutes, see your doctor. No matter what your age or your state of cardiovascular health you should see your

---

Remedies with 🫖 *are made using an infusion. Those with* ☕ *are made using a decoction. Instructions for both methods are on pages 4 - 7. Variations and other procedures are contained in the text following the description of that remedy.*

doctor if your nose is still bleeding after 20 - 30 minutes of treatment. There's a lot of blood circulating in your head and you can loose a lot of it through your nose in 20 minutes.

Archangel *(Lamium album, also known as Blind Nettle, White Dead Nettle)*

Drinking an infusion of archangel a popular remedy for bleeding injuries during the Middle Ages.

Houseleek *(Sempervivum tectorum, also called hen-and chickens or singreen)*

Just because seventeenth century English physician and herbalist, Nicholas Culpeper, was one of the most influential herbalists of his time, doesn't mean that his recommendations were always sensible. "Bruise a few houseleek leaves and place the bruised leaves on the crown of your head," was one of his remedies for a bleeding nose. Try it if you like, but don't expect more than strange looks from your family if you try this foolish folk remedy.

Knotgrass *(Polygonaceae spp, including Polygonum douglasii, P. aviculare, and P. sachalinense) also known as knotweed*

This is another of Nicholas Culpeper's recommendations for bleeding from the nose. At first glance it looks like it might be more effective than placing bruised houseleek leaves on the crown of your head, but not more pleasant! This remedy requires you to spray the juice extracted from knotgrass into your nostrils. Avoid this remedy if you suffer from hay fever or any pollen induced allergy.

Periwinkle (Vinca major)

Like Culpeper's knotgrass remedy, this oldie recommends applying the juice from periwinkle to the inside of your nostrils.

Lady's Bedstraw (Galium verum)
also known as Cheese Rennet

This oldie sounds practical, stuff your nostrils with lady's bedstraw.

Some old-fashioned remedies whose origins have been lost in time

● eat plums and drink whey[1]

● eat grapes and raisins—since grapes and raisins are high in iron, an important mineral in the clotting process, this folk remedy may actually work.

Especially for Children

● pinch the nose to stop the bleeding

● make a twist in a tissue dampen it, dip it in salt and then insert into the child's nose (the salt is supposed to help the blood vessels contract)

● place a cold cloth on the nose or the back of the neck

Red String

In Uganda traditional healers tell you to place a piece of folded paper between your gum and upper lip, tie a red string around your little finger, and remain quiet.

---

[1]   *watery liquid left after separation of curd from milk*

Yarrow [1] *(Achillea millefolium)*

Legend has it that Achilles stopped the bleeding of his fellow soldiers wounds by applying yarrow leaves. At about the same time that Achilles was supposed to be using yarrow on his fellow soldiers Chinese physicians were using a native yarrow plant to treat bleeding problems.

Folk healers are still recommend yarrow to staunch the flow of blood. Drinking an infusion of yarrow and using decocted yarrow leaves to pack the nose are the two recommended treatments.

---

[1] *avoid during pregnancy*

Blood Pressure

If you are not convinced that high blood pressure is dangerous, try this experiment. Find a balloon and blow it up. That's right, keep blowing, keep blowing, keep on, just a little bit more... KABOOM! That's what can happen when your veins, arteries and capillaries are under too much pressure as they try to transport your blood around your body.

And when they go KABOOM! you'll have more to worry about than scaring the cat. Explosively high blood pressure can mean a stroke or aneurism. So keep an eye on your blood pressure. High blood pressure is called the silent killer because it is only by monitoring it that you can tell whether or not your blood pressure is high.

Low blood pressure is not as dangerous as high blood pressure. Low blood pressure may mean that you feel dizzy or light headed when you get up quickly after sitting or lying down. But don't ignore low blood pressure either. Talk to your doctor if you notice any of the symptoms of low blood pressure.

Remedies with ☕ are made using an infusion. Those with ♨ are made using a decoction. Instructions for both methods are on pages 4 - 7. Variations and other procedures are contained in the text following the description of that remedy.

Barberry *(Berberis vulgaris)*

Folk healers in the former Soviet Union recommend drinking a decoction of barberry to control high blood pressure.

Bach Flower Remedies

These remedies are believed to counteract the reasons for high blood pressure, rather than the symptoms.

Try

Oak and Elm - if you are overwhelmed by responsibilities

Impatiens - if you are irritable and impatient

Agrimony - if you suffer from hidden anxieties

Vervain - if you are over enthusiastic or under strain

Vine - if you are ruthless and driven by ambition

Rockwater - if you set impossibly high standards

Beech - if you refuse advice

Holly - if you are angry and have a desire for revenge

Mimulus - if you have a fear of poverty

Star of Bethlehem - if you are suffering from shock or grief

Vine, Rockwater and Beech - if you find it difficult to relax

Cinnamon [1] *(Cinnamomum zeylanicum in the west, C. cassia in China, C Cassia from the bark = rou gui or from twigs gui zhi)*

Japanese folk healers recommend a liberal sprinkling of cinnamon on your food to reduce blood pressure.

---

[1] *avoid during pregnancy*

Rice diet

The Romany people, sometimes called Gypsies, recommend this diet to control high blood pressure. Whether or not it works, give it a miss—there are safer ways to reduce high blood pressure. A day or two of the diet won't do any harm, it's low fat, low salt and high in fibre. But high blood pressure is dangerous enough, you don't want to add malnutrition to your worries by using this restricted and highly unbalanced diet.

250 grams (8 ounces) steamed, unsalted brown rice

1. Add 680 grams (1½ pounds) fruit or fresh fruit juices

2. When cool add 100 grams (3 ½ ounces) honey

3. Divide this mixture into 7 portions

4. Each morning eat 5 grams (½ teaspoon) fresh yeast and one portion of the rice mixture

5. Through out the day eat five more portions of the rice mixture at regular intervals

6. Before you go to bed eat another 5 grams (½ teaspoon) of fresh yeast and the final portion of the rice mixture

7. Do not drink anything after eating the final portion at night

Cocoa *(Theobroma cacao)*

Philippine folk healers recommend people suffering high blood pressure eat—that's right, eat—dry cocoa powder. Try 5 grams (1 teaspoon) four times a day if you're game.

Garlic [1] *(Allium sativum)*

Traditional Chinese medical practitioners follow their ancient ancestors and recommend garlic, and lots of it, to treat high

---

[1]   *avoid during pregnancy and if breast feeding*

blood pressure. Eat 3 - 10 cloves of garlic a day to keep high blood pressure (and vampires) at bay.

Coconut *(Cocos nucifera)*
Horseradish *(Amoracia rusticana)*
and Garlic [1] *(Allium sativum)*

Hawaiian healers recommend eating garlic and horseradish if you are suffering from high blood pressure. Oh, they tell you to drink fermented coconut water too!

Red Clover *(Trifolium pratense)*

Another Hawaiian remedy for high blood pressure, drinking an infusion of red clover.

Goldenseal [2] *(Hydrastis canadensis)*

Cherokee (Native American) medicine men recommend drinking an infusion of goldenseal for low blood pressure. A dash of red pepper added just before drinking gives this remedy a zing.

Chive *(Allium schoenoprasum)*

During the Middle Ages, people all over northern Europe ate chives to reduce high blood pressure and strengthen the heart.

---

[1]   avoid during pregnancy and if breast feeding
[2]   avoid during pregnancy

Hawthorn Berries (Crataegus oxycantha, C. monogyna, C. pinnatifida called Shan zha in China)

Irish folk healers recommend drinking an infusion of hawthorn berries to lower high blood pressure. Use just 10 grams (2 teaspoons) ripe hawthorn berries to make this infusion.

Ylang-Ylang (Cananga odorata) also called Canangium odoratum

A massage using ylang-ylang oil (1 - 2 drops of ylang-ylang oil diluted with 10 millilitres of good quality vegetable or nut oil) is Indonesian and Philippine folk healers' recommendation when high blood pressure is the problem.

Kiwi Fruit (Actinidia sinensis) also called Chinese Gooseberry

Not many folk healers' recommendations taste as good as this one does. When a Kiwi Fruit was called a Chinese gooseberry few people in the west knew or cared what a Chinese gooseberry was. Our neighbours across the Tasman did some research, improved on an already good product and in a streak of marketing genius, renamed these furry, egg-shaped treasures, Kiwi Fruit—and a world wide phenomenon was born.

No matter what you call them, they are delicious. They are also low in kilojoules and high in potassium. It's the potassium that get Kiwi fruit a guernsey in high blood pressure sufferers' diets. The potassium helps to correct the electrolyte imbalance high blood pressure sufferers sometimes develop.

Body Odour

Body odour is an equal opportunity affliction, it will alienate your friends and enemies. The problem is sweat doesn't smell, but (and this is a very big but) when sweat hits your skin it meets up with bacteria living on your skin. It's this combination that results in the characteristic, offensive odour.

The bacteria, and the odours they create, cling to your skin and clothing, so good old-fashioned soap and water is your best bet for avoiding (and get rid of) body odour.

You should also know that the same foods that turn your breath into a dangerous weapon at 20 paces can make their way into your sweat. That means you'll need to lay-off the garlic, onions and curry if you have an especially difficult time getting rid of body odour.

Give these folk remedies a try, even if you don't think you have a problem, sometimes you are the last to know.

Chinese Salad

This old Chinese remedy for getting rid of body odour uses a decoction of coriander seeds and leaves, orange peel, a date, some parsley and a few drops of peppermint oil to make a

---

Remedies with ☕ are made using an infusion. Those with ♨ are made using a decoction. Instructions for both methods are on pages 4 - 7. Variations and other procedures are contained in the text following the description of that remedy.

fragrant wash that should banish the most persistent body odour.

70 grams (3 ½ tablespoons) coriander seeds

2 litres (2 quarts) water

1. Bring to the boil
2. Simmer 90 minutes, or until water is reduced by one-half
3. Add 10 grams (2 teaspoons) finely grated orange peel and 1 pitted date, finely chopped
4. Simmer an additional 15 minutes
5. Remove from heat
6. Add 5 grams (1 teaspoon) dried coriander leaf, some finely chopped fresh parsley and a drop or two of peppermint oil
7. Steep 30 minutes, stirring occasionally
8. Strain through a fine sieve
9. Store in a jar or bottle with a tight fitting lid
10. Warm 125 millilitres (½ cup) and rub the liquid wash over your body (including genital region)

Fennel *(Foeniculum officinale)*

Fennel was one of Hildegard of Bingen's favourite medicinal plants. This famous German abbess and herbalist recommended drinking an infusion of powdered fennel seed to banish body odour.

Ginger *(Zingiber officinalis)*

In India ginger is considered a physical and spiritual cleanser. This tasty remedy for foul body odour should help spice up your life in more ways than one. Chew on small pieces of peeled ginger or add it to your food.

Goosegrass *(Galium aparine) also known as Cleavers*

This old-fashioned, natural deodorant has been used for generations to keep house, clothes and body smelling sweetly. Put goosegrass clippings in your cupboards and drawers, between your mattress and box spring and in your airing cupboard.

Powdered alum

Use alum to make this inexpensive, old-fashioned deodorant. Buy the alum from your pharmacist.

2.5 grams (½ teaspoon) powdered alum
300 ml (½ pint) warm water
Apply as you normally would deodorant

Essential Oils

Add a few drops of any of the following essential oils to your bath to help reduce body odour.

Thyme *(Thymus vulgaris)*

Marjoram *(Origanum marjorana)*

Geranium *(Pelargonium odorantissimum)*

Verbena *(Lippia citriodora)*

Lavender *(Lavandula angustifolia)*

Sandalwood *(Santalum album)*

Angelica *(Angelica sinesis, also known as dang gui)*

Cinnamon *(Cinnamomum zeylanicum in the west, C. cassia in China, C Cassia from the bark = rou gui or from twigs gui zhi)*

Turnip (Brassica rapa)

Turnip juice is a Japanese folk remedy for body odour. Splash 5 millilitres (1 teaspoon) of turnip juice under each armpit.

Blind or Stinging Nettle [1]
(Urtrica dioica or U. urens)

If you happen to cross paths with a travelling band of Gypsies, ask them if you can buy some of their nettle beer. Drinking it is supposed to do wonders for problem body odour.

---

[1]   *stinging comes from formic acid and histamine which are found in the fine hairlike needles of the leaves.*

Boils

They're ugly and they're painful and those are their good points. If boils are treated improperly they can be dangerous too.

The inside story on boils
(Only for the strong stomached)

Boils form when a bacterial infection starts to brew under your skin without an escape route. Instead of dying a noble death these selfish creatures just keep multiplying until they become critically over populated.

If the crowding wasn't bad enough the other by-product of overpopulation — garbage also builds up. In the case of boils the garbage is pus, a ghastly concoction of dead cells and their living relatives' waste matter (You were warned that this required a strong stomach, but you wanted to know).

Together the bacteria and pus are responsible for the painful, red, hot to the touch, swollen boil.

Remedies with 🫖 *are made using an infusion. Those with* ♨ *are made using a decoction. Instructions for both methods are on pages 4 - 7. Variations and other procedures are contained in the text following the description of that remedy.*

When you treat a boil your objective is to bring the matter to a head, literally. You want to draw the bacterial cells—and the waste they produce when they grow and multiply—to the surface so they can drain out of your body. Otherwise all this poisonous junk will travel inward where it will eventually reach your blood stream.

This is why you never squeeze a boil. Squeezing can force the poison into, rather than out of, your body. Instead apply a compress or poultice to draw the gunk to the surface and allow it to drain naturally.

If you notice any red lines on your skin—especially if the lines look as if they come from the boil—or if you feel sick or feverish, it may mean that the poisons have already worked their way into your blood stream and you should see your doctor immediately.

Finally always have your doctor treat boils on children and the elderly. Their immune systems may not be able to handle the infection as well as an adult's can. Be safe rather than sorry.

Lucerne (Medicago sativa known as Alfalfa in North America)

Spain introduced alfalfa to the New World. The conquistadors brought it along with them to feed to their horses. About 200 years ago South American folk healers started using alfalfa medicinally. They recommend eating alfalfa sprouts to help clear boils. Just ask for double sprouts on your salad sandwich and you should be right.

Mustard *(Brassica hirta)*

This poultice uses mustard's ability to generate heat and draw the poison to the surface. Combine mustard seeds with a little water and mash, making a paste. Protect your skin with a thin layer of petroleum jelly before applying the paste of mustard seeds to the skin around the boil. Hold the poultice in place with a cloth or gauze bandage and leave the whole mess on for several hours, 24 if possible.

Pukatea *(Laurelia novae-zelandiae)*

An infusion of pukatea bark is a traditional Maori wash for treating boils.

Linseed [1] *(Linum ustatissimum)*

This poultice uses a decoction of ground linseed. Apply the warm, softened linseed to the boil, hold it in place with gauze. Re-apply when the poultice cools, continue until boil opens at the surface.

Fenugreek [2] *(Trigonella foenum-graecum)*

Or try this poultice, it uses fenugreek seeds. Make decoction of fenugreek seeds and use as per linseed poultice above.

Potato *(Solanum tuberosum)*

This is a novel way to use leftovers. Make a poultice from warm mashed potato. Apply to the boil and repeat as necessary until the boil clears.

---

[1]   use sparingly as linseed oil contains prussic acid, don't use artists' or craft linseed oil

[2]   avoid during pregnancy

Pot Marigold[1] *(Calendula officinals)*

Calendula oil is an Ayurvedic remedy for boils. Dilute 1 - 2 drops of calendula oil with 10 millilitres of good quality vegetable or nut oil and massage it gently in and around the boil.

White Mangrove *(Avicennia marina)*

In Zaire, formerly called The Congo, they burn white mangrove wood and mix the resulting ash with fresh or salt water to make a poultice to use on boils.

Purple Coneflower *(Echinacea augustifolia)*

Native Americans used the purple coneflower in many remedies including this wash for boils, a decoction of purple coneflower roots. Repeat as necessary until boil clears.

Lavender[2] *(Lavandula angustifolia)*

Use 1 - 2 drops of lavender oil diluted with 10 millilitres of good quality vegetable or nut oil on the boil and the skin around it, massage gently.

Burdock *(Arctium lappa)*

For centuries the Romany people, sometimes called Gypsies, have used this cold decoction of burdock root as a poultice to draw boils.

30 grams (1 ounce) burdock root
1. Soak overnight in 750 millilitres (3 cups) cold water
2. In the morning, bring the liquid to the boil

---

[1] *do not confuse with French Marigold, Tagetes patula*
[2] *avoid high doses during pregnancy*

3. Simmer 15 minutes

4. Cool

5. Strain, discarding solids

6. Mix the liquid with enough fullers earth (buy this at your pharmacy or natural products store) to make a paste

7. Apply paste to boil, after one hour remove with cold water and apple vinegar

8. Re-apply as necessary

Sassafras *(Sassafras albidum)*

The Hungarian Romany people use the membrane from the inside of an egg to draw a boil. They also recommend drinking an infusion of sassafras to help clear a boil.

Dandelion *(Taraxacum officinale also known as pu gong ying)*

This is an ancient, traditional Chinese treatment for boils, a poultice made from decocted dandelion leaves. Apply while still warm, hold poultice in place with a cloth or gauze bandage.

Slippery Elm Bark *(Ulmus fulva)*

Two Native American tribes, the Menoiminee and Potawatomi, use powdered slippery elm bark mixed with enough water to make a paste to treat boils. Apply as needed.

Morning Glory *(Ipomoea pes-caprae)*

Throughout Brazil and Jamaica, Morning Glory leaves are used to make poultice to draw the pus out of boils.

Finely chop fresh-picked, washed Morning Glory leaves

1. Grind using 60 millilitres (3 teaspoons) ice water
2. Apply the ground leaves to the boil
3. Wrap with gauze or cloth
4. Change the poultice every 45 minutes, 3 - 4 times in succession
5. Repeat daily until boil opens to the surface

Breast Discomfort

One of the reasons regular breast self-examination (BSE) is so important is that breast tissue is heavily influenced by hormonal changes. This means that during a woman's normal hormonal cycle breast tissue changes with the level and type of hormone fluctuations. Regular BSE is even more important in the role it plays in early diagnosis of breast cancer.

Monthly Breast Self-Examination is almost like getting free life insurance.

That's because BSE is the best and most reliable way of identifying benign and cancerous changes in your breasts. Any form of cancer is easier to cure if diagnosis is made as soon as possible after the cancerous growth begins.

Do your BSE at the same time each month. Most doctors recommend one week after your menstrual period begins.

If you find a lump or other change in your breasts, DON'T PANIC! Nine out of ten breasts lumps are not due to cancer. But do have your doctor examine any lumps or other irregularities you find. Only your doctor can tell if a lump requires further testing.

Remedies with ☕ are made using an infusion. Those with ♨ are made using a decoction. Instructions for both methods are on pages 4 - 7. Variations and other procedures are contained in the text following the description of that remedy.

After skin cancer, breast cancer is the most common form of cancer in women. One in 15 Australian women will develop breast cancer during their life. Because breast cancer is so common it is also the subject of many myths.

● The cause of breast cancer is unknown, but some risk factors have been identified. While breast cancer can occur in women of any age, it is most common in women over forty.

● In fact, increasing age is the most important risk factor, and all women are at risk as they grown older. Research also shows that if you have already had breast cancer or if you have a family history of breast cancer you have a slightly higher risk of developing breast cancer than the general population.

● The influence of other factors is not so clear. Some factors which may increase your risk of developing breast cancer include not having children or having them at a late age, a diet high in animal fat and some forms of benign breast disease.

● A bump or blow to your breast cannot cause breast cancer, nor can you catch breast or any other form of cancer from someone.

● And contrary to common belief, breast feeding neither causes nor protects you from breast cancer.

Ask your doctor to show you how to conduct a self examination. Can you really afford to turn down free life insurance?

Normal changes in breast tissue include those that precede a women's menstrual cycle, accompany pregnancy, the birth of a baby as well as benign lumps and cysts. Because these changes occur in sensitive breast tissue the discomfort they cause can be great even if their seriousness is not. So try one of these folk remedies to soothe the pain.

Remember that whatever mum eats or drinks baby will too. Babies' systems can be more sensitive than an adults'. Don't use any folk remedy when pregnant or when nursing without consulting your doctor.

Apricot *(Prunus armeniaca)* and Wheat

Combine 1 - 2 drops each apricot and wheat germ oil with 20 millilitres of good quality vegetable or nut oil, for a soothing massage oil to use on painful breast tissue. Heat the oil mixture in a bowl of warm water for extra soothing.

Camphor *(Cinnamomum camphora)*

Mix 1 - 2 drops of camphor oil with 20 millilitres of olive oil and use it to massage 'hard breasts' but do not use if you are nursing.

Potatoes *(Solanum tuberosum),* Turnip *(Brassica rapa),* French beans *(Phaseolus vulgaris)*

Use any of these to make a comforting poultice to relieve mastitis pain. Cook the vegetables until they are mushy. Mash with a little of the water they have cooked in and apply the warm mash to painful breasts.

Basil [1] *(Ocimum basilicum)*

In India they call basil "Tulsi". It is a sacred religious herb with a long tradition—having been used for nearly 2500 years, since early Vedic times. A massage with 1 - 2 drops of basil diluted with 10 millilitres of good quality vegetable or nut oil can soothe breast discomfort. Do not use this remedy while breast feeding.

Tapioca and Milk

In Argentina folk healers recommend using a poultice of tapioca made in milk to soothe breast discomfort.

1. Make the tapioca according to package directions and apply while still warm. Spread the tapioca on several layers of gauze or a piece of muslin
2. Apply the gauze to the breast (tapioca against the skin)
3. Cover the poultice with a towel
4. Remove the poultice when it cools, repeat as often necessary

---

[1]   *do not use essential oil in any form during pregnancy*

Breastfeeding

In the forties and fifties bottle feeding was all the rage. It was convenient and oh so modern. In the nineties the tide has turned and a whole generation of women who were raised on bottles are breastfeeding their own children. After all, it's convenient and they will tell you "It's oh so modern!"

Not all women can breastfeed, but if you can it really is the best for your child. Breast milk is nutritionally perfect. Breast milk also helps pass on immunity to your baby. Nursing mothers associations in every state provide information, advice and support to breast feeding mothers.

Fennel [1] *(Foeniculum officinale)*

Fennel has a long association with breastfeeding. Dioscorides recommend nursing mothers chew fennel seeds to increase milk production. Later Nicholas Culpeper included fennel in his seventeenth century herbal, also praising the plant's ability to increase milk production. In Latin America today, folk healers tell nursing mothers who want to increase their milk production to drink a milk infusion of fennel seeds.

Remedies with ☕ are made using an infusion. Those with ♨ are made using a decoction. Instructions for both methods are on pages 4 - 7. Variations and other procedures are contained in the text following the description of that remedy.

---

[1]   *avoid during pregnancy*

5 grams (1 teaspoon) fennel seeds

250 millilitres (1 cup) very hot milk

1. Steep covered, 10 - 15 minutes
2. Strain, discarding solids
3. Drink 250 millilitres (1 cup), 3 times a day

Fenugreek [1] *(Trigonella foenum-graecum)*

In India nursing mothers traditionally eat fenugreek seeds, a wee bit all day long, believing it will increase their milk production.

Goat's Rue *(Galega officinalis)*

An infusion of goat's rue also has a reputation for stimulating the flow of milk.

Spinach *(Spinacia oleracea)*

In Spain folk healers tell expectant and nursing mothers to drink spinach juice if they want to improve the quality and quantity of their milk. You can make spinach juice with a juice extractor, and it can't hurt. More that 85 millilitres (1/3 cup) at a time can upset your tummy, and it will have a very strong flavour, so you will probably want to mix it with another juice, carrot or a nice sweet fruit juice. If your baby starts to look like Popeye, you're drinking too much spinach juice.

Jasmine *(Jasminum officinale)*

A massage with jasmine oil is believed to increase the flow of milk. Unfortunately steam distilled jasmine oil is no longer

---

[1] *avoid during pregnancy and if breast feeding*

available as the process is very expensive. Jasmine oil is now extracted with organic solvents. This oil is suitable for perfumery applications but is unsuitable for aromatherapy due to the toxicity of many organic solvents.

Stay clear!

Castor *(Ricinus communis)*

Don't try this remedy, having a castor bean tree any where near small children is too dangerous. The beans are highly toxic and the oil is a very strong purgative. But in the Cape Verde Islands they say that a poultice made from the leaves of the castor-bean tree can bring on the flow of milk. The remedy is said to be so successful that even women who have never borne children or who have not nursed a child for years can produce milk.

Bronchitis

It feels like a little irritation at the back of your throat. It might be a hanger-on from a cold that you just can't seem to shift. You try to ignore it, but you can't, so you try to clear your throat, very gently. Instead you set-off a chain reaction, a coughing fit that threatens to bring down the walls, and seems to go on for ever. Yep, you've got it again.

It, is bronchitis and it's a classic good news, bad news situation. There are two types of bronchitis, acute and chronic. Acute bronchitis usually comes on after a cold or flu. There is not much you can do to make it go away. It's usually caused by a virus so antibiotics won't have any effect. Even so, it will probably be gone in a week or two. Sometimes bronchitis is caused by a bacterial infection, when that's the case antibiotics can help.

Chronic bronchitis is a sign of irreversible damage to the lungs—usually from long-term exposure to irritants, like cigarette smoke. Chronic bronchitis can, if untreated lead to emphysema, so don't waste time getting treatment for chronic bronchitis.

Remedies with ☕ are made using an infusion. Those with ♨ are made using a decoction. Instructions for both methods are on pages 4 - 7. Variations and other procedures are contained in the text following the description of that remedy.

No matter what type of bronchitis you suffer from, you'll feel better if you can get some relief from the exhausting cough.

Scots Pine *(Pinus sylvestris),* Lavender [1] *(Lavandula angustifolia)* and Honey

For centuries, the Romany people, who are sometimes called Gypsies, have treated chest complaints with a drink made of pine resin, lavender oil and honey mixed in warm milk. You can buy pine resin at health food stores.

5 millilitres (1 teaspoon) pine resin
1 drop of lavender oil
5 millilitres (1 teaspoon) honey
250 millilitres (1 cup) warm milk
Drink 85 millilitres (1/3 cup), 3 times a day

Balsam *(Myroxylon balsamum var. pereira)*

A traditional Peruvian treatment for chest complaints calls for balsam resin, gently rubbed on the chest, neck and back at night. You can buy balsam from a health food store or a natural pharmacy. Wash the resin off the next morning, it's sticky.

Chaparral *(Larrea divaricata L. tridentata)*

The Native Americans in the south west of what is now the USA drank an infusion of this native plant's flowers to treat chest complaints.

---

[1]   *avoid high doses during pregnancy*

Catnip *(Nepeta cataria)*

For about 2000 years, traditional Chinese herbalists have recommended drinking an infusion of catnip for chest complaints.

Elecampane *(Inula helenium)*
also called scabwort, horseheal

Traditional Indian Ayurvedic physicians recommend drinking a cold infusion of elecampane. Use cold water and steep covered 8 to 10 hours to make this infusion.

Ma Huang [1] *(Ephedra simca)*

Native Americans of the Utah tribe drank a decoction of dried ephedra for chest complaints.

Fenugreek [2] *(Trigonella foenum-graecum)*

A drink of decocted fenugreek seeds was the recommendation when you suffered from chest complaints in ancient Greece. If you find the decoction too bitter add a little honey.

Fig *(Ficus carica)*

The ancient Romans used fresh and dried figs as laxatives and recommended drinking fresh fig juice to soothe a nagging chest cough.

2 - 3 fresh figs for each dose use a juice extractor
Drink 3 - 4 times a day

---

[1] restricted herb in Australia and New Zealand probably due to the presence of the alkaloid ephedrine

[2] avoid during pregnancy

Steam Inhalations

Steam inhalations are popular folk remedies for many chest complaints. These remedies have an added benefit, the lovely scent that helps to restore both mind and body to natural health. The basic procedure for any steam distillation is the same.

Add the herb, essential oil and any other ingredients to a pot of boiling water or put the ingredients in a basin and pour boiling water over them. Cover your head with a large towel and bend over the pot. Inhale the rising steam for 5 to 15 minutes, repeat three or four times day.

Scots Pine *(Pinus sylvestris)*,
Eucalyptus *(Eucalyptus globus)*,
Elecampane *(Inula helenium)* also called
Scabwort, Horseheal

Use separately or together, in what ever ratios you prefer and follow the procedure above for steam inhalations.

Eucalyptus *(Eucalyptus globus)*

European settlers learned about the healing powers of eucalyptus from Australian Aborigines. Aboriginal traditional remedies often called for burning a medicinal plant's leaves and inhaling the scented smoke. The Europeans used the leaves to make a steam inhalation.

Rosemary *(Rosmarinus officinalis)*

The Egyptians recommend rosemary oil in massage therapy for chest complaints. Use 1 - 2 drops of rosemary oil with 10 millilitres of good quality vegetable or nut oil and massage the oil into the upper body.

Dandelion *(Taraxacum officinale, also known as pu gong ying)*

This ancient Chinese treatment for chest complaints uses a decoction of dandelion roots.

Wall Germander [1] *(Teucrium chamaedrys)*

In medieval times, an infusion of wall germander flowers was a popular drink for people suffering from chest complaints.

Thyme *(Thymus vulgaris)*

Chest complaints were also treated with a drink of infused thyme leaves and flowers during medieval times.

Red Clover *(Trifolium pratense)*

During the Middle Ages they switched to drinking an infusion of red clover.

Garlic [2] *(Allium sativum)*

This simple and tasty treatment goes back 2000 years when the Romans recommended eating finely chopped garlic at all meals to ease chest complaints. Chop or crush the garlic and add to your food at every meal. You can skip breakfast if you're a delicate sort.

---

[1] *use sparingly*
[2] *avoid during pregnancy and if breast feeding*

Angelica *(Angelica archangelica)*

A decoction of fresh angelica root is an old fashioned European drink for chronic chest complaints.

Peach syrup *(Prunus persica)*

Some Native American tribes use a syrup made from a decoction of peach kernels and bark to treat bronchitis.

1. Pound 170 grams (⅔ cup) peach bark
2. Split 170 grams (⅔ cup) peach kernels
3. Add 2 cups each apple cider vinegar and water to the peach bark and kernels
4. Steep covered for 5 days, store the container in a warm place, but out of the direct sunlight
5. Shake the container several times each day
6. After five days bring the liquid to the boil
7. Simmer gently for 30 minutes
8. Add 125 millilitres (½ cup) brandy or whisky as a preservative
9. Use 20 millilitres (1 tablespoon) every 3-4 hours
10. Store in a well-sealed bottle or jar discard any unused liquid after 1 month

Bruises

Ouch! You bump into a chair, trip in the garden or get bumped playing sport. It hurts for a little while, then you forget all about it. Until a day or two later when, YUCK! you notice a large, dark blue blotch. Bruises aren't dangerous, just unsightly. Your primary concern should be getting rid of the dreadful reminder of your clumsiness as quickly as possible.

Allspice *(Pimenta diocia) also known as Jamica pepper, pimento*

For centuries Guatemalan folk healers have used a poultice of crushed allspice to treat bruises. Crush some allspice in a mortar and pestle and add enough water make a paste.

Apply to the bruise holding the paste in place with gauze or cloth bandage, repeat as needed.

Archangel *(Lamium album) also known as Blind Nettle, White Dead Nettle*

Drinking an infusion of archangel was one of Nicholas Culpeper's recommendations for getting rid of bruises. 🫖

Remedies with 🫖 are made using an infusion. Those with 🫖 are made using a decoction. Instructions for both methods are on pages 4 - 7. Variations and other procedures are contained in the text following the description of that remedy.

Comfrey [1] *(Symphytum officinale) also called Knitbone*

Ancient Greek herbalists wrote about the ability of comfrey to bind and close wounds and recommended using a decoction of comfrey roots to make a poultice to heal bruises rapidly. Apply warm 3 or 4 times a day, hold in place with a gauze or cotton bandage.

Mustard *(Brassica hirta)*

Some folk healers recommend the heat of a mustard plaster to help heal a bruise quickly. Grind mustard seeds with enough water to make a paste. Protect your skin with a thin layer of petroleum jelly before applying the mustard plaster to the bruise. Hold the mustard seeds in place with a gauze or cotton bandage, leave in place for 24 hours, repeat as necessary.

Cabbage *(Brassica oleracea)* and Clay

This cabbage is one of grandma's favourite healing plants. To help heal a bruise, try a cabbage leave poultice or a cabbage leaf poultice alternating with a clay pack wrap.

Cocoa *(Theobroma cacao)*

American folk healers recommend applying cocoa butter to cuts, bruises and wounds.

---

[1] restricted herb in Australia and New Zealand due to presence of alkaloid, shown to cause liver damage in rats

Pot Marigold [1] *(Calendula officinalis)*

The aromatherapy remedy for bruises is calendula oil, mix 1 - 2 drops of calendula oil with 10 millilitres of good quality nut or vegetable oil and gently massage into the bruise.

Cayenne Pepper *(Capsicum frutescens)*

In Taiwan, folk healers use this ointment on bruises and swollen, painful joints.

1. One part ground cayenne pepper and five parts petroleum jelly
2. Melt the petroleum jelly in a double boiler
3. Mix in the cayenne
4. Cool
5. Use on bruised or swollen areas

Figwort *(Scrophularia nodosa)*

In the middle ages a poultice made from a decoction of figwort was a popular remedy for bruises. Apply warm twice a day, hold the poultice in place with a gauze or cotton bandage.

Golden rod *(Solidago virga aurea)*

The European herbalist Arnoldus de Villa Nova recommended drinking a decoction of golden rod and using a little of the liquid as a wash to treat bruises.

---

[1]   *do not confuse with French Marigold, Tagetes patula*

Potato (Solanum tuberosum)

With their wandering lifestyle the Romany people have had to develop quick and easy remedies for every day ailments. When a child had a bad bruise this treatment wouldn't take more than a few seconds out of Mum's dinner preparations, all she had to do was take a slice of potato and place it on the bruise.

Parsley (Petroselinum crispum)

If you don't like walking around with a slice of potato on your bruise try another Romany remedy, a poultice of crushed parsley leaves. (If you planned this right you could make a meal out of your bruise treatments). Crush a handful of parsley leaves and apply directly to the bruise, leave in place for a few hours and repeat as necessary.

Oat (Avena sativa)

This poultice is a stable boy's remedy for bruised shins. Mix rolled oats with enough boiling water to make a thick paste. Apply while still warm, directly on the bruise. Hold it in place with a gauze or cotton bandage. Repeat as necessary.

Turnip (Brassica rapa)

Japanese folk healers recommend using a turnip poultice to reduce the swelling and discolouration of a bruise.

1. Apply grated turnip directly on the bruise
2. Hold the poultice in place with a gauze or cotton bandage
3. Leave the poultice in place for about 30 minutes
4. Repeat every day until the bruise is gone

Burns

If you play with matches, or strong chemicals, or electrical equipment, or hot food from the microwave, or . . . . you're bound to get burned.

You can treat most first and second degree burns yourself. First degree burns will be red and painful, but won't blister. Second degree burns will blister, ooze and are very painful.

Third degree burns require immediate medical attention. You also need to be more concerned about second degree burns that cover a large area, burns on infants and on people over 60 and if the burn is on your face—especially your eyes—or if the burn takes more than two weeks to heal.

The first and most important thing to do when you are burnt, is to wash the area with cool water and lots of it (see special information on chemical burns below). Don't use ice water, it can add to the damage done by the burn. If the burn is especially painful keep it under water, it will be less painful that way. Don't use butter or other oil, or any food on a burn, that's an open invitation to infection. The oozing fluid from a blister is a direct route to your blood stream.

Remedies with 🫖 *are made using an infusion. Those with* 🍲 *are made using a decoction. Instructions for both methods are on pages 4 - 7. Variations and other procedures are contained in the text following the description of that remedy.*

Only use folk remedies on mild, first degree burns, mild sunburns, etc. On second degree burns wait until the blister has healed and no raw flesh remains before using any folk remedy.

Chemical burns need special attention

Chemical burns are dangerous. Even after you have washed the chemical off of your skin, the chemicals can continue to damage your skin as they work their way through deeper and deeper layers of skin tissue.

If you splash strong acidic or alkaline solution on your clothes, remove your clothes immediately and use a shower or hose to rinse the chemicals off of your skin. This is not the time to be modest. If you don't remove your clothing the chemical will stay against your skin and continue to burn.

Never work with strong chemicals without proper safety equipment, including eye protection, gloves, long sleeves and trousers, etc.

To be truly prepared for a chemical burn you'll need to know what kind of chemical you are using and have a neutralising solution on hand whenever you are working with strong chemicals. Alkaline and acidic liquids can burn your skin. Battery acid, is one example of a strong acid, while lye is an example of a strong alkali. Using the wrong solution on a chemical burn can do more damage than the original burn. In some cases even water can worsen the problem.

Continued next page

Chemical burns need special attention
Continued from previous page

Clearly label the neutralising solution, not just with the solution's name but with what it is used for, if you spill something in your eye you may have to depend on someone else to read it.

Finally, if you splash a chemical in your eye don't be mingy with the water. Rinse with running water for 5 - 10 minutes, at least. If there is no access to running water hold your eye open and gently pour at least 10 litres of water over your eye.

Archangel *(Lamium album, also known as Blind Nettle, White Dead Nettle)*

More than 300 years ago, Nicholas Culpeper, English physician and herbalist recommended using an infusion of archangel as a treatment for burns.

Pot Marigold [1] *(Calendula officinalis)*

An old fashioned remedy for burns, recommends using ten drops of calendula tincture in 250 millilitres (1 cup) water as a wash for burns. After a burn has begun to heal the traditional Indian recommendation is to massage calendula oil (dilute 1 - 2 drops of calendula oil with 10 millilitres good quality nut or vegetable oil) on the healing skin, it's supposed to reduce scaring.

---

[1]   *do not confuse with French Marigold, Tagetes patula*

St John's Wort *(Hypericum perforatum)*

Another old fashioned remedy, this one uses a tincture of St John's Wort in 250 millilitres (1 cup) warm water as a swab for burnt skin.

Aloe *(Aloe vera)*

The gel that oozes from a freshly broken aloe leaf is soothing when applied to any painful skin condition, including burns.

Comfrey [1] *(Symphytum officinale) also called Knitbone*

Make a infusion of comfrey and use the liquid as a wash and the leaves as a poultice. Strain and retain both liquid and softened leaves and allow to cool. Use liquid as a wash and apply the cool, softened leaves directly to the burn as a poultice. Hold the poultice in place with a gauze or cotton bandage. 🫖

Elder [2] *(Sambucus nigra)*

Since the Middle Ages a poultice of crushed elder berries has been a popular European treatment for burns. Crush a handful of elder berries and apply them directly to the burn. Hold the poultice in place with a gauze or cotton bandage.

Slippery Elm Bark *(Ulmus fulva)*

A paste of powdered slippery elm bark and water is another old fashioned treatment for burns. Moisten 30 grams of powdered slippery elm bark with enough water to make a thick

---

[1] restricted herb in Australia and New Zealand due to presence of alkaloid, shown to cause liver damage in rats

[2] do not use during pregnancy

paste. Apply to the burn and hold in place with a gauze or cotton bandage. Repeat as necessary.

Garlic [1] *(Allium sativum)*

Use the medicinal properties of garlic to soothe the pain and help the skin heal quickly. Apply purchased garlic oil or crush garlic and suspend in olive or sunflower oil. Apply directly to the burn.

Tea *(Camellia sinensis var. sinensis, China Tea; C. Sinensis var. assanica, Assam Tea)*

Most teenagers who have tried this remedy on their holiday sunburn, know that lying in a bath tub filled with cool tea is soothing and helps to reduce a sunburn's sting.

Acorn *(from oak, Quercus robur)*

The Iroquois, a league of Native American nations, washed burns with the liquid from a decoction of acorns.

24 cracked acorns
750 millilitres (3 cups) water
1. Bring to the boil
2. Simmer until the volume is reduced by half
3. Strain, discarding acorns
4. Wash the burn with the liquid several times a day

Chaparral *(Larrea divaricata L. tridentata)*
also known as Creosote Bush

The resin from this plant, a native of the south west of what is now the USA was used by Native Americans to treat burns.

---

[1]   *avoid during pregnancy and if breast feeding*

Cocoa *(Theobroma cacao)*

Mexican folk healers recommend rubbing cocoa butter into burns.

Lavender [1] *(Lavandula angustifolia)* or Peppermint [2] *(Mentha piperita)*

These two oils have a reputation for soothing the sting of a burn. Try rubbing a few drops of either oil (diluted with 10 millilitres of good quality vegetable or nut oil) into the burn.

Eucalyptus *(Eucalyptus globus)*

Eucalyptus plays an important role in many Australian Aboriginal healing practices. Eucalyptus gum, collected either as a sticky semi-liquid or a solid crystalline substance, was boiled until the gum dissolved and the resulting water was used as a soothing, healing wash.

Wineberry *(Aristotelia serrata)*

The Maori alused a decoction of wineberry leaves or bark to treat burns. Wineberry is known to contain alkaloids, a class of chemical often found to have analgesic (pain killing) properties. Use the normal amount of water if using leaves, use double if you are making a decoction of wineberry bark.

Kanono *(Coprosma australis)*

Kanono was also a popular Maori healing plant. Its leaves, bark and young shoots were used in infusions to help heal

---

[1]   avoid high doses during pregnancy

[2]   avoid during pregnancy and if breast feeding do not give in any form to very young babies

ailments as diverse as bruises, stomach ache, and bladder stoppages. A poultice of kanono leaves was used to hurry broken bones to knit. The Maori applied juice extracted from kanono leaves to soothe painful skin injuries.

Harakeke, New Zealand Flax
(Phormium tenax)

According to James Neil, a follower of Samuel Thompson's Botanic Eclectic system of medicine, New Zealand flax was one of the most useful native New Zealand plants. He wrote that the gum found in the folds of the flax leaves, when dissolved in water, could be used to help burns and other painful skin sores heal.

Bursitis

You don't need to know what bursae are, you don't need to know where they are, you don't even need to know what they they are supposed to do. When your bursae stop working you'll know everything you need to know about bursae. When they are working these little sacs of lubricating fluid allow your joints to work smoothly and painlessly. When they don't it's pure torture.

One of the problems with bursitis is that it comes and goes. You make an appointment to see the doctor, when your appointment rolls around the pain is gone. Not only is this frustrating, it makes it difficult for your doctor to treat and for you to monitor the success of your treatment. Relief from the pain is the bottom line. If bursitis didn't hurt you wouldn't really care about bursae at all.

Hydrotherapy - Cold Compress

Apply a cold compress to the joint during the first few days of a flare-up, when swelling and pain are worst. Leave it on overnight and for 20 minutes during the day, renewing it whenever it no longer feels cold.

Remedies with 🫖 *are made using an infusion. Those with* 🍲 *are made using a decoction. Instructions for both methods are on pages 4 - 7. Variations and other procedures are contained in the text following the description of that remedy.*

Replace the cold compresses with hot compresses once improvement begins. For acute inflammation, use an ice-pack or when you don't have one, a bag of frozen peas (it will accommodate the irregular surface of the human elbow, shoulder or knee). Smear your skin with olive (or any cooking oil) to prevent frostbite. Apply the cold (or hot compresses) three times daily, using the following cycle. On for five minutes, off for five minutes. On for ten minutes, off for ten minutes. On for 15 minutes, off for 15 minutes.

Epsom salts

Australian folk healers tell you to soak your arm in hot water in which you have dissolved epsom salts and then massage your sore arm with olive oil and salt.

Housemaid's Liniment

Take 1 teaspoon each of the essential oils of lavender, marjoram, eucalyptus and rosemary and mix with 5 teaspoons of sunflower oil. Use the fragrant oil to gently massage the knee several times a day.

Chamomile *(Chamaemelum nobile, Roman, or C. recutita, German)*

Use chamomile oil (1-2 drops of chamomile oil diluted with 10 millilitres of good quality vegetable or nut oil) to gently massage the affected area.

Canker Sores
(mouth ulcers)

That's it, you've done it now. You couldn't wait for the pizza to cool and you've burnt your lip. If you're lucky you will have a few days of mild discomfort and then it will all be forgotten. If you're not so lucky in a few days you will wake up with a white, flat sore on the inside of your lip right where the burn was. It's a canker sore (sometimes called a mouth ulcer) and the only mystery is why you keep getting them.

Eating food that's too hot. Biting your lip, or your tongue, or indulging in your favourite, extra-crusty french bread. For most people these are minor irritations, but for you they mean torture, because you get canker sores.

No one knows exactly why people get canker sores, and no one knows why some people get them and others don't. But if you get them you'll be interested in trying one of these folk remedies. They may help ease the pain and send the canker sores back to wherever they come from.

Remedies with 🫖 *are made using an infusion. Those with* ♨ *are made using a decoction. Instructions for both methods are on pages 4 - 7. Variations and other procedures are contained in the text following the description of that remedy.*

Lady's Mantle [1] *(Alchemilla vulgaris)*

For centuries Europeans have sipped an infusion of lady's mantle to help heal canker sores. Save some of the liquid to use as a mouth wash too. 🫖

Plum *(Prunus spp.)*

The Japanese gargle with fresh plum juice to treat canker sores. Use a juice extractor to remove the juice from two fresh plums. Swish the juice around your mouth for a few minutes making sure that the juice contacts the canker sore. If the sore is especially bad you can soak a piece of cotton wool in fresh plum juice and hold it against the sore with your tongue.

Watercress *(Nasturtium officinale)*
and Carrot *(Daucus carota)*

This special watercress soup is a popular folk remedy with folk healers.

200 grams (½ pound) each chopped watercress and chopped
2 litres (2 quarts) water
1. Bring to the boil
2. Simmer until the liquid is reduced to ⅓ - ¼ of the original volume
3. Eat

Lemon *(Citrus limon or C. medica, var. limonum)*

Equal parts lemon and water. It's simple. It's supposed to be effective. It's supposed to promote healing if applied directly to the canker sore. It probably hurts like the dickens, but so

---

[1]   *avoid during pregnancy*

does a canker sore, if it helps to heal the canker sore quickly, may be it's worth a try.

Rose *(Rosa canina)*

English physician and herbalist Nicholas Culpeper recommended drinking an infusion of rose-hips to heal canker sores.

Cellulite

Either cellulite doesn't exist or it's the worst calamity to affect women in the last millennium. It all depends on who you ask. If you've got it you know that it's real, real ugly!

Even people who believe that cellulite is real (because they've seen the puckery, orange-peel effect with their own eyes, on their own thighs!) can't agree on whether there is any physical or chemical difference between the fat in cellulite and fat under normal, beautiful smooth skin. The best recommendation anyone can give you is to keep your weight within the normal range for your height. And give some of these folk remedies a try, because every little bit helps.

Beetroot (Beta vulgaris)

Beetroot is supposed to help your liver break down fats in your diet. Use a juice extractor to make fresh beetroot juice and drink 125 millilitres (4 fluid ounces) every day.

Celery (Apium graveolens)

Celery is supposed to help remove excess fluid from your system. Eat a lot of it and eat it raw.

Remedies with 🫖 are made using an infusion. Those with ☕ are made using a decoction. Instructions for both methods are on pages 4 - 7. Variations and other procedures are contained in the text following the description of that remedy.

Cucumber *(Cucumis sativus)*

Cucumbers are supposed to help your kidneys eliminate waste more efficiently. Eat a large cucumber salad every day.

Saunas

Saunas are a Scandinavian tradition. They help cleanse the skin and get the blood flowing. Most Middle European and Slavic countries use dry or wet heat in ritual or social baths. Many Native Americans use sweat lodges in their religious festivals. Most cultures agree that there is something about a steam bath or sauna that is good for you.

Some old-fashioned remedies

Lemon *(Citrus limon or C. medica, var. limonum)*

Boil a lemon rind in 250 millilitres (1 cup) water for 30 minutes. Let it steep overnight. Drink the liquid first thing in the morning, drink it instead of coffee or tea.

Onion *(Allium cepa)*

Make some rich onion soup, add a generous sprinkling of dried sage and eat it for lunch.

Lettuce *(Lactuca sativa)* and Chervil *(Anthriscus cerefolium)*

This infusion is supposed to help eradicate cellulite.

30 grams (1 ounce) lettuce leaf
15 grams (1/2 ounce) chervil

600 ml (1 pint) boiling water
1. Steep covered 10 minutes
2. Drink 250 millilitres (1 cup), 3 times a day

Patchouli (Pogostemon cabin-labiatae)

Massaging the whole body with this fragrant essential oil is a favourite cellulite remedy throughout Asia. It's especially popular in Japan, China and Malaysia. Dilute 1 - 2 drops of patchouli oil with 10 millilitres of good quality vegetable or nut oil and massage the whole body with special attention on cellulite prone areas. Don't go overboard though, patchouli can be overpowering in confined quarters.

Ivy (Glechoma hederacea)

Use common household ivy to make this soothing poultice.

150 grams (5 ounces) ivy leaves chopped
300 grams bran
1. Add enough warm water to form a paste
2. Apply while still warm to areas of the body where cellulite is a problem (usually upper legs, buttocks, etc.)
3. Repeat once a week

Or try this recipe for a soothing compress made from a decoction of ivy.

150 grams (5 ounces) chopped ivy leaves
1 litre (1 quart) water
1. Bring to the boil
2. Simmer 10 minutes
3. Strain, discarding solids
4. Soak a cotton towel in the liquid
5. Apply while still warm to affected area

Chapped Hands

Your age shows first on your face, but your hands are not far behind in the 'Giving away your age stakes'. If you want people to think that you are younger than you really are you'll need to take care of your hands. Moisture is the key to soft skin, moisture, not water. When you wash your hands you remove your skin's natural oils, the oils that should be holding the moisture in your skin. Without this oil the moisture evaporates. The result is? The cracked, red, rough, painful, skin called chapped hands. If you have chapped hands wash them enough to keep them clean, but no more, and always moisturise after washing.

If your hands look and feel more like sandpaper than skin try one of these folk remedies now, your hands will thank you for it.

Mudpacks

Sure mudpacks are ugly, but they make your skin look beautiful. Most women already know how good a mudpack makes the skin on their face look and feel. Treat your hands to the same tender loving care. Using clay-rich earth to treat dry

---

Remedies with ☕ are made using an infusion. Those with ♨ are made using a decoction. Instructions for both methods are on pages 4 - 7. Variations and other procedures are contained in the text following the description of that remedy.

and chapped skin is a longstanding folk remedy for dull, lifeless skin. Mud helps to draw impurities from your pores and gently remove the top layer of dead cells. Use the same mud based products you use on your face for your hands, or look for products especially formulated for hands and feet.

Vinegar, Honey and Petroleum Jelly

Folk healers in the U.S. state of Vermont recommend washing your hands in vinegar then applying equal parts of honey and petroleum jelly.

Borax and Oatmeal Powder

Or try this old-fashioned remedy, rinse your hands in a very dilute solution of borax, 5 grams (1 teaspoon) borax in 1 litre (1 quart) water. Then dust them with oatmeal powder.

Milk

This is another 'beauty' treatment that most women will already know because of its age-old reputation as a miracle worker for tired skin. Milk baths are the ultimate indulgence. For a fraction of the cost, treat your hands to the luxury of a milk bath. After all your hands do all the work. Don't they deserve to be pampered once in a while? Soak your hands in a bowl of milk each night and feel the difference in the morning.

Wheatgerm Oil

If your hands have gone beyond chapped, to sore, cracked and splitting skin, all is not lost. Treat them to a nightly massage with wheatgerm oil and you'll be helping them to heal quickly. Don't wash the oil off before going to bed or you won't get the maximum benefit. Just wear a light pair of cotton gloves to bed, the gloves will protect your bedding and your hand can get the benefit of the rich moisturising treatment all night long.

Flaxseed *(Linum usitatissimum)*

This remedy, made from flaxseed, takes a lot of work but it's worth the effort.

1. Soak 40 grams (2 tablespoons whole or crack flaxseed in 250 millilitres (1 cup lukewarm water for 12 hours
2. Bring to the boil
3. Simmer 20 - 30 minutes
4. Strain, discarding the gluey residue and seeds
5. Add 500 millilitres (2 cups) apple cider vinegar and 30 millilitres (2 tablespoons) glycerine
6. Heat again, to boiling, remove from heat
7. Mix well, using an egg-beater
8. Store in an airtight bottle, in a cool place out of direct sunlight
9. Rub the mixture into your skin morning and night.

Groundsel *(Senecio vulgaris) also known as common groundsel or ragwort)*

This European remedy dates back to the seventeenth century. Make an infusion from groundsel leaves and flowers. Use the strained liquid as a soothing wash and save the softened leaves and flowers to make a poultice to use on knots and warts.

Chapped, dry hands often means hang-nails (ingrown nails and damaged cuticles) too, a little problem that can be very painful. If you are troubled with hangnails, try one of these folk remedies.

Harakeke, Native Flax *(Phormium tenax)*

The Maori used the gum from native flax (and other similar plants) to soothe and promote healing, in the treatment of burns and inflamed skin conditions. Modern researchers are trying to incorporate extracts from flax roots into a soothing soap to use on chapped, inflamed skin. The Maori placed a high value on the healing properties of native flax and modern research is confirming their view. Could native flax be another aloe vera, just waiting to be 'discovered'?

Kanono *(Coprosma australis)*

Kanono was a popular Maori healing plant. Its leaves, bark and young shoots were used in infusions to help heal ailments as diverse as bruises, stomach ache, and bladder stoppages. And a poultice of kanono leaves was used to heal broken bones. The Maori applied the juice extracted from kanono leaves to soothe painful skin complaints, like chapped hands.

White Deadnettle *(Laminum album)*

During the Middle Ages a poultice of infused white deadnettle leaves was used to treat infected hangnails. Use the warm, softened leaves on your infected hangnail to draw the poisons out.

Pot Marigold [1] *(Calendula officinalis)*

This popular remedy has been used in England for years. It's suppose to help soften and heal hangnails and to soothe and heal cracked, sore skin on your hands, and feet.

1. Melt a small jar of petroleum jelly in a double boiler
2. Add six clean, crushed marigold flowers, head and all
3. Simmer the petroleum jelly and marigold flowers for several hours
4. Strain and allow to cool then return warm petroleum jelly to the jar
5. Apply to hangnail

---

[1]   *Do not confuse with French Marigold, Tagetes patula*

Chapped Lips

If you think that returning from a ski weekend with chapped lips will make you look cool, think again. You'll only look careless. Take care of your lips while you are on the slopes. In fact it's cold, dry air that causes cracked, swollen, peeling lips so take good care of your lips all the time, but be especially kind to your lips during the winter.

If you do get chapped lips try one of these folk remedies, they're sure to bring a smile back to your face.

Cocoa Butter

In Mexico folk healers recommend putting a thin film of cocoa butter on chapped lips.

Lemon (Citrus limon or C. medica, var. limonum)

In France it's lemon to the rescue. They mix the lemon pulp left after juicing with a little glycerine to make a healing and moisturising surface treatment for chapped lips.

Remedies with 🫖 are made using an infusion. Those with ♨ are made using a decoction. Instructions for both methods are on pages 4 - 7. Variations and other procedures are contained in the text following the description of that remedy.

Blind or Stinging Nettle [1]
(Urtrica dioica or U. urens)

The Romany people, who are sometimes called Gypsies, swear by their old-time remedy, a healing paste made from nettle tops. Be sure to simmer the nettles for a long time, to make them very soft and to remove all the formic acid. Otherwise this 'remedy' could end-up burning like the dickens.

1. Simmer a handful of nettle tops in water until they are reduced to a pulpy mass
2. Strain, discarding liquid
3. Allow the pulp to cool then spread on chapped lips

Some of the following old-fashioned remedies are found in the family lore of many cultures.

Goose Grease, Butter

One of the first ways people re-moisturised chapped lips was with butter or goose grease. Adding soothing medicinal plants was the ancient version of making a 'new and improved' product. Chickweed and mallow were especially popular soothing plants for this sort of treatment.

Beeswax

If you know a beekeeper, ask for some yellow beeswax straight from the hive. Store it in a cool, dry place and rub a little over your lips every now and then.

---

[1] *stinging comes from formic acid and histamine which are found in the fine hairlike needles of the leaves.*

Petroleum Jelly

It's not nearly as romantic as beeswax, but petroleum jelly is a multi-functional treatment for any sore skin condition. Petroleum helps protect your lips from the elements, moisturises dry lips and soothes chapped lips.

Olive Oil, Castor Oil or Honey mixed with Rosewater

Use any of these mixtures to protect your lips and hasten healing.

Aromatherapy

To ease pain of chapped lips add a drop of chamomile, calendula, lavender or myrrh oil to 10 ml (2 teaspoons) vegetable oil and apply gently to painful chapped lips.

Something in the air . . .

Aromatherapy is catching on in the least likely places. Japanese companies were the first to try scenting the air in office buildings to improve staff performance. Invigorating lemon scents were tried. Now some American companies are trying it out, experimenting with different scents at different times of the day. The Smell and Taste Treatment and Research Foundation in the U.S. city of Chicago, Illinois has looked at the influence of scent on people's ability to concentrate and found that appealing fragrances can help

---

Cholesterol

Yesterday you couldn't spell cholesterol, today your doctor told you have to keep an eye on yours. It's no wonder you're confused. You've probably heard that "cholesterol . .

. . . is necessary for a healthy body."

. . . causes heart attacks and strokes."

. . . is good"

. . . is bad"

. . . isn't just cholesterol it's LDL, HDL, dietary and serum cholesterol"

What's important, what's not? Is it good or is it bad?

Cholesterol is necessary for a healthy body, so that must mean it is good. But it also causes heart attacks and strokes, so that must mean it is bad. The truth is somewhere in between and it all depends on what kind of cholesterol you are talking about.

Cholesterol is vitally important to the production of hormones, cellular components and the insulating sheaths around your nerves, but your body is perfectly capable of

Remedies with ☕ are made using an infusion. Those with ♨ are made using a decoction. Instructions for both methods are on pages 4 - 7. Variations and other procedures are contained in the text following the description of that remedy.

producing all the cholesterol it needs—without any help from your diet. Your body doesn't need any more. When you insist on eating extra cholesterol your body doesn't make more stuff out of it. No, your body is happy to leave this extra cholesterol to its own devices, let it travel around your blood stream, looking for a nice cosy nook or cranny in which to settle and make some mischief.

That's why diet is important in controlling cholesterol levels. Eat too much of it and these cholesterol conventions can block the flow of traffic in your veins and arteries (these traffic jams are best known for the heart attacks and strokes they can cause).

Eating high cholesterol foods can raise your serum cholesterol. Eating saturated fats also raises blood cholesterol, while some research has shown that eating unsaturated fat can lower cholesterol. However you look at it, a low fat diet then is one of the best things you can do for your body.

There are few true folk remedies for cholesterol, and when you think about it, that's just what you would expect. It's only recently that humans have lived in conditions where levels of cholesterol in our diet are a problem. But there are some traditional cultures that suffer few cholesterol related complaints.

Vegetarian cultures don't have problems with cholesterol. Animal products are the main culprits in the cholesterol caper. No-nos from the plant kingdom include coconut milk and palm oil, both of which are high in saturated fats. They should therefore be treated as if they were animal fat in a cholesterol control diet. Cultures that are not vegetarian but that eat meat sparingly, and consume a large proportion of

Who's who in the cholesterol game?

Watching your cholesterol is just like watching a football match, you've got to know who is playing to understand what's going on.

● Dietary cholesterol is the cholesterol in the food you eat.

● Serum cholesterol is what's in your blood. It's what your doctor measures.

● Your serum cholesterol (which should be 200 or below) is made up of low-density lipoprotein (LDL) and high-density lipoprotein (HDL). This is the part where people get confused. Much of what is reported in the popular press concerns these two components of serum cholesterol and their relative roles in atherosclerosis.

● LDL is the culprit in heart disease, it's the fat that collects in your arteries. When your arteries are clogged heart attacks and strokes follow.

● HDL is sometimes called 'good cholesterol' because it helps to remove the LDL deposited in your arteries and veins.

their calories as complex carbohydrates—especially pectin producing fruit, vegetables, grains and pulses—also seem to be better protected from cholesterol related problems. Traditional African and South American cultures get a gold star in this category, with oats, corn, carrots, cabbage and broccoli in their diets thought to be especially beneficial.

Some non-vegetarian cultures also have significantly lower levels of cholesterol than most western populations. Two of the most interesting are Inuit still living traditional lives in what is now the US state of Alaska and Japanese eating traditional diets. Both eat a significant proportion of their protein as fish. The Inuit also eat a large amount of animal fat (from marine mammals) yet they do not suffer from the effects of high cholesterol levels, while Japanese living in the west and switching to a western diet end up suffering the same levels of high cholesterol, heart attacks and strokes as those seen in western populations.

So, eating pectin producing fruits and pulses along with fish is good for you. This type of diet seems to keep cholesterol levels low and help protect you from any stray cholesterol that does end-up travelling through your veins.

Garlic [1] *(Allium sativum)*

Garlic is one of the oldest known medicinal plants. According to practitioners of traditional Chinese medicine, eating 3 - 10 cloves of garlic a day helps to control cholesterol levels and western research has confirmed that garlic can reduce fat in the blood stream

---

[1]   *avoid during pregnancy and if breast feeding*

Great veins - pity about the breath

Many people are hesitant to take up a garlic based remedy because they are worried about the effect of all that garlic on their breath.

If you want to up your consumption of garlic to lower your cholesterol levels or for another remedy in which it features, but are wary of the effect the garlic will have on your breath, you can try garlic capsules, which usually contain garlic powder. Or you may want to give deodorised garlic oil, usually sold in gelatine pearls, a go.

Some folk healers and herbalists believe that the therapeutic effect of garlic is lost when the oil is deodorised. But that may not be as much of a problem as it seems. Compared to a clove of garlic, garlic oil is highly concentrated. That's because of the type of garlic used and the process by which it is made. So when you take deodorised garlic you are getting very much more than would be possible to take as fresh garlic.

Colds

They call it the common cold but it's really an uncommon nuisance. Forget wet feet, wet hair, or getting wet on a cold day. You catch a cold when two simple conditions are met, your guard is down (your immune system is susceptible to attack) and you are exposed to the cold virus.

That's where the simplicity ends. It's unlikely that medical science will discover a cure for the common cold in the foreseeable future. The common cold is actually caused by lots of different cold viruses. Each of these viruses is changing all the time. So while you might think that one cold feels just like all the others, the cold you catch today is different from the one you caught last year or the one you will catch next year.

Don't waste your time and money going to see a doctor when you catch a cold. He or she won't give you a script for antibiotics, they don't have any affect on a virus. Antibiotics work against bacterial, not viral diseases. The Doc will tell you to do what you were going to do anyway. "Take it easy; take some aspirin or paracetamol to reduce the fever; drink plenty of fluids. Blah, blah, blah". Here's the most important thing you

---

Remedies with ☕ *are made using an infusion. Those with* ☕ *are made using a decoction. Instructions for both methods are on pages 4 - 7. Variations and other procedures are contained in the text following the description of that remedy.*

need to know about a cold. Unless you are already ill and therefore have a weakened immune system, your cold will go away in about seven days. Even if you do nothing at all!

What can you do to make having a cold more bearable? Years ago, when dual Nobel Prize winning chemist Linus Pauling, began to talk about Vitamin C and its role in a healthy, strong, immune system most people just laughed. Today the benefits of Vitamin C are acknowledged by conventional and alternative health practitioners alike.

Just how Vitamin C works and the extent of its powers are not known. We do know that Vitamin C can help your body stay healthy and strong. It can also help your body return to health when challenged by viral and bacterial diseases, stress or environmental pollutants.

Make sure that you get a good dose of Vitamin C every day. Increase the amount when you are likely to be exposed to any disease causing organisms or when you are under stress. Then take an extra dose when a cold strikes and boost your body's ability to banish the bugs from your system - pronto!

While you are at it try one of these folk remedies from around the world, they will soothe your system and help you return to a normal, happy state of health.

Homoeopathic remedy, Allium cepa

It's no accident that this traditional homoeopathic remedy takes its name from the botanical or scientific name for onions. Allium cepa is in fact made from onions. You'll need to buy homoeopathic remedies from a homoeopathic pharmacy or from a homoeopath. One 30c pill every hour for four or five hours is the usual recommendation.

Homoeopathy

Homoeopathy began in Germany when Dr Samuel Hahnemann noticed that when he took cinchona, which was used to treat malaria, he experienced the same symptoms that malaria produced. From this experience he developed the first principle of homoeopathy, "Treat like with like". By this Hahnemann meant that illness should be treated with substances that produce in healthy people the physical symptoms of the disease you are treating.

The second principle of homoeopathy is 'minimum dose'. Hahnemann found that many people got worse when treated with what he considered a normal dose of a medicinal substance. So he began diluting his treatments. When he did this, he found that the more dilute the treatment the better the treatment seemed to work.

According to the homeopathic beliefs a remedy becomes more potent as its dilution increases (higher dilution = lower concentration) because energy builds up in the molecules in the dilution process. The first step in making a homoeopathic remedy is to make the mother tincture. These are usually made by extracting the active principle from the plant or animal source using a small amount of alcohol. The mother tincture is the most concentrated. It is from successive dilutions of the mother tincture that a homoeopathic remedy is prepared. *continued over page*

Homoeopathy
continued from previous page

Homeopathic remedies are made in two standard dilution scales. The X or Decimal scale and the C or Centesimal scale. 1X means that the mother tincture has been diluted once at a 1:10 dilution. For the C scale each dilution is made at the 1:100 ratio. Each dilution in the X scale is 10 times as dilute (in the C scale 100 times as dilute) as the preceding dilution. It is important that the dilutions are made successively rather than in a single step, this means that the 1X (or 1C) is diluted to make 2X (or 2C) and 2X (or 2C) diluted to make 3X.

Potency	Effective Concentration
1X1	drop of mother tincture to 10 drops of alcohol
2X	drop of mother tincture to 100 drops of alcohol
3X	drop of mother tincture to 1000 drops of alcohol
1C	drop of mother tincture to 100 drops of alcohol
2C	drop of mother tincture to 10,000 drops of alcohol
3C	drop of mother tincture to 1,000,000 drops of alcohol

Onion *(Allium cepa)*

If you like, think of this remedy as the 'DIY' version of the homoeopathic remedy allium cepa, because you'll be making a very dilute onion infusion.

If you live alone or have a very understanding spouse you can get double duty from you medicinal onion. Place half an onion on your bedside table. Inhaling the onion vapours through the night is said to reduce mucus formation and speed recovery.

1. Dip a slice of freshly cut onion into a glass of hot water.

2. Remove the onion after only 2 or 3 seconds

3. Cool and sip this throughout the day.

Allspice *(Pimenta diocia,*
also known as Jamica pepper, pimento)

In the Caribbean, folk healers recommend drinking a hot allspice infusion. Some people think that allspice is a mixture of spices, but it isn't. Allspice berries have a flavour that tastes like a combination of cloves and nutmeg with a hint of peppery hotness.

Boneset *(Eupatorium perfoliatum)*

This plant, a native of North America takes its name from its use to treat 'breakbone' or Dengue fever. It was a favourite herb with Native American tribes because of its ability to induce sweating. Many tribes used sweating for medicinal and spiritual purposes. For colds they recommended drinking an infusion made from boneset dried leaves and flower tops.

Chaparral *(Larrea divaricata L. tridentata)*

Drinking an infusion of chaparral flowers was another Native American cold treatment.

Burdock *(Arctium lappa)*

Early Chinese physicians and traditional Ayurvedic healers both recommended drinking a decoction made from burdock roots to treat colds.

Bayberry *(Myrica cerifera)*

Nineteenth century American herbalist, Samuel Thomson recommended drinking a decoction of bayberry root for colds because of its ability to heat the body.

Lemon *(Citrus limon or C. medica, var. limonum)*

Even if breathing these vapours doesn't reduce the symptoms of your cold, the clean, fresh lemon scent will brighten your day. Take 30 ml (1 ounce) lemon juice and add to 1 litre boiling water. Cover your head with a towel and lean over the container and breathe in the vapours, repeat twice a day.

Celery *(Apium graveolens)*

Drinking an infusion of celery seeds is a traditional cold remedy in India.

Cinnamon [1] *(Cinnamomum zeylanicum in the west, C. cassia in China, C Cassia from the bark = rou gui or from twigs gui zhi)*

In the twelfth century the German abbess and herbalist, Hildegard of Bingen recommended drinking an infusion of cinnamon to treat a cold.

Cinnamon [2] *(Cinnamomum zeylanicum),*
Clove *(Syzgium aromaticum),*
Lemon *(Citrus limon or C. medica, var. limonum)*
and Honey

As useful as Hildegard of Bingen's infusion may be, this French folk remedy sounds even better. It starts as a simple

---

[1]   avoid in pregnancy

[2]   avoid in pregnancy

If you can't be famous, will infamous do?

The nineteenth century American herbalist Samuel Thomson founded the 'Physiomedical theory of health', developed his 'Improved System of Botanic Practice of Medicine' and sold his *New Guide to Health or Botanic Family Physician.* Thomson's membership system was a sort of herbal friendly society, through which members could buy Thomson's herbal remedies.

Thomson's system lives on today, though not in the way he would have liked. He patented his medical system so that he could sell it. But he wanted to prevent buyers using the system for their own gain. Seeing a good way to make a quick buck others followed suit, patenting their unique concoctions and selling them to the unsuspecting public. Unfortunately while these recipes were unique, few had any medicinal value. The travelling hucksters that sold the treatments didn't explain to customers that the patents were granted for unique recipes, but they had no requirement to prove the efficacy of a unique concoction.

The term Patent Medicines lives on as a shorthand way of describing something that promises the buyer everything but delivers nothing, except a large profit to the seller. Not what Samuel Thomson had in mind at all when he began selling his 'Improved System of Botanic Practice of Medicine'.

decoction of cinnamon and cloves. You add a little bit of lemon juice and some honey and the secret ingredient . . . whisky, so it's guaranteed to pack a wallop.

One small stick of cinnamon and a few cloves

500 ml (2 cups) of water

1. Bring to the boil
2. Simmer 5 minutes, remove from heat
3. Add 10 millilitres (2 teaspoons) lemon juice and 15 ml (½ tablespoon) dark honey
4. Add 40 millilitres (2 tablespoons) whiskey
5. Stir well, cover and let steep 20 minutes
6. Strain, discarding solids
7. Drink 125 ml (half a cup) every 3 to 4 hours

Mustard (Brassica hirta))

The ancient Romans recommended a mustard footbath to treat colds. In the 2000 intervening years this remedy has never gone out of favour with folk healers. Pour hot water over about 30 grams (1 ounce) bruised mustard seeds and soak your feet in the water for a warming treatment that is sure to get your circulation going.

If the cold has settled in your chest, that old-time favourite, a mustard plaster, won't go awry. Try this variation on the standard plaster — the bran helps spread the mustard seed over a larger area.

1. Mix 20 grams (1 tablespoon) dry mustard with an equal amount of bran or oatmeal
2. Add enough hot water to make a paste and apply to the chest
3. Cover the plaster with a towel to hold in the heat and protect your clothes

For extra benefit, go to bed with a hot water bottle and call in sick the next morning.

Elder [1] *(Sambucus nigra)*

Late last century the juice of ripe elderberries was a favourite cold remedy. They didn't know it then but elderberry juice contains Vitamin C, the 'modern, high-tech remedy' for colds that folk healers have been recommending for centuries.

Ephedra simca [2] *(ma huang)*

Was ephedra the first plant our ancient ancestors used medicinally? No one will ever know, but it could have been. We do know that ephedra is one of the oldest plants to be used medicinally. Its use is recorded in the oldest Chinese herbals. It's fitting then, that infusions and decoctions of ephedra have been used to treat an ailment that has bugged humans for ages. Use fresh ephedra for an infusion, dried ephedra for a decoction.

or

Ginger [3] *(Zingiber officinalis)*

When Shen Nung compiled his *Pen Tsao Ching* ('Classic of herbs'), he recommended ginger for treating colds. Ginger mulled in beer is an old-fashioned remedy that is supposed to help you sleep, though it would be hard to separate the influence of the beer from that of the ginger. If you don't fancy a little ginger with your beer, eat fresh ginger. Nibble on a little throughout the day, or add about 5 grams (1 teaspoon) powdered dried ginger to any drink.

---

[1] do not use during pregnancy

[2] This is a restricted herb in Aust and NZ, and can only be sold by registered practitioners in the UK

[3] use sparingly during pregnancy

Peppermint [1] *(Mentha piperita)*
or Spearmint [2] *(Mentha spicata)*

Keep a small bottle of either of these oils in your medicine cupboard. When a cold strikes, add a couple of drops of oil to a cup of lukewarm water and drink it. Put a few drops of either oil on a handkerchief and inhale the aroma. It will help to clear your head.

Vervian [3] *(Verbena officinalis)*

Drinking an infusion of this indigenous North American plant is an old-fashioned folk remedy for colds. You can use the root, leaves or flowers to make this infusion.

Catnip *(Nepeta cataria)*

In the Middle Ages an infusion of catnip was a popular cold remedy.

Garlic [4] *(Allium sativum)*

As a medicinal plant, garlic has almost as long a pedigree as ephedra does. If you work closely with the public (or are in love with a vampire) and can't indulge in daily doses of garlic you may want to look into commercial garlic preparations, many of which used deodorised garlic. But you should know that some researchers believe that the process of deodorising the garlic reduces garlic's medicinal properties.

---

[1]   *avoid during pregnancy and if breast feeding, do not give in any form to very young babies*

[2]   *avoid during pregnancy and if breast feeding, do not give in any form to very young babies*

[3]   *avoid during pregnancy*

[4]   *avoid during pregnancy and if breast feeding.*

Yes, that catnip

If you're wondering if the catnip used in human herbal remedies is the same catnip that makes your normally serene, sedate and aloof cat go positively goofy, the answer is yes.

Ageing hippies can forget any ideas they may have about reliving the hazy days of their lost youth. Catnip does not affect humans the way it affects cats. You might even say that it has the opposite effect.

A cat that is sensitive to catnip, and not all cats are, is energised by the herb. It puts them into a state called 'catnip euphoria'. In contrast catnip has a soothing, almost tranquillising, effect on humans.

While Fluffy can join you in this herbal remedy don't experiment on Fluffy or Fido using herbal remedies. Dogs and cats often react violently to medications, including herbal remedies, which are safe for humans. This is not only because of the size differences between the species but of physiological differences as well.

There are herbal remedies especially developed for dogs and cats though, so shop around. You may even be able to find a herbal veterinarian!

Honey and Lemon (Citrus limon or C. medica, var. limonum)

This is probably the best folk practice for soothing a cold's symptoms. Dilute the juice of one lemon with hot water and drink warm. If you like add a couple of cloves, a dash of cinnamon, or a few slivers of ginger, for a little extra zip.

Honey and Eucalyptus *(Eucalyptus globus)*

Almost as well known as honey and lemon is honey and eucalyptus. Mix 5 millilitres (1 teaspoon) honey with a 250 millilitres (1 cup) hot water and 3 drops of eucalyptus oil. Drink 2 or 3 times a day.

Peach *(Prunus persica)*

Some Native American tribes use a syrup made from a decoction of peach kernels and bark to treat colds.

1. Pound: peach bark 170 grams (⅔ cup)
2. Split: peach kernels, 170 grams (⅔ cup)
3. Add: 500 millilitres (2 cups) each apple cider vinegar and pure distilled water
4. Steep: 5 days in a warm place, shake several times each day
5. Simmer: Gently until the volume is reduced by ½
6. Add: 250 millilitres (½ cup) brandy or whisky as a preservative
7. Use: 20 ml (1 tablespoon) every 3 - 4 hours
8. Store: in a well-sealed bottle or jar in a cool location, out of direct sunlight
9. Discard unused portion after 1 month

Pukatea *(Laurelia novae-zelandiae)*

Drinking an infusion of pukatea bark is a traditional Maori way to soothe sore throats from colds and flu.

Kawakawa *(Macropiper excelsum)*

The Maori also chewed kawakawa leaves to soothe sore throat pain.

Chicken Soup

Perhaps the most famous folk remedy for colds is chicken soup. Most cultures have a traditional recipe but when you have a cold only one recipe will do. Your Mum's recipe! Be prepared and get the recipe before you catch a cold. Better yet, call your Mum and ask her to make some for you. While Mums and Nans have been singing the praises of hot chicken soup for generations, science has confirmed that there really is something to it. It seems that the warm soup, the steam (and a good sized dollop of TLC) encourages the flow of mucus, which helps to open your sinuses and flush the germs out of your respiratory system—so enjoy.

Willow [1] *(Salix alba)*

Herbalists and folk healers have been telling people to drink a decoction of willow bark to reduce fever, inflammation and pain for thousands of years. Modern herbalists recommend an infusion of powdered willow bark. Western medical practitioners recommend a cousin of the active ingredient in willow bark. Instead of having you drink a decoction of willow bark they will have you take it in tablet, capsule or soluble form, and they'll call it aspirin.

Red Currant *(Rubes sativum)*

Early American pioneer women treated colds with a remedy that might catch on at the pub. To help the patient sleep and hasten recovery they added a little bit of red currant jelly to a glass of whisky, which the patient was to drink just before

---

[1] *Treat willow as you would aspirin, do not take if you are pregnant and do not give to children under two or to children suffering with a cold, flu or chicken pox*

sleep. Of course the bigger the glass of whiskey, the better this remedy worked!

Acupressure

These two remedies are said to work on everyone, but are especially useful on children under 2 years of age, on whom herbal remedies shouldn't be used. The remedies probably originated in acupressure therapy

Press into the pad of each toe with your thumb. Hold for 20 - 30 seconds. Do this on each foot until tenderness decreases. Repeat this technique every half hour on infants.

Or, rotate the big toe on each foot and press in with your thumb all around each big toe, from the base of the toe to the tip.

A remedy that smells of superstition?

Umbilical Cord

In Malta mothers preserve their baby's umbilical cord in powder. When the baby gets a cold, the cord is given to the child to smell, which is believed to help cure the cold.

Cold comfort from a cold cold-remedy

Snow

It is said that the Inuit people (sometimes called Eskimos) have hundreds of words for snow. This one would probably translate as AACHOOOH! It seems that when the Inuit catch a cold instead of sniffling, they sniff snow. The icy cold snow contracts the swollen nasal membranes, expels mucus and in due course, makes the cold disappear.

My herbal is older than yours

A herbal is a book that contains information about the medicinal use of plants. Botanists have specific requirements for classifying a plant as a herb, while herbalists generally refer to any plant used for medicinal purposes as a herb.

It is traditional to trace herbal remedies to four classical herbal cultures, Chinese, Indian, European and Native American — or new world. The real story is of course more complex. For example: European, which includes Egyptian, could be subdivided into Greco-Roman, Greco-Arabic and Egyptian.

The oldest culture to use plants medicinally rarely gets a mention in the list of traditional herbal cultures. That's because Australian Aborigines rely on an oral tradition to pass their cultural wisdom from one generation to the next. As well, it is often forbidden to write about sacred Aboriginal practices or to discuss them with the uninitiated.

So when the Chinese get credit for the oldest herbal tradition, it would be more accurate to say that theirs is the oldest surviving written record of herbal remedies. The oldest existing Chinese herbal, *Pen Tsao Ching*, is said to have been written about 3400 BC, during the reign of the emperor Shen Nung. Not everyone accepts that *Pen Tsao Ching* is quite that old. Some say it is more likely to date from around 1000 BC. If this is true it would mean that the three traditional herbal cultures

continued over page

My herbal is older than yours
continued from previous page

were developing their practices at about the same time in different parts of the world.

China has the longest unbroken practice of traditional use of medicinal plants. Today in China herbal medicine exists right alongside western medicine. The development of traditional Chinese medicine has been influenced by Taoist philosophy and incorporates acupuncture, herbs, massage, diet and exercise.

It's possible that traditional Indian medicine, called the Ayurveda, or the 'science of life' is even older than Chinese herbalism. Ayurvedic medicine was incorporated into the Hindu sacred and cultural writings called the Vedas. Vedic writing is believed to go back to 10,000 BC, although no texts exist from that time. Nevertheless, Ayurvedic medicine was already well developed in 1000 BC as Vedic texts of that time demonstrate. Like traditional Chinese medicine, the Ayurveda includes more than simple herbal remedies, it also includes diet, exercise and mental practices called yogas.

The Ebers Papyrus, an Egyptian herbal written on a papyrus scroll almost 20 metres (65 feet) long dates back to about 1500 BC. It records the use of almost 1000 medicinal plants

Greco-Roman herbalism is usually dated from the time of Galen (130 -200 AD) and Dioscorides (first century

continued over page

My herbal is older than yours
continued from previous page

AD). Galen, who was Marcus Aurelius' physician, wrote a recipe book that contained about 130 remedies. Dioscorides wrote what is called the first true herbal, *De Materia Medicia*, which included information about 500 plants. Despite the relative lack of detail in both of their writings these works were held as the highest authority on herbalism until about the sixteenth century. Greco-Roman herbal traditions were preserved during the Dark Ages (641 to 1096, the fall of Alexandria to the First Crusade) by the church, generally within monasteries and abbeys. Outside these cloistered environments however, herbalism continued to develop.

While folk herbalism continued developing it suffered because practitioners did not have access to the historic knowledge held within the closed society of the church. Without the sanction of the church, folk healing's reputation also suffered. Eventually folk medicine came to be seen as superstition, even in some cases witchcraft.

During this period Europe stagnated while the Arab world flourished. In their conquests, Arab armies didn't just seize North Africa. They gained access to Greek and Roman medical texts, which the Arab physicians studied and built upon. The Arab physician Ib-Sina (known as Avicenna in the west) used Aristotelian and Galenic principles in his attempt to incorporate all known medical knowledge into his *Kitab al-Qanun* or *Canon of Medicine.*

continued over page

My herbal is older than yours
continued from previous page

The 100 years beginning in 1530 could be called the Age of Herbals. By this time most European cultures had a herbal with realistic, lifelike drawings of the plants a distinguishing feature. John Gerard's *Herball* [sic] *or Generall Historie of Plantes* [sic] (1597) and Nicholas Culpeper's *The English Physician* (also called *The Complete Herbal*, 1651), are two of the best known from that era.

In the New World, European settlers arrived with their minds open to herbalism and folk wisdom. Native American herbal practices were adopted, copied and combined with the traditional herbal remedies they had brought from all over Europe. As a result, a rich hybrid herbal culture began in the new world. This environment eventually resulted in Samuel Thomson's *"Improved System of Botanic Practice of Medicine"*, and his *"New Guide to Health or Botanic Family Physician"*, a system through which member families could buy their herbal remedies.

Until the twentieth century herbal medicine and what we now call conventional western medicine existed side by side. During the twentieth century medicine has increasingly taken the scientific, mechanistic approach to healing. Recently however, the older remedies have been attracting attention from conventional camps. In the end the best remedies come from an open mind and a combination of conventional and folk practices.

Cold Sores

Like colds, cold sores are caused by a virus. The difference is that you body can kill all the viruses that cause your cold, but the cold sore virus knows all the good hiding places in your body and once you've got it, you've got it for good.

The virus that causes a cold sore is a member of a group called the Herpes viruses. All the viruses in the herpes clan have a common habit. Unlike many viruses herpes viruses don't fight it out to the bitter end when they are attacked by the cells of your immune system. They hide, usually in a nearby nerve cell. The virus doesn't do any harm there, it just hangs out until it the time is right. It's the viruses nerve-cell hideaway that is responsible for the unmistakable tingling that signals another outbreak is on the way.

Herpes simplex I and *II* are kissing cousins. *H. simplex I* is usually responsible for cold sores on the lips, *H. simplex II* plays the role of the villain in genital herpes, but either one can be transmitted to either location. And infection by one type does not give you immunity to infection by the other.

The other common herpes virus *Herpes zoster* (also known as *Varicella zoster*) is responsible for chicken pox. True to its

Remedies with are made using an infusion. Those with are made using a decoction. Instructions for both methods are on pages 4 - 7. Variations and other procedures are contained in the text following the description of that remedy.

family traditions, this herpes virus hangs around long after the fact. Instead of cold sores, *H. zoster* causes shingles. If you think a cold sore is painful, you ain't felt nothing yet. The good thing is that *H. zoster* is less outgoing than its simplex relatives. Many people who have had chicken pox are never bothered by shingles. Therein lies one of the mysteries of the herpes clan; some people are infected but never experience an outbreak, others experience infrequent outbreaks, others have frequent outbreaks.

Cold sores give colds a bad rap. It would be just as correct to call the painful blisters common to the three main herpes viruses wind sores, stress sores or sun sores, since wind, sun and stress are also common triggers for an outbreak. What these triggers have in common is that they tax the immune system. So anything you do to boost your ability to fight disease will help you keep the virus at bay and speed your recovery from any outbreak you do suffer.

Anyone who has ever had a cold sore would agree that it's better to avoid one than to get rid of one. So try this home remedy, it has a reputation for keeping a cold sore at bay.

Ice

Some people swear by this old-fashioned remedy, which they say sends the virus back to its hideaway before it causes a sore. When you first feel the telltale tingling that comes before an outbreak apply ice to the spot for 15 - 20 minutes. Repeat frequently.

Once a sore has started the best thing you can do is let your body's defence department get to work. Keep this in mind while you are suffering. Your immune system always wins in the contest between herpes and you. The virus will eventually give up and go back to its hideaway. But that doesn't mean you have to make it comfortable when it's holidaying on your face. *These remedies will make retreat look like a very good idea and keep other viral or bacterial interlopers from setting up camp at the site of the sore.*

Lemon *(Citrus limon or C. medica, var. limonum)*

Make a solution of equal parts lemon juice and water. Apply the solution to the cold sore.

If you are desperate and very, very brave, dip a piece of cotton wool in pure lemon juice and apply it to the sore.

Glycerine

Put a few drops of glycerine and thymol in warm water and use as a rinse. Thymol comes from thyme oil and is a common ingredient in antiseptic mouth washes.

Eucalyptus *(Eucalyptus globus)* and Olive Oil

Or let the antiseptic qualities of eucalyptus hasten your recovery. Mix eucalyptus oil and olive oil in warm water and use as a rinse.

Biochemic Tissue Salts

For cold sores try Nat Mur *(sodium chloride)*. Buy it at health food store (some chemists carry tissue salts too). They are usually available in 6x potency, but you may want to consult a natural health practitioner for precise recommendations.

It's probably a good thing that you don't feel extremely attractive with a giant cold sore sitting on your lip.

Herpes viruses have split personalities. When they're dormant they are shy and retiring, hanging-out in their nerve-cell hiding place, not bothering anyone. But when they come out to play, they are too friendly for most people's liking.

So keep your hands away from the cold sore, and keep your lips to yourself too. You can pass on the virus by kissing someone when you have an active cold sore or by sharing a drinking glass with them. Don't share towels or flannels either as the virus can lie in wait there too.

Sage[1] *(Salvia officinalis)*
and Ginger[2] *(Zingiber officinalis)*

Use an infusion of sage and ginger as your own homemade antiseptic mouthwash. Use lukewarm, and repeat frequently.

Plum *(Prunus spp.)*

The Europeans use fresh plum juice as a wash and topical treatment for cold sores.

---

[1] *avoid therapeutic doses in pregnancy. Small amounts used in cooking are quite safe.*

[2] *use sparingly during pregnancy*

1. Take 60 ml (2 tablespoons) plum juice
2. Hold it in your mouth for a couple of minutes touching the sore areas with the juice on the tongue and apply the juice to the sores with cotton wool

---

Don't prolong the pain

Stress is your enemy and the cold sore's friend. Stress puts an unnecessary burden on your immune system and reduces your body's ability to fight the virus.

So relax. If a cold sore is the worst thing you have to worry about, you've got it pretty good. With a positive state of mind you'll spend less time worrying, you'll get fewer cold sores and those that you do get will heal faster, which will help you worry less, so you'll get fewer cold sores, and those you get will heal faster, so you will worry less. . . .

Colic

It's hard to know who suffers most from colic, the baby or the baby's parents, but colic has been tormenting families since the dawn of human civilisation. A feed doesn't help, nor does a change of nappies. Walking and patting the baby's back helps for a few minutes, if that. You'd be forgiven for thinking that nothing soothes a colicky baby.

Mum and Dad are at their wit's end. They won't believe you if you tell them that no matter how horrible parenthood seems today, there will eventually be an end to colic. Most babies outgrow colic by the age of four months. But you want relief and you want it NOW!

Theories about what causes colic vary. Mum's diet for breast-fed babies and intolerance to the formula for bottle fed babies are prime contenders. It also may be that some babies' digestive systems haven't quite got the hang of eating just yet. For bottle fed babies you may want to try a different shape or style teat [1] as babies can sometimes have trouble with different shapes causing them to take in too much air when nursing.

Remedies with ☕ are made using an infusion. Those with ♨ are made using a decoction. Instructions for both methods are on pages 4 - 7. Variations and other procedures are contained in the text following the description of that remedy.

---

[1] *nipple in the USA*

You don't need to know what causes colic to know what causes the baby such distress — trapped gas bubbles.

The best remedy then is anything that helps to move the bubbles through the system (so that it can escape and relieve the pressure). Like an adult, a baby only has two exits from its digestive system. One at the top the other at the bottom. If the colic is centred in the stomach burping will send the gas out the mouth. If the gas is trapped in the intestines it will have to make an even less glamorous exit, through the bottom.

Beat the burp

Burp a nursing bub frequently, every 30 millilitres (ounce) or so. This gets the gas out before it gets a chance to get trapped in the intestines.

Massage

A gentle massage is the oldest and best remedy for colic. It works like a crowd controller at a major sporting event, herding the bubbles on their way through the intestines for a speedy exit. Here are a few techniques you can try separately or in succession.

● Lay the baby on your lap, on the floor, or on a cushion on your changing table. Put a few drops of olive oil on your hands and rub them together briskly to warm the oil. Massage the baby's tummy from the base of the ribcage to the bottom of the tummy. Do this 6 -10 times.

● Hold your baby's feet and push them gently, so that his or her knees bend, travelling up towards the tummy. Hold position for 30 seconds. Release and gently pat legs, rocking them from side to side with your hands.

● Massage the tummy in a clockwise direction. Make a full circle with your right hand, a half circle with left hand. Do this 6 -10 times.

Chamomile [1] *Chamaemelum nobile, Roman, or C. recutita, German)*

This remedy brings the added benefit of aromatherapy to the massage remedy described above. Dilute 1 or 2 drops of chamomile oil with 10 millilitres of good quality vegetable or nut oil and use in the massage therapy described above.

Gripe Water

This old-fashioned patient medicine for babies with colic probably does more for an anxious parent's indigestion than for a baby's colic — but if it works for your baby, don't knock it.

If your baby is still suffering from colic after he or she has started on solid food you may want to try one of the following remedies.

Carrot

Mashed carrot is probably already on the menu. Fennel is a popular herbal remedy for stomach upsets in young and old alike. Cook a carrot and an equal sized piece of fennel (bulb) until soft. Mash and add a little honey before feeding it to your baby.

---

[1]   *avoid excessive doses and the oil in any amount during pregnancy*

Chervil (Anthriscus Cerfolium)

Last century chervil was the favourite French remedy for colic. The dried leaves were crumpled and sprinkled on bread, and the fresh leaves were cut up and sprinkled on cooked foods.

If you two-year old is still suffering from colic, you have every mother's sympathy. Along with that sympathy you also have the option of trying one of the following herbal infusions. Remember to use a reduced dose, 10 millilitres or so instead of the normal adult's dose. Though it's unlikely you'll be able to get your child to take more than that anyway.

Chamomile [1] (Chamaemelum nobile, Roman, or C. recutita, German)

In the nineteenth century an infusion of chamomile flowers was a popular remedy for colic.

Grandma's Drink

Take a teaspoon each of aniseed, caraway and fennel seeds, pour boiling water in a cup and mix, leave it for 10 minutes then strain and drink warm.

Marjoram (Origanum marjorana)

The ancient Greeks used an infusion of marjoram to relieve colic.

---

[1]   *avoid excessive doses and the oil in any amount during pregnancy*

Dill *(Anethum graveolens)*

Traditional Chinese physicians have used an infusion of dill seeds to treat colic for over a thousand years. Use 5 grams (1 teaspoon) finely ground dill seeds in 250 ml (1 cup) water and give 1 teaspoon 3 times a day.

Fennel [1] *Foeniculum officinale)*

During the third century BC Hippocrates recommended fennel for colicky children.

1. Grind a few fennel seeds to a fine powder
2. Add a few drops of water
3. Feed 1 teaspoon of the watery mixture to the child

For older babies boil ¾ teaspoon of fennel seeds in a little milk, strain and cool before giving to the child.

Umbilical Cord

If you had any success ridding your child of a cold with the Maltese cold remedy (that uses a preserved umbilical cord) get out your baby's preserved umbilical cord again, and try this Sicilian remedy for colic. Like Maltese mothers, Sicilian mothers also preserve their baby's umbilical cord in powder. According to Sicilian folk traditions having a colicky baby smell their preserved umbilical cord, is a magical cure for colic.

---

[1]   *avoid during pregnancy*

Conjunctivitis

'Pink-eye', it sounds so nice and sweet, even soft. Too bad it's a stand-in for such an irritating condition. If you have ever suffered with conjunctivitis you'll know that rather than being nice, soft or sweet, conjunctivitis feels like a piece of sandpaper rubbing against your eye.

There are two types of conjunctivitis, one caused by an allergic reaction, the other caused by an infection. Whatever the cause, both types usually go away after a few days of tender loving care. Meanwhile, try one of these soothing folk remedies to make the time pass more comfortably.

If your conjunctivitis doesn't go away in a few days, or if the discharge is heavy, yellow or green in colour and accompanied by pain, consult your doctor immediately, it's probably not conjunctivitis.

You must strain these remedies very carefully to remove any solids from the solutions, use boiled or distilled water to make the solutions and use impeccably clean equipment. Remember, never reuse any cotton wool or cloth that has touched your eye without thoroughly washing in very hot water.

Use an ultra-fine sieve to strain, any remedy used on the eye.

Remedies with ☕ are made using an infusion. Those with ☕ are made using a decoction. Instructions for both methods are on pages 4 - 7. Variations and other procedures are contained in the text following the description of that remedy.

Eyebright *(Euphrasia officinalis)*

With a name like eyebright it's not surprising that this plant has been used to treat eye complaints for generations. It has in fact been used since the sixteenth century. Originally the juice, extracted from the whole plant, was diluted and used to wash the eye.

Scottish Highlanders, with a flair for the dramatic, took the leaves and flowers and made a milk infusion, which they applied to the eye with a feather.

Now you can buy a tincture of eyebright at most health food or traditional medicine stores. Use 1 drop of the tincture in ten drops of boiled or distilled water. Use the diluted tincture to bathe your eyes, an eye cup is the most convenient way to do this. Use the tincture three times a day until the redness is gone.

Parsley *(Petroselinum crispum)* *and Chervil* *(Anthriscus cerefolium)*

For centuries the French have used chopped parsley and chervil leaves to soothe conjunctivitis.

Jequirity [1] *(Abrus precatorius)*
also known as Indian Liquorice

This plant was introduced to Brazil three hundred years ago. It has become a popular medicinal plant and this cold infusion of jequirity seeds makes a soothing eye wash. Handle the seeds carefully, and do not take internally under any circumstances.

---

[1]   *Seeds contain a toxic albumen which can be fatal*

2.5 grams (½ teaspoon) powdered seeds

1. Soak 24 hours in 1 litre (1 quart) cold water

2. Strain, using a fine sieve to remove all the seeds, discard solids

3. Bathe affected eyes with the wash 3 times a day for 3 days

---

I spy with my itchy, red eye

Old-fashioned remedies used for infections in babies' eyes have included squirting breast milk in their eyes, washing the baby's eyes with a cotton towel that been dipped into cool tea and dropping a few drops of the tea into the eye. And believe it or not a drop of lemon juice in 60 ml (two tablespoons) boiled water has even been used as a remedy for conjunctivitis.

Tea also gets a mention for adults' eyes, this time Indian tea. Warm tea bags were to be laid on closed eyelids. This was intended to relieve pain and reduce under-eye puffiness.

Another food based remedy was apple juice, extracted from cooked apples. The juice was applied to a piece of cotton wool and used to wipe sore eyes. Grated raw potato and potato juice were also used to soothe and reduce swelling in irritated eyes.

Fumitory *(Fumaria officinalis)*

This popular European remedy for treating conjunctivitis is an eyewash made from an infusion of dried fumitory.

Turmeric (Curcuma domestica)

Be warned, if you want to try India's traditional Ayurvedic practitioners' recommendation — to use a piece of clean cloth soaked in turmeric powder solution to wipe away the discharge that collects in the corner of irritated eyes — you'll have to have a good explanation ready when people ask you about the bright orange stain on your skin.

Constipation

You feel sluggish, all clogged up. You wonder why, it doesn't seem to make sense. Then some sixth sense tells you to count the days since your last bowel movement. Suddenly everything becomes clear. You're constipated. Most constipation is self inflicted, either a result of what you eat; a high fat diet, with plenty of highly refined foods, or what you don't eat; fluids, complex carbohydrates and fibre.

Occasional constipation is not a worry. Chronic constipation (and the diet that cause it) is linked to varicose veins, hernias and bowel cancer. So check your diet (and change it if needs be). If you want to get things moving, try one of the following folk remedies as well.

Boneset (Eupatorium perfoliatum)

Native Americans used an infusion of boneset to treat constipation. 🫖

Cascara (Rhamnus purshiana)

Native Americans on the west coast of what is now the USA drank a decoction of cascara bark to treat constipation. You'll

---

Remedies with 🫖 are made using an infusion. Those with ☕ are made using a decoction. Instructions for both methods are on pages 4 - 7. Variations and other procedures are contained in the text following the description of that remedy.

need to speak very slowly and enunciate very carefully if you want to use this herb's other name, 'chittem bark'. Otherwise, you may embarrass yourself. Say it too quickly and you'll know why some people believe this name developed as 'genteel' way of describing the herb's effect. Cascara is sometimes used in over-the-counter and prescription laxatives because its active principle is from a class of chemicals called anthraquinones. Anthraquinones are responsible for causing contractions of the muscles of the bowel. Why not make your own cascara decoction to hurry things along, so to speak.

Coffee *(Coffea arabica, C. liberica, C. robusta)*

America's nineteenth century herbalists recommended an infusion of coffee beans as a remedy for constipation. It sounds suspiciously like a cup of coffee, doesn't it?

Sesame *(Sesamum indicum or S orientale)*

For thousands of years Egyptian folk healers massaged the stomach with sesame seed oil to relieve constipation.

Celery *(Apium graveolens)*

Two thousand years ago the Greek physician, Dioscorides and the Roman naturalist, Pliny described the medicinal virtues of celery. Relieving constipation is just one of the many healthful uses to which celery has been put since. What could be easier than chomping down on a calorie free stalk of celery?

Plum *(Prunus spp.)*

For centuries the Romany people, sometimes called Gypsies, have used this special recipe to make a plum jam, which they use to treat constipation.

2 kg (4.5 pounds) ripe plums

1 litre (1 quart) water

1. Boil the plums in the water for one hour, stirring occasionally
2. Then remove the pits and let the fruit simmer another 15 minutes
3. Remove from heat and allow to cool
4. Then add:

    100 grams (3.5 ounces) honey

    20 ml (1 tablespoon) apple vinegar

    100 grams (3.5 ounces) tamarind jam
5. Store in sterilised, tightly sealed glass containers
6. Take 20 grams (1 tablespoon) of the jam each morning on an empty stomach

Soybean *(Glycine max)*

The Japanese prefer to drink a decoction of black soybeans to relieve constipation.

40 grams (2 tablespoons) cleaned black soybeans

1 litre (1 quart) water, boil until the water is reduced by half.

1. Add 20 grams (1 tablespoon) kelp
2. Mix well and strain
3. Drink one cup three times a day

Franzensbad Springs Water

In the latter part of the Middle Ages these springs in the Central European kingdom of Bohemia became the treatment of choice for constipation. There are three springs in Franzensbad—Franzens-quelle, Salz-quelle, and Wiesen-quelle — all of which are naturally carbonated and rich in sodium sulphate. You can buy Franzensbad water at natural food stores.

Since constipation is a fairly common ailment there are a lot of home remedies for this uncomfortable condition.

Linseed [1] *(Linum ustatissimum)*

Soak a tablespoonful of linseed in boiling water for 2 hours. Add honey and drink the sweetened mixture.

Stinging Nettle [2] *(Urtrica dioica)*

Boil young stinging nettles in milk. Remove the nettles, and drink the milk every morning on rising. Use 40 grams (2 tablespoons) dried powered nettle in 1 cup milk. Bring to the boil, strain then drink.

Hot Water

This is one of the simplest home remedies for constipation — drink a glass of hot water first thing in the morning.

---

[1] use sparingly as linseed oil contains prussic acid, don't use artists' or craft linseed oil

[2] stinging comes from formic acid and histamine which are found in the fine hairlike needles of the leaves.

Folk remedy the real reason for trendy drink?

Many people concerned about the amount of caffeine in their diets (and maybe about the regularity of their bowels as well) have switched to drinking hot water (plain or if you're daring — with a slice of lemon). The approved trendoid name for this drink is 'Crystal Tea'.

Fig Paste

This fig paste is similar to popular fruit leathers. It's more like a snack than a medicine so it should be popular with children of all ages.

100 grams (3 ½ ounces) figs
100 grams (3 ½ ounces) sultanas
20 grams (1 tablespoon) of powdered senna pods (buy from your health food store or natural pharmacy)
20 - 40 grams (1 -2 tablespoons) ground linseed
Mix everything together, grind into a paste and shape into a roll, cut off a slice and eat as needed

Wheat and Linseed

Cook freshly ground whole wheat (30 grams or 1 ounce) a small chopped onion and a crushed clove of garlic together in 125 millilitres (½ cup water). When soft, add chopped parsley and a spoonful of olive oil. For more stubborn constipation, add ground linseed. Take 15 grams (3 teaspoons) once a day.

Soybeans, an Asian favourite makes its mark in the west

Westerners can be forgiven for thinking they have discovered something new and wonderful when they first taste soybeans. While no one would deny this versatile legume is indeed wonderful, it is no newcomer. The soybean has been a staple on Far Eastern tables for centuries. In fact in ancient China soybeans were classified as one of five sacred grains.

Throughout Asia soybeans are eaten fresh, roasted, fermented and dried. They find their way into sweet and savoury dishes, snack foods, condiments, main courses and deserts. It is often soybean sprouts that turn up as the ubiquitous bean sprout in Asian cooking. Throughout the world, soybean flour, which is high in protein and low in carbohydrates, is mixed with wheat flour when extra protein is needed to boost the protein level in low protein wheat varieties.

From soybean seeds we get soybean oil and soybean milk. Soybean oil is a bland edible oil which is useful for cooking and the production of margarine precisely because the refined soybean oil is bland. It does not dominate with a flavour of its own. Soybean milk is used in Chinese and Japanese cooking and is a popular invalid food throughout Asia. It is a boon to anyone anywhere that cannot tolerate dairy milk in their diet.

Soybeans of course are the essential ingredient in soy sauce, used in South East Asian, Chinese and

continued over page

Soybeans, an Asian favourite makes its mark in the west

continued from previous page

Japanese cooking. Soybeans are also required for two other staples of traditional Japanese diets — miso and tofu.

Despite their long and varied history, soybeans have only recently made their way in significant amounts onto traditonal western tables.

Vegetarians discovered that soybeans, with twice as much protein per gram as meat, make an excellent base for making meat substitutes. Soybean milk was taken up by people wanting to reduce or eliminate milk in their diets. But it was the growing popularity of Asian foods that was the real catalyst for getting soy onto the tables of the average westerner. As more and more people learnt about the health benefits of traditional Asian diets, miso, tofu, soy milk, even toasted soybean 'nuts' started appearing on tables everywhere.

Corns and Calluses

Corns and their siblings, calluses, are nature's way of saying "You're a slave to fashion." This can be a very painful lesson. Once a callus starts it will only get worse and it may eventually turn into a 'hard core' callus otherwise known as a corn. You probably don't need to be told that a corn is even more painful than a callus. So stop them before they start and your feet will thank you for it.

There are times when, and places where, having a callus is beneficial. If you go without shoes you'll develop calluses to protect the normally tender skin on your feet. Soft calluses, usually found between the toes, form when the bones in the toes rub against each other. Unless you are planning to have your toes boned (and this would make it considerably more difficult to walk) these soft calluses are doing more good than harm. Only treat them if they bother you.

Houseleek *(Sempervivum tectorum, also called Hen and Chickens or Singreen)*

For centuries the Romany people, who are sometimes called Gypsies, have treated corns and calluses with a poultice made from the juice of crushed houseleek. They apply the juice to

Remedies with ☕ are made using an infusion. Those with ♨ are made using a decoction. Instructions for both methods are on pages 4 - 7. Variations and other procedures are contained in the text following the description of that remedy.

the corn, cover with a slightly crushed whole houseleek leaf then put a bandage over the whole thing, to hold it in place.

Don't be callous about a callus

If you have diabetes or any circulatory problem you need to be especially careful with any treatment to your feet.

One of the long-term effects of diabetes is decreased circulation in the body's small blood vessels. Reduced circulation means wounds and infections are slower to heal. So avoid any treatment that breaks the skin. The same goes for people with any other medical conditions that reduce circulation.

Of course the situation for circulatory problems holds for the whole body, it's just that problems on the feet can go unnoticed till a minor problem turns into a major disaster.

Soap and Water

Wash your feet daily with soap and warm water, rubbing well between the toes. Dry well and dust with powder. This will prevent soft corns coming up between the toes, and any existing corns will be less painful.

Castor Oil and Turpentine

A mixture of castor oil and turpentine was used to harden feet and hands and make them less susceptible to corns and calluses. If there were corns, they used a pumice stone (porous lava) to remove the hard skin.

A corny cure for wool stockpile?

Unwashed wool is a favourite country remedy for corns. City folk who want to duplicate this treatment will have to do a bit of extra work. A purchased plaster, even if it's made from wool, won't be the same as unwashed wool.

The proper name for unwashed wool is 'greasy wool' and the grease in greasy wool is wool fat. Wool fat is pure, natural lanolin.

Lanolin is one of the best natural moisturising fats available. So city folk will need to apply a bit lanolin to the corn or callous before putting on the plaster if they want to give this remedy a fair trial.

The effect of dags on the remedy's efficacy has yet to be measured.

Lemon *(Citrus limon or C. medica, var. limonum)*

If this remedy doesn't get rid of your corn it may make your feet smell better.

1. Squeeze lemon juice into a container, save peel
2. Take the lemon peel and boil in 250 millilitres (1 cup) water for 30 - 40 minutes
3. Apply the boiled lemon peel to the corn, inside of the peel towards the skin
4. Hold in place with a cotton bandage and leave on overnight
5. Apply the juice to the hard skin twice a day

Tomato *(Lycopersicon esculentum)* or Pineapple *(Ananas comosus)*

These remedies take advantage of the naturally acidic nature of tomatoes and pineapples, one to soften corns. Bandage a small piece of either fruit against your corn.

Madonna Lily *(Lilium candidum)*

The petals of the madonna lily, soaked in brandy and applied rough side down were frequently used to 'draw' whitlows and boils. The crushed bulb of the madonna lily was used to remove corns.

Tincture of iodine

Try painting corns with tincture of iodine to soften them and make them easier to remove.

Drastic measures . . .

Cashew Nut *(Anacardium occidentale)*

In the West Indies they use the caustic juice from between the cashew nut and its shell to treat corns. This strong, acrid liquid dissolves away the hard skin of the corn (and probably more than that) as the juice has a more than passing resemblance to strong carbolic acid. A careless or forgetful folk healer might never have to worry about corns again, they might not have any toes left.

Cuts and Scrapes

Back in the schoolyard cuts and scrapes were badges of honour. Cuts and scrapes are rarely serious but they can damage an adult's ego, after all they signal a level of clumsiness that most of us would like to think we left in the schoolyard.

Whatever your age, the first thing you need to do for a cut or scrape is stop the bleeding. Use a clean cloth and apply pressure to the wound. If the bleeding doesn't stop in a few minutes see if you can position your body so that the wound is above the heart. Of course this works best when the wound is on your arm or leg, and no-one would suggest you should stand on your head to stop the bleeding from a cut to your abdomen. When the bleeding has stopped clean the wound to reduce the risk of infection and scaring. Everyone should have a basic knowledge of first aid.

Don't use any folk remedy on an open wound, wait until the skin has started to knit together. You don't want to add a nasty infection to your list of worries.

Remedies with 🫖 are made using an infusion. Those with 🍲 are made using a decoction. Instructions for both methods are on pages 4 - 7. Variations and other procedures are contained in the text following the description of that remedy.

Spit and Rub

This remedy has been used by Mums since, well, probably since the first Mum. It won't kill you, but it's not recommended. It is better than doing nothing, but only just. Its one advantage . . . this remedy can be used anywhere, no special equipment required!

Pot Marigold [1] *(Calendula officinalis)*

An infusion of pot marigold leaves and flowers was a common wound dressing in the trenches of World War I. It might not have worked but it probably made the trenches a lot more homely. Don't use it on bullet wounds though. This remedy maybe more appropriate for a minor scrape or cut.

Aloe *(Aloe vera)*

The first recorded use of aloe to treat cuts, scrapes and wounds was in 332 BC during Alexander the Great's conquest of Egypt. According to some historians Alexander was so impressed with the healing powers of aloe that he wanted sole access to the plant, believing this would give his army an unbeatable edge over his rivals' soldiers.

Alexander ordered his men to capture the island (off the coast of what is now Somalia) where the plant was found.

You won't have to mobilise an army or travel to the west coast of Africa to get the benefit of aloe's healing properties, just grow an aloe plant in your kitchen. Apply the gel that oozes from a freshly broken leaf to your cuts and scrapes.

---

[1]   do not confuse with French Marigold, Tagetes patula

Lemon Balm *(Melissa officinalis) also known as Sweet Balm and Bee Herb*

A poultice of lemon balm was a favourite wound treatment of both the ancient Greek physician Dioscorides and his contemporary, the Roman naturalist Pliny. Soften roots, stems and leaves in boiling water and apply to the wound.

Comfrey [1] *(Symphytum officinale) also known as Knitbone*

Comfrey's scientific name, Symphytum, comes from the Greek word meaning 'to grow together' so its ability to aid healing should come as no surprise. Use a decoction of the roots for a poultice to help stop bleeding and aid healing.

Chamomile [2] *(Chamaemelum nobile, Roman, or C. recutita, German)*

In seventeenth and eighteenth century England chamomile was a favourite remedy for cuts, bruises and wounds. When you make this infusion, instead of putting in one for the pot, you'll make one to drink and another to use as a soothing compress. Soak a clean towel in the liquid and apply to the wound while you sip the warm infusion.

Geranium *(Pelargonium odorantissimum)*

In the Middle Ages a dressing made from geranium leaves was a popular wound treatment. The leaf was lightly crushed and applied to the cut.

---

[1]   restricted her in Australia and New Zealand due to presence of alkaloid, shown to cause liver damage in rats

[2]   avoid excessive doses and the oil in any amount during pregnancy

Harakeke, New Zealand Flax
(Phormium tenax)

The Maori knew the value of this versatile plant. Native flax was used in a variety of ways against a range of ailments. This included using the plant gum to stop bleeding from cuts and scrapes. One of the more inventive uses was in the treatment of new born Maori babies. The Maori took advantage of the plant's styptic property when they washed newborn babies in water containing native flax gum.

Kanono *(Coprosma australis)*

The Maori also used an infusion of kanono leaves to treat cuts and scrapes.

Heath Tea Tree *(Leptospermum ericoides)*

A poultice of heath tea tree leaves was a traditional New Zealand way to help sores and wounds heal more quickly. Red Tea Tree, Kahikætoa, Mænuka *(L. scoparium)* was used by the Maori as a substitute for tea.

Metrosideros *(Metrosideros albiflora)*

An infusion of metrosideros bark is a traditional New Zealand way to help wounds heal more quickly.

Purple Coneflower [1] *(Echinacea augustifolia)*

Native Americans used the purple coneflower for a whole range of ailments, including cuts and scrapes. They used a decoction made from the root to clean and help heal broken skin.

---

[1]   restricted her in Australia and New Zealand due to presence of alkaloid, shown to cause liver damage in rats

If you doubt the dual role food and medicinal plants played in our ancestors' lives, read on. These remedies should be used with caution, and never on an open wound as the food that they feature can carry bacteria.

Whey

When people made their own cheese at home concentrated whey was often used on wounds. A light dusting with calcium powder and an application of soft white cheese finished it off.

If cheese making is not your hobby and you don't live near a dairy maybe you make bread.

Wheat and bran

Soak wheat or bran in fresh milk. Mince the grain and use it to cover the wound. You don't have to mince the bran just soak and apply. Dust the wound with calcium powder and after two days of treatment apply pulped cabbage leaves.

Parsnip *(Pastinaca sativa)*

Boil a couple of parsnips in water, cool to lukewarm, then wash the cut with the water. Mash the parsnip and apply the warm pulp to the wound, holding the poultice in place with a bandage.

Apple *(Malus pumila)*

Or if you don't like parsnips, crush a raw apple and apply the pulp to the wound.

Lemon (Citrus limon or C. medica, var. limonum)

For a pleasant, fragrant treatment, dilute 1 or 2 drops of lemon oil in 10 ml of good quality vegetable or nut oil. Apply the diluted lemon oil to a wound that has begun to heal, it's supposed to help reduce scaring.

Good ideas gone wrong

As wise as many of our ancestors may have been some things they did make you shudder, like using fresh cow dung, puffball dust, powdered grass, mouldy bread, butter, mutton fat and cobwebs on cuts!

When at sea, tobacco was often stuffed into cuts, the cigarette paper stuck on top to hold the cut skin together. It probably didn't do any more harm than smoking the tobacco did.

Dandruff

If, in the middle of January, someone asks you how the skiing was (and you haven't just returned from the Swiss Alps) you probably have dandruff — and a not too subtle friend. Dandruff is just dry skin that has flaked off, either because your scalp is dry or because the sebaceous glands on your scalp are blocked. Dandruff is not contagious, it's not the worst thing that can happen to you, but it can destroy your self-confidence and take the shine off the best of days.

When it comes to hair care, folk remedies are right at home with the best commercial products. Check the ingredients list on any 'new' natural formula product. If you leave out the emulsifiers, artificial colours and fragrances you'll find many ingredients in folk remedies right at home in commercial, natural, hair care products.

Stress can make dandruff worse, but what are you worrying about, try one of these folk remedies to get rid of your reputation for being a little flaky.

Remedies with 🫖 are made using an infusion. Those with ☕ are made using a decoction. Instructions for both methods are on pages 4 - 7. Variations and other procedures are contained in the text following the description of that remedy.

Sesame *(Sesamum indicum or S. orientale)* and Ginger [1] *(Zingiber officinalis)*

For treating dandruff Egyptian folk healers recommend this mixture.

Two ginger roots, finely grated

1. Extract 5-10 ml (1 - 2 teaspoons) of ginger juice with a juice extractor or by squeezing the grated ginger between two layers of gauze or cheesecloth
2. Mix the ginger juice with 90 ml (3 ounces) sesame seed oil and 2.5 ml (½ teaspoon) lemon juice
3. Rub into your scalp using a flannel, repeat 3 times a week

Chaparral *(Larrea divaricata L. tridentata)*

Native Americans of the Puma tribe in what is now the US state of Arizona used an infusion of chaparral to treat dandruff. Wash your hair as you would normally then apply the infusion to your hair and scalp. Rub it well into your scalp. Rinse after 2 - 3 minutes.

Some old-fashioned remedies found in many cultures

Yogurt

This remedy was a favourite not so long ago, in fact your grandmother may have used when she was a girl.

1. Wash and rinse your hair, then rub natural yoghurt well into your scalp and leave it for about 15 minutes
2. Rinse thoroughly
3. Wash your hair

---

[1]   *use sparingly during pregnancy*

Rosemary *(Rosmarinus officinalis)*

This old-fashioned remedy stops the flakes and adds shine to your dry hair too. Dilute 1 - 2 drops rosemary oil with 10 millilitres of good quality vegetable or nut oil and apply to your scalp.

Hops *(Humulus lupulus)*

Hops are essential for brewing beer and for making this dandruff treatment, which calls for an alcohol infusion of hops.

375 grams (1 ½ cups) of cut, fresh hops

Add 550 millilitres (2 ¼ cups) of brandy

1. Put in a bottle with a tight lid
2. Shake daily for 2 weeks
3. Strain the liquid through a clean muslin cloth or fine filter paper
4. Wash your hair normally and thoroughly rinse with plain water
5. Apply the hops infusion to your scalp, rubbing it well into your scalp, leave on for 2 - 3 minutes
6. Rinse thoroughly

Beer

A quicker and easier way to treat your hair with hops, is to use a beer rinse on your freshly shampooed hair. Use a can or stubby, your favourite brand will do. Leave in 2 - 3 minutes then rinse well or you'll smell like a brewery.

Apple *(Malus pumila)*

An apple today will keep the dandruff flakes at bay . . . mix 30 ml (1 ounce) pure apple juice and 60 millilitres (3 table-spoons) warm water. Massage the mixture into your scalp three times a week, after shampooing your hair. Leave on for 2 - 3 minutes then rinse well.

Rosemary *(Rosmarinus officinalis)*

Or use an infusion of rosemary, as a scalp tonic. It will smell yummy! If you like, add a pinch of borax to the infusion. Massage the tonic into your scalp and leave on for 2 - 3 minutes then rinse well.

Nasturtium *(Tropaeolum majus)*

For a more colourful treatment try this infusion of nasturtium leaves and flowers. Massage this springtime tonic into your scalp after shampooing your hair. Leave the tonic on for 2 - 3 minutes, then rinse well.

Depression

Depression is a word that has come to be used lightly. They might say they are depressed when they are feeling down because of some disappointment or loss in their life. What they are really saying is that they have a case of the blues.

That is not depression. Depression is more than feeling sad. Depression is more serious than normal grief in response to a loss. When your sadness lingers long after your psychological wound should have healed, when the depth of your psychological pain is out of proportion to the actual hurt you experienced, or when just getting out of bed seems like too much trouble, you are experiencing depression. Depression is a serious clinical, psychological condition, often with a chemical cause. It requires immediate treatment from a qualified medical practitioner.

Everyone, however feels down occasionally. Grief and sadness are normal, healthy responses to loss, disappointment or trauma in your life. And, sometimes, without any obvious cause, you just feel like singing the blues. Whenever your personal blue Monday hits, a dose of one of the folk remedies that follow, taken along with a friend's shoulder on which to cry may be just the thing you need to soothe your soul.

Remedies with ☕ are made using an infusion. Those with ☕ are made using a decoction. Instructions for both methods are on pages 4 - 7. Variations and other procedures are contained in the text following the description of that remedy.

Saffron *(Crocus sativus)*

Saffron was introduced to Europe by Arab traders. Chinese physicians are reported to have used saffron to treat depression for well over a thousand years. They recommend taking extracts of saffron in small doses.

Golden saffron

Saffron has always been associated with luxury — a tradition that holds to the present day, one that is justified on price alone. Saffron, the stamen of a particular species of crocus, is the world's most expensive spice. About 170,000 individually hand-harvested stamens are required to make 1 kilogram (2.2 pounds) of the spice.

The ancient Egyptians, Greeks and Romans all wrote of using saffron for a range of mystical, religious, medicinal and culinary purposes.

If you're feeling down and need a special pick-me-up buy some saffron and the best seafood you can afford. Use them to make yourself a rich pot of bouillabaisse or a warming paella, two traditional European dishes that feature saffron. A special meal makes a tasty way to add some of saffron's sunny yellow spirit to your life.

Chicory *(Cichorium intybus)*

When you're feeling down, European folk healers recommend drinking an infusion of chicory.

Evening Primrose *(Oenothera biennis)*
also known as Tree Primrose

American folk healers recommend drinking an infusion of evening primrose to chase the blues away.

St John's Wort *(Hypericum perforatum)*

This herb's medicinal use can be traced back to Pliny (the Roman naturalist) and Dioscorides (the Greek physician) both of whom sang its praise. The herb gets its name from the belief that the herb released its blood-red oil on 29 August, the anniversary of the saint's beheading. Drinking an infusion of St John's wort flowers is recommended by some folk healers when the problem is believed to be caused by nervous depression.

Bach Flower Remedies

These popular remedies, available from most natural pharmacies and health food stores, are believed to address the psychological cause behind ailments, try:

Olive - if the depression follows an illness or longstanding exhaustion

Mustard - if sudden depression is accompanied by repressed anger

Willow - if the depression is caused by resentment or bitterness

Gorse - if depression is caused by feelings of hopelessness

Larch - if depression is due to lack of confidence

Centaury - if depression is caused by putting other

people's interests before your own

Sweet Chestnut - if depression causes extreme despair in those who are spiritually minded

Walnut - if depressed due to impending changes in life, or if you have lost interest in life

Some oldies but goodies, with a reputation for raising the spirits.

Pennyroyal *(Mentha pulegium)*
also known as Pudding Grass

Drinking an infusion of pennyroyal, a member of the mint family, has a reputation for soothing the psyche and brightening the spirit.

Cola *(Cola nitida) sometimes written Kola*

Don't be surprised if this medicinal plant's name sounds familiar. Its name has been shanghaied by the ubiquitous soft drink, Coca-cola™. The original recipe for Coca-cola included extracts of cola and coca (the source of cocaine). The cola nut (which is actually a seed) contains caffeine, so it has a stimulating effect. Caffeine effect on the central nervous system is what gives the cola nut its reputation as an antidepressant.

Cola is traditionally used in South America and tropical Africa to treat depression, especially cases associated with weakness and debility.

If you don't want to get your cola from a soft drink make your own cola nut decoction, if you can find the cola nuts, that is.

1. Collect cola nuts and grind to a powder
2. Take 5 - 10 grams (1 - 2 teaspoons) of the powder
3. Add to 250 millilitres (1 cup) water
4. Bring to the boil, simmer gently 15 minutes

Lady's Slipper *(Cypripedium calceolus)*

This herb has been used in England for well over one hundred years to brighten the spirit and reduce stress, emotional tension and anxiety. Use dried, powdered dried lady's slipper root to make your infusion.

Apple Cider Vinegar

Mix 5 millilitres (1 teaspoon) cider vinegar and a little honey in a small wineglass of warm water, drink first thing in the morning and last thing at night.

Orange Juice

At breakfast, drink a glass of orange juice extracted from fresh fruit.

Chervil *(Anthriscus Cerfolium)*

Use it in salads to brighten the spirit.

Rosemary *(Rosmarinus officinalis)* and Sage [1] *(Salvia officinalis)*

Use plenty of these herbs in cooking.

---

[1]   avoid therapeutic doses in pregnancy, small amounts used in cooking are quite safe.

Walnut *(Juglans regia)*

Eat plenty of them during the day.

Pot Marigold [1] *(Calendula officinalis)*

Grow pots of this bright flower on windowsills, verandahs and balconies. Their colourful display helps to cheer the spirit.

Lavender [2] *(Lavandula angustifolia)*

Place a lavender pillow beneath your head at night.

Ylang-Ylang *(Cananga odorata also called Canangium odoratum)*

Aromatherapists believe the essential oil distilled from the yellow flowers of this sixty-foot perennial tropical plant can balance the mind and soothe the spirit. It's claimed to be especially useful when combined with professional massage therapy.

Rose *(Rosa canina)*

The ancient Egyptians, Arabs, Greeks and Romans all used rose medically, but it was folk healers in southern Europe that started using rose oil medicinally. It is claimed to be especially useful for post-natal depression.

Oat *(Avena sativa)*

The thought of greeting another cold winter's morning with an equally dismal bowl of porridge has probably dampened

---

[1]   *do not confuse with French Marigold, Tagetes patula*
[2]   *avoid high doses during pregnancy*

e spirits of a fair few school children. So you may be surprised to find that porridge once had a reputation as a remedy for depression! It may be that the Middle Ages were so dreary that a bowl of hot, stodgy porridge was cheering by comparison. Whatever the reason, European folk healers still believe in a bowl to revive the spirits of people suffering from depression and nervous exhaustion.

Vervian [1] *(Verbena officinalis)*

This herb's many common names shows how useful it has been throughout the ages. 'Simpler's joy' reflects the plant's popularity with herbalists or 'simplers' as they were also called during the Middle Ages. From the legend that vervian's was used to stop the bleeding of Christ's wounds, we have the 'herb of the cross'. The Druids used vervian in various religious and arcane rituals. Vervian itself comes from the Celtic 'fer faen', meaning to drive away. Celtic folk healers recommended drinking an infusion of vervian drive away depression.

---

[1]   *avoid during pregnancy*

Dermatitis or Eczema

These two painful skin conditions are often lumped together, because they're both caused by an extreme reaction to some irritant, allergen or toxic substance. Don't be fooled by the name 'contact dermatitis' either. The inflamed skin of contact dermatitis is not restricted to the site of contact with the irritating substance. Food and other allergens can also cause dermatitis and eczema.

One thing you don't have to worry about is catching dermatitis or eczema, they are unsightly but not contagious. The skin can be weepy, red, and cracked or extremely dry either way it's itchy and irritating, so try one of these folk remedies to soothe the pain and hasten healing.

Pot Marigold [1] *(Calendula officinalis)*

For centuries Indian physicians have used calendula oil to treat inflamed skin conditions like dermatitis and eczema. Dilute 1-2 drops of calendula oil with a good quality vegetable or nut oil before gently applying it to the irritated skin.

Remedies with ☕ *are made using an infusion. Those with* 🍵 *are made using a decoction. Instructions for both methods are on pages 4 - 7. Variations and other procedures are contained in the text following the description of that remedy.*

---

[1]   *do not confuse with French Marigold, Tagetes patula*

Geranium *(Pelargonium odorantissimum)*

Folk healers on the island of Madagascar have used geranium oil to treat inflamed skin conditions since ancient times. Dilute 1-2 drops of geranium oil with 10 millilitres of good quality vegetable or nut oil and apply to the irritated skin.

Cabbage *(Brassica oleracea)*

Soothing cabbage leaves were Grandma's favourite remedy for any painful skin condition. Fresh, washed cabbage leaves pounded to soften.

1. Steam the leaves to soften further
2. Apply several layers of the steamed cabbage leaves, holding them in place with a bandage
3. Repeat every morning and night

Centaury *(Centaurium erythraea)*

The ancient Greeks were the first to write about the wound healing properties of this plant. They applied centaury's pink flowers directly to the irritated skin.

Juniper *(Juniperus communis)*

During the Middle Ages juniper oil was a favourite remedy for weeping, inflamed skin conditions. Dilute 1-2 drops juniper oil in 10 millilitres good quality vegetable or nut oil and apply to the inflamed skin.

Lavender[2] *(Lavandula angustifolia)*

The Egyptians taught the Romans about the medicinal qualities of lavender oil and both found it to be a soothing treat-

---

[2]   *avoid high doses during pregnancy*

ment for irritated skin. Dilute 1-2 drops of lavender oil with 10 millilitres of good quality vegetable or nut oil and apply to the irritated skin.

Couchgrass (Agropyron repens)
Blind or Stinging Nettle [1]
(Urtrica dioica or U. urens)
and Dandelion (Taraxacum officinale).

For centuries the Romany people, who are sometimes called Gypsies, have drunk the juice extracted from the roots of these plants to treat eczema.

1. Grind equal amounts of each plant's roots in a mortar and pestle
2. Press the ground roots through a gauze cloth to extract the juice
3. Drink 1 teaspoon, 3 times a day

Fumitory (Fumaria officinalis)

Since the seventeenth century an infusion of fumitory has been drunk to treat skin problems.

Goldenseal (Hydrastis canadensis)

For centuries Native Americans have been using an infusion of goldenseal as a wash to soothe irritated skin, colonists took up the practice as well.

---

[1]   stinging comes from formic acid and histamine which are found in the fine hairlike needles of the leaves

Kanono *(Coprosma australis)*

Kanono was a popular Maori healing plant. Its leaves, bark and young shoots were used in infusions to help heal ailments as diverse as bruises, stomach ache, and bladder stoppages. And a poultice of kanono leaves was used to heal broken bones. The Maori applied the juice extracted from kanono leaves to soothe painful skin complaints.

Neroli bigarade *(Citrus aurantium var. bergamia)*
also called Neroli or Bitter Orange

This member of the citrus family originated in India, its name 'neroli' comes from the Sanskrit word, "nagaranga". The plants were taken out of India by Portuguese sailors some 500 years ago. Neroli oil is extracted from the neroli flowers in an intricate process called enfleurage. Neroli oil is believed to have cell regenerative properties. In Sicily it is gently massaged on painful skin conditions, like eczema. Dilute the neroli oil with a good quality vegetable or nut oil 1 or 2 drops of neroli oil to 10 ml vegetable or nut oil.

Oat *(Avena sativa)*

Add a muslin envelope filled with about 500 grams (about 1 pound) oatmeal or oat bran to your bath water for a soothing and relaxing treatment.

Olive *(Olea europaea)*

Soak strips of linen in olive oil and apply to the irritated skin to reduce scabbing.

Chamomile [1] *(Chamaemelum nobile, Roman, or C. recutita, German)*

Dilute 1-2 drops of chamomile oil in 10 millilitres almond oil and rub gently into the painful, irritated skin.

Carrot *(Daucus carota)*

Strange but true, an old-fashioned way to treat inflamed skin conditions calls for boiled, grated carrots, mashed and applied to the inflamed skin.

Bilberry *(Vaccinium myrtillus)*

Drink the juice or chew a few dried berries to help irritated, cracked skin heal.

Goat's Milk

Many folk healers believe goat's milk to be a valuable addition to the diet of people suffering from painful skin conditions.

Burdock *(Arctium lappa)*

Nothing goes to waste in this folk remedy for irritated skin. You drink the liquid from the decoction of burdock root, using any left over liquid as a soothing wash for painful skin. Don't throw away the softened burdock root though. Extract the liquid from the softened root and combine it with petroleum jelly to make a soothing ointment. Crush the root into a pulp and extract the juice. Mix the extracted juice with petroleum jelly and apply to the irritated skin.

---

[1]   *avoid excessive doses and the oil in any amount during pregnancy*

Linseed [1] *(Linum ustatissimum)*
or Rose *(Rosa canina)*

Add either of these to your bath water. They are said to soften the skin and soothe the mind.

Sulphur and Sweet Cream

In the former Soviet Union folk healers apply sulphur and sweet cream to irritated skin two times a day.

---

[1] *use sparingly as linseed oil contains prussic acid, don't use artists' or craft linseed oil*

Diabetes

It almost sounds like a dieter's dream. Your doctor says, "I'm sorry Mr Smith, you body can't metabolise sugar or carbohydrates." You ask, "Does that mean I can eat all the sweets I want and never get fat?" No, the opposite in fact. Diabetes is the result of your body's inability to metabolise sugar and other carbohydrates, it doesn't mean that you can gorge on your favourite sweets.

Diabetes can be caused by insufficient, inefficient or ineffective insulin. But the resulting un-metabolised or partially metabolised carbohydrates don't pass out of your body, they collect in it. And uncontrolled, these carbohydrates and the by products of their partial metabolism can build up to dangerous, even deadly levels.

Never use any folk remedy in place of your doctor's treatment. Always discuss any folk remedy with your doctor before trying it. Be sure to count any carbohydrates, sugar or fats in a folk remedy as part of your dietary intake.

Remedies with ☕ *are made using an infusion. Those with* 🍲 *are made using a decoction. Instructions for both methods are on pages 4 - 7. Variations and other procedures are contained in the text following the description of that remedy.*

Bran

Native South Africans rarely suffer from diabetes. Some researchers attribute this to their higher than average consumption of wheat and sorghum bran — about 50 grams (about 2 ounces) every day.

Yoga

Some exercises in Hatha yoga are believed to help balance the body's natural metabolic processes. Consult a skilled yoga therapist if you want to incorporate yoga into your diabetes treatment.

More than an exercise, a way of life

Yoga has been a part of Indian culture for 4000 years. Yoga comes from a Sanskrit word meaning yoke or union, and it is more than an exercise regime. It is a system of spiritual, mental and physical training closely allied with the traditional Indian medical system the Ayurveda. While true yoga incorporates spiritual training it is not necessary to subscribe to the spiritual beliefs of yoga to participate and get some of the benefits of this ancient technique.

The underlying philosophy behind yoga stresses the influence of mind over body, and holds that mental and spiritual development are necessary to reinforce the benefits that the physical exercises can bring.

Goat's Rue *(Galega officinalis)*

Goat's rue has a reputation for lowering blood sugar levels so it's a natural for people suffering from diabetes. Folk healers recommend drinking an infusion of goat's rue and careful monitoring of your blood sugar levels.

Jambul *(Syzygium cumini)*

India's traditional physicians recommend diabetics drink an infusion of jambul seeds.

Brussels Sprouts *(Brassica oleracea)*

Folk healers recommend drinking Brussels sprout juice to help control diabetes. Use a juice extractor to make the juice. It will have a strong, green and possibly sulfurous taste, so blend it with carrot or apple juice to make it palatable.

French Beans *(Phaseolus vulgaris)*
also called haricot beans

The juice from fresh French beans is believed to stimulate the production of insulin. Drink 150 ml (5 fl oz) a day or try it in combination with Brussels sprout juice.

Diarrhoea

Strange food or water, infection, improperly cooked food, improperly stored food, allergies or nerves—whenever diarrhoea strikes, you can count on it being inconvenient. When you are doubled-up in pain and forced to remain within a short run of your toilet, it's hard to believe that this is happening for your own good.

Diarrhoea is your body's way of getting rid of unwelcome guests, usually viral or bacterial invaders. Despite the pain and inconvenience the best way to deal with diarrhoea is to let nature take its course. It will be over in a few days and your system will be better for the purge. If you're not willing (or able) to ride out the storm, try one of the following folk remedies.

Apple (Malus pumila)

Ancient India's traditional Ayurvedic healers were ahead of their time when they first started recommending eating apples to relieve diarrhoea. Modern research has shown that your intestines can transform the pectin in apples to provide

Remedies with 🫖 are made using an infusion. Those with 🍲 are made using a decoction. Instructions for both methods are on pages 4 - 7. Variations and other procedures are contained in the text following the description of that remedy.

When diarrhoea means danger

Dehydration is always a risk with diarrhoea, but if you are healthy dehydration is easy to prevent and to remedy, just remember Fluids - Fluids - Fluids. When it comes to infants and young children the elderly and the chronically ill — or anyone who can't or won't drink the volume of liquids required to replenish fluids lost from diarrhoea — dehydration can be deadly!

Because dehydration can strike quickly, consult your doctor immediately when anyone in these groups suffers from diarrhoea.

Other danger signs:
● if the diarrhoea lasts longer than a day or two

or

● if the diarrhoea is accompanied by fever, severe cramping, a rash or jaundice

Consult your doctor immediately, the diarrhoea may be caused by a more serious infection.

a soothing, protective coating for the irritated intestinal lining caused by diarrhoea. Pectin also adds bulk to your stool. This slows the passage of the stool through your intestines and helps to relieve diarrhoea.

For babies that have started on solid foods, try finely grated apples, followed by oatmeal or porridge. For older children, try apple followed by raw oat flakes, but be sure that they chew thoroughly and do not give them anything else to eat for a few hours.

Bayberry *(Myrica cerifera) also known as Wax Myrtle*

During the eighteenth century, settlers in what is now the US state of Louisiana drank an infusion made from wax scraped from bayberry plants to relieve diarrhoea. Later, during the nineteenth century, the American herbalist Samuel Thomson refined the recipe and recommended drinking an infusion of powdered bayberry root. 🫖

Blackberry *(Rubus ulmifolius)*

Two thousand years ago Romans drank a decoction of blackberry leaves and bark to relieve diarrhoea. Folk healers still recommend this remedy. 🍲

Banana [1] *(Musa)*

In parts of Central America eating mashed, cooked banana is the standard way to put an end to diarrhoea. It's a good practice too, because bananas can help soothe irritated intestinal lining. And because bananas are high in potassium eating bananas can help restore electrolyte imbalances caused by the dehydration that often accompanies diarrhoea.

Chaparral *(Larrea divaricata L. tridentata)*

Some early American colonists followed the Native American's practice of drinking an infusion of chaparral to relieve diarrhoea. 🫖

---

[1]   because all cultivated bananas are sterile hybrids, they do not have exact species names.

Cinnamon [1] *(Cinnamomum zeylanicum in the west, C. cassia in China, C Cassia from the bark = rou gui or from twigs gui zhi)*

Another remedy from America's past. This one comes from nineteenth century herbalists, who prescribed powdered cinnamon to people suffering from diarrhoea. Their recommendation, sprinkle a little cinnamon on everything you eat and drink an infusion of powdered cinnamon—2.5 grams (half a teaspoon) powdered cinnamon in one cup boiling water—after every meal.

Persimmon *(Diospyros kaki)*
also known as Chinese Date Plum

Native Americans of the Seminole tribe recommended drinking either persimmon juice or an infusion made from near ripe persimmons to relieve chronic diarrhoea.

To make the infusion
1. Cut six near ripe persimmons into sections
2. Steep in 3 cups of boiling water 20 minutes
3. Strain discarding solids
4. Drink 2 cups over a 4 hour period

Cardamom *(Elettaria cardamomum)*

A traditional Chinese remedy for children suffering from diarrhoea is to sprinkle ground cardamom onto everything the child eats.

---

[1]   *avoid in pregnancy*

Clove *(Syzgium aromaticum)*

Another traditional Chinese treatment for diarrhoea, for adults this time, is to drink an infusion of clove flowers.

Catnip *(Nepeta cataria)*

During the Middle Ages drinking an infusion of catnip was the primary remedy for diarrhoea in children. [1] Do not use herbal remedies on children under two years of age.

Barberry *(Berberis vulgaris)*

Another popular remedy from the Middle Ages, this time from Spain, eating barberries.

Fennel [2] *(Foeniculum officinale)*

For centuries Africans treated diarrhoea by chewing on fennel seeds. Chew about 5 grams (1 teaspoon) fennel seeds 2 or 3 times a day.

Honey

In Colombia local folk healers recommend eating honey to stop diarrhoea.

Jambul *(Syzgium cumini)*

For centuries India's traditional physicians have recommended drinking an infusion made from dried jambul seeds to treat diarrhoea.

---

[1] *Herbal remedies are not recommended for children under 2 years of age. Doses for children should be adjusted based on the child's age and weight. Consult a qualified herbalist for detailed recommendations.*

[2] *avoid during pregnancy*

Koromiko *(Hebe salicifolia and H. stricta)*

These two well known and documented remedies for dysentery and diarrhoea were a godsend to Maori troops during World War II. Large quantities of dried koromiko, a traditional Maori remedy for diarrhoea were shipped to the Maori troops on the North African front.

Heath Tea Tree *(Leptospermum ericoides)*

A decoction of heath tea tree fruit was a traditional New Zealand treatment for diarrhoea.

Kanono *(Coprosma australis)*

Drinking an infusion of kanono bark in small amounts, was another Maori way to banish a stomach ache.

Korokio *(Corokia buddleioidea)*

The Maori also used a decoction of korokio as a general tonic, and drinking a decoction of korokio is a traditional New Zealand remedy for a stomach ache.

Pomegranate *(Punica granatum)*

A drink of tangy pomegranate juice is an old Egyptian remedy for diarrhoea. Extract the juice from a pomegranate and drink a spoonful every hour or so, throughout the day.

Ginger [1] *(Zingiber officinalis)*

A glass of ginger ale is an old-fashioned diarrhoea remedy that is still popular in England today.

Icelandic moss *(Chondrus crispus)*

Iceland's inhospitable climate means it is a country with few natural plant resources to exploit for folk remedies. They didn't let that stop them though. They used what they could and experimented with almost everything. They collected Icelandic moss (actually a lichen) to make a decoction, and drank the resulting liquid to remedy diarrhoea.

Rabassum *(Pelargonium reniforme)*

The Dutch, who appropriated this remedy from indigenous South Africans, called the plant 'rabassum'. A milk decoction is the preferred preparation. Soldiers suffering from diarrhoea during the Boer war were treated with this remedy.

Rhubarb *(Rheum rhaponticum)*

If you like rhubarb you might not hate having diarrhoea in the future. Another traditional Chinese recommendation for putting an end to diarrhoea is to eat boiled rhubarb stalks.

Some more old fashioned remedies to the rescue . . .
- Drink lots of fresh, clear water
- Barley water with a dash of lemon—an old stand by
- Plain boiled white rice with mashed bananas—especially good for children

---

[1]   *use sparingly during pregnancy*

● A small bowl of plain natural yoghurt, it will kill off unwanted bacteria and replace beneficial bacteria -restoring your intestines to their normal healthy state

● A drink of sloe-gin—another ancient 'quick fix'

● Drink port and brandy—it's supposed to warm and settle the stomach

● A gentle massage, clockwise on the abdomen - helps to soothe the ache of severe diarrhoea, use 1 or 2 drops of geranium, sage, lavender, peppermint or clove oil diluted with 10 millilitres of a good quality vegetable or nut oil when you do the massage described above - and add the benefit of aromatherapy to the soothing massage.

Diverticulosis

You won't find a lot of folk remedies for diverticulosis. Like high cholesterol, diverticulosis is a 'modern' disease. Our ancestors didn't have to worry about diverticulosis because their diets protected their colons from the sorts of irritations that encourage the development of the little pouches called diverticula, that give this twentieth century disease its name.

In the US almost 50 percent of people over 60 years of age will have some level of diverticulosis. Australian colons are probably no healthier. That is not as grim as it appears at first. You can form diverticula without suffering any serious symptoms of diverticulosis. But that doesn't mean you are completely off the hook either. The biggest danger with diverticulosis is that it can develop into a serious, painful and potential life-threatening condition known as diverticulitis.

So, while our ancestors can't help us with remedies for diverticulosis, they (or more accurately their dietary habits) can help us prevent diverticulosis from developing into diverticulitis. You won't have to do anything weird, just adopt a healthy, high fibre diet that includes plenty of fluids. That ought to help keep your colon healthy and happy.

Remedies with 🫖 *are made using an infusion. Those with* ☕ *are made using a decoction. Instructions for both methods are on pages 4 - 7. Variations and other procedures are contained in the text following the description of that remedy.*

Heat and diet

English folk healers apply heat locally and put the patient on a low-residue diet: lean meat; eggs; bran; cooked white cereals; white bread; rice pudding; fruit juices; strained cooked fruits or vegetables; cottage or cream cheese; milk; sugar; potato soup; tea and coffee.

Food to avoid: raw fruit and vegetables; pork; veal; spices; fried or fatty food; whole wheat cereal or bread.

Wild or Atlantic Yam (Dioscorea villosa)

Drinking a decoction of wild yam root is the traditional treatment for diverticulosis in Spain and Greece.

Dry Hair

If you've ever wanted to shout, "Don't talk to me! I'm having a bad hair day," you won't need to be told that dry, brittle, fly-away hair robs you of your vitality and natural beauty. So if you think of the scarecrow in the *Wizard of Oz* every time you catch your reflection in the mirror, it's time you did something about your dry hair. Try one of the following folk remedies to bring your hair back to life. Many can be made with ingredients found in any well stocked kitchen.

Old favourites from the kitchen pantry

Rosemary *(Rosmarinus officinalis)*

Dilute 1-2 drops rosemary oil with 10 millilitres of good quality vegetable or nut oil and massage into your hair. If you also suffer from dandruff, rub some of the diluted rosemary oil into your scalp.

Remedies with 🫖 are made using an infusion. Those with 🍲 are made using a decoction. Instructions for both methods are on pages 4 - 7. Variations and other procedures are contained in the text following the description of that remedy.

Avocado (Persea americana) *and Banana* (Musa[1])

Banana and avocado both have reputations for conditioning dry hair. Massage either or both into your hair and leave the whole mess in for one hour before washing your hair as you would normally.

Onion (Allium cepa)

Save clean, onion skins from golden and brown onions until you have about 750 millilitres in volume (2 ½ cups) of lightly packed dry onion skins. Use these to make an infusion and use the infusion as a rinse to soften and add shine to your dry hair.

2.5 cups clean dry onion skins

1 litre (1 quart) water

1. Steep 60 minutes
2. Strain, use as a rinse after shampooing
3. Rinse again with clear water after the onion skin infusion

Yoghurt and Egg

If your hair is fine and hard to control, try this protein rich treatment.

1. Combine 1 egg and ½ cup yoghurt (This recipe is for short hair, increase amounts for long hair) Mix well and rub into scalp
2. Leave in hair 10 minutes
3. Rinse well

---

[1]   because all cultivated bananas are sterile hybrids forms they do not have exact species names

Olive *(Olea europaea)*

This old favourite is especially good for dry, fly-away hair. Pour some olive oil into a small bowl and heat gently. Massage the warmed oil into your scalp and through your hair until it is completely covered. Comb through and massage again. Cover your head with a plastic cap and cover that with a warmed towel. Leave on as long as you can, overnight if possible. Then shampoo thoroughly.

Mayonnaise

Egg yolks and oil, either can be used as a nourishing treatment for dry hair. Put them together, in the form of mayonnaise, and they work even better than they work separately. Massage mayonnaise into your hair and scalp. Cover as described for the olive oil treatment above, and leave on for several hours, then shampoo thoroughly to remove all the mayonnaise.

Beer

This is the teenager's favourite and has been since your Mum's (and maybe even her Mum's) day. Before commercial treatments and hair conditioners became a growth industry, a beer rinse was THE way to get your hair looking healthy and shiny. It was an absolutely necessary part of every girl's beauty routine for important occasions. If you want to give it a try, rinse your hair with a can or stubby of beer. Leave the beer on for a few minutes. Do not drink the beer dripping from your hair and do rinse well with cool water.

Dry Skin

Dry skin can strike any time, but it seems to plague most people during the winter, when heated homes, shops and offices rob your skin of its natural oils. Dry skin is irritating and it's not attractive either. It's flaky, itchy and if you ignore it, it's cracked, red and raw. When you want to turn sandpaper back into supple skin, turn to a folk remedy for welcome relief.

Apple (Malus pumila)

Vermont folk practitioners recommend using apple cider vinegar on dry skin. Apply the cider vinegar with a piece of cotton wool six times a day.

Sandalwood (Santalum album)

The name sandalwood comes from the Sanskrit word 'candana' meaning burning incense-wood. Sandalwood figured in ancient Indian and Chinese medical and religious practices. The oil has antiseptic properties and it is very soothing. Dilute sandalwood oil with 10 millilitres of good quality vegetable or nut oil and massage it into your skin before your bath.

Remedies with ☕ are made using an infusion. Those with ☕ are made using a decoction. Instructions for both methods are on pages 4 - 7. Variations and other procedures are contained in the text following the description of that remedy.

Ylang-Ylang *(Cananga odorata also called Canangium odoratum)*

The fragrant oil from yellow ylang-ylang flowers is a favourite in 'oriental' style fragrances. Ylang-ylang is also used throughout Asia as a moisturiser for dry skin. Dilute 1-2 drops of the oil with 10 millilitres of good quality vegetable or nut oil and massage into dry skin.

Jasmine *(Jasminum officinale)*

Called the 'king of the oils', jasmine originated in the Middle East in the ancient kingdom of Persia. It was taken to Europe in the sixteenth century. Dilute 1-2 drops of jasmine oil with 10 millilitres of good quality vegetable or nut oil and massage gently into dry, itchy skin.

Lavender [1] *(Lavandula angustifolia)*

Dilute 1-2 drops of lavender oil with 10 millilitres of good quality vegetable or nut oil and gently massage into the skin.

Elder [2] *(Sambucus nigra)*

In Britain during the Middle Ages an extract of elder flowers, applied directly to dry skin, was a popular remedy for dry skin. You can buy the extract from a natural pharmacist or health food store.

Oat *(Avena sativa)*

Use oatmeal instead of soap — it's easy, natural, inexpensive and it helps you shed dull, flaky skin.

---

[1]   avoid high doses during pregnancy
[2]   do not use during pregnancy

Earache

Earaches are more common in children than in adults and some children seem to suffer more earaches than others. You get an earache when the tubes that connect the back of your throat to your middle ear are blocked. Colds, allergies, sinus problems, sudden changes in atmospheric pressure and ear infections are common causes. If an earache lasts more than 24 hours you need to see your doctor.

But what do you do while you are waiting? Try one of these folk remedies to soothe the pain and make the time pass more quickly.

Chickweed (Stellaria media)

Seventeenth century English physician and herbalist, Nicholas Culpeper recommended using chickweed leaves to treat earaches. He told his patients to apply a few drops of the juice extracted from fresh chickweed leaves into a sore ear.

Remedies with 🫖 *are made using an infusion. Those with* 🍲 *are made using a decoction. Instructions for both methods are on pages 4 - 7. Variations and other procedures are contained in the text following the description of that remedy.*

Mullein *(Verbascum thapsus)*

Or try 6 to 10 drops of mullein oil in the sore ear, three or four times a day. Protect the ear with a plug of cotton wool. (Dilute 1 - 2 drops of mullein oil with 10 millilitres of good quality vegetable or nut oil before applying).

Drop it!
The warm spoon technique

How do you get the folk remedy to the site of the action? A clean eye dropper is your best bet, but if you don't have one, all is not lost.

One simple way to get a few drops of liquid into your ear is to use a spoon. That's right a spoon, but not the way you think. To get just a few drops into your ear dip the spoon into the liquid and use the spoon to transfer the few drops that adhere to the surface of the spoon to your ear. If you need to warm the liquid, heat the spoon before dipping it into the liquid.

Or try a piece of cloth, dipped into the liquid then use the wet cloth to transfer the liquid to your ear.

A piece of cotton wool works in much the same way. A small piece of cloth or cotton wool can also be used to trap the liquid in your ear. It will also keep the inner ear warm, protecting it from wind. For some reason an earache always hurts more when it's cold and windy. Just twist the cloth or cotton wool into a small plug and put it in the ear, but not too deeply or tightly.

Witch Hazel *(Hamamelis virginiana)*

Try a few drops of witch hazel in the sore ear.

Onion *(Allium cepa)*

Or peel and grate an onion and collect the juice. Apply 2 - 3 drops of the warm onion juice into the sore ear. Use the warm spoon technique described on the previous page to warm and apply the onion juice.

Salt *(Sodium Chloride)*

Heat 125 grams (½ cup) of table salt in the oven. When the salt is warm put it into a cotton sock and hold the warm salt against the sore ear. If the salt is too hot, cover your ear with a towel and then apply.

Olive *(Olea europaea)*

Place 2 drops of heated (not hot) olive oil into the sore ear. Use the warm spoon technique described on the previous page to warm and apply the olive oil.

Sweet Almond *(Prunus dulcis var. dulcis)*

Sweet almond oil is the most commonly recommended oil for easing the pain of an earache. Warm the oil and apply using the warm spoon technique described described on the previous page. Then plug the ear with a piece of cotton wool to prevent the oil from seeping out. After applying the warm oil gently massage the base of the ear, where it joins the cheek.

Parsley *(Petroselinum crispum)*

Parsley oil and parsley juice are old-fashioned remedies for earaches. Dilute the oil (1-2 drops of parsley oil with 10 millilitres of good quality vegetable or nut oil) or use the juice full strength. Place some of the diluted oil or full-strength juice onto a piece of cotton wool. Use the cotton wool to plug the sore ear.

Goldenseal *(Hydrastis canadensis)*

Native Americans used goldenseal oil to soothe earaches. Dilute 1-2 drops of the oil with 10 millilitres of good quality vegetable or nut oil and place a couple of drops in the sore ear.

Boric Acid and Vodka

In the former Soviet Union folk healers treat a sore ear with a mixture of boric acid and vodka. They recommend putting 3 drops of the following mixture into the sore ear three times a day.

640 milligrams (10 grains) boric acid
30 millilitres (1 ounce) vodka

Of course vodka alone can be used to dull the pain. Apply 30 millilitres (1 ounce) to the lips and swallow swiftly - shouting Na zdorovye! (Cheers!) may help.

Ear Infection

The same tubes that, when they were blocked gave you an earache, can also become infected.   If they do, the pain will be even worse. You may even experience some temporary hearing loss and nausea. Your doctor can usually clear an ear infection, quick smart. Untreated ear infections can lead to permanent hearing loss so don't fool around with an ear infection.

While you are waiting for your appointment try one of these folk remedies, they may help to ease the pain and suffering while you wait.

Lemon *(Citrus limon or C. medica, var. limonum)*
or Onion *(Allium cepa)*

A wad of cotton wool dipped in the juice of either lemon or onion and used to plug the sore ear is an old-fashioned treatment for painful ear infections.

St John's Wort *(Hypericum perforatum)*

Another old favourite, try a few drops of this oil warmed and applied in the sore ear.

Remedies with 🫖 *are made using an infusion. Those with* 🍲 *are made using a decoction. Instructions for both methods are on pages 4 - 7. Variations and other procedures are contained in the text following the description of that remedy.*

Onion (Allium cepa)
or *Mustard* (Sinapis arvensis)

A popular remedy in the seventeenth and eighteenth century was to apply mashed up onion paste behind the sore ear. If this smelly solution didn't work the next step often was to use a mustard plaster behind the sore ear.

1. Grind mustard seeds with a little water
2. Coat the skin of the affected area with petroleum jelly (this prevents the mustard from blistering or irritating the skin)
3. Apply the paste to the sore area, holding it in place with gauze and adhesive tape. Leave on for an hour or two

Ground Ivy (Glechoma hederacea)

Dilute 1-2 drops of ivy oil with 10 millilitres of good quality vegetable or nut oil and drop a few drops of this mixture into the sore ear. Plug the ear with a wad of cotton wool.

Aluminium Acetate $Al(CHOOH)_3$
in Vinegar

Folk practitioners in New England dilute aluminium acetate solution in vinegar and apply a few drops in to the sore ear.

Turmeric (Curcuma longa)
and *Baking soda* (Bicarbonate of soda, Sodium Bicarbonate $NaHCo_3$)

India's traditional Ayurvedic physicians mix turmeric with an equal amount of baking soda and apply a tiny amount of the mixture to the outer ear to help dry up any fluid discharges.

Interesting but probably worthless

Smoke

Turkish healers blow tobacco smoke in the patient's ear for instant relief.

Wied-il-ghajn

Beginning in the late nineteenth century and continuing into this century, Maltese mothers took a child suffering with an ear infection to Wied-il-ghajn. She would bring several other mothers with her to help with the 'cure'.

First she would bury her child, up to his or her chin, in the sand. Then she would hide behind rocks and call to the other mothers who had accompanied her to the spot, and who had stayed near the child, "Give me my child".

The other mothers replied, "This is not your child". They repeated themselves three times then the child was taken out of the sand and his or her chemise buried in that spot. They believed that this treatment would solve problems with ear infections and ear defects.

Basil [1] *(Ocimum basilicum)*

In El Salvador herbalists believe placing basil flower tops in the ear will treat deafness.

---

[1] *do not use essential oil in any form during pregnancy*

Ear Wax

When your mum told you "Don't put anything smaller than your elbow in your ear" you either laughed and promptly forgot the advice or you tried for half an hour or so to get your elbow anywhere close to your ear.

Now you're an adult and while you remember your mother's advice you are plagued with itchy, sticky ear wax that just won't go away. Trying to forget it doesn't work, it only seems to make it worse. Sometimes it gets so bad, the wax builds up and reduces your hearing.

The advice about not putting anything into your ear was good advice. But not the whole story. You shouldn't ever put anything hard or sharp into your ear. Your eardrum is delicate and easily damaged. But you can use something to soften the wax and allow it to drain from your ear easily, and if you do, use one of these folk remedies, naturally.

Remedies with 🫖 *are made using an infusion. Those with* 🍲 *are made using a decoction. Instructions for both methods are on pages 4 - 7. Variations and other procedures are contained in the text following the description of that remedy.*

Olive *(Olea europaea)*

What could be easier? Put a few drops of olive oil in each ear 3 times a day for a week or so. Put a wad of cotton wool into each ear for a few minutes after putting in the oil, to stop the oil from draining out of your ear.

Bitter Almond [1] *(Prunus dulcis var. amara)* and Olive Oil *(Olea europaea)* with Lemon *(Citrus limon or C. medica, var. limonum)*

Soften ear wax with a few drops of either almond or olive oil added to few drops of lemon juice. Put the mixture into a small bowl or bottle and heat by immersing it in hot water. Be sure that the mixture is no more than body temperature, you want to loosen the wax so it drains naturally, not burn it out. Use an eyedropper to put a few drops of the mixture into the ear 2 or 3 times a day.

Peppermint [2] *(Mentha piperita)* Clove *(Syzgium aromaticum)* or Pot Marigold [3] *(Calendula officinalis)*

Add 1 drop of any of these fragrant oils to 5 millilitres (1 teaspoon) of almond oil. Put a drop or two into your ear and plug with cotton wool.

---

[1] Bitter almonds are not for eating, not only because of their bitter, unpleasant taste but because the kernels and crude oil of bitter almonds contain prussic acid, HCN (also known as hydrogen cyanide). Bitter almonds are grown primarily for their oil while sweet almonds are grown for their edible nuts. Avoid during pregnancy and if breast feeding

[2] avoid during pregnancy and if breast feeding do not give in any form to very young babies

[3] do not confuse with French Marigold, Tagetes patula

Sesame *(Sesamum indicum or S. orientale)*

In Egypt, folk healers use warm sesame seed oil to soften and remove ear wax.

They warm the oil first, to just body temperature, and apply the warm oil using an eye dropper.

Emphysema

This is bad news—no doubt about it. Unfortunately many people's emphysema is self inflected and smoking is the number one cause. So stop smoking, NOW! That is the most important thing you can do for yourself, your friends and your family. Keep away from others people's smoke, allergens and, as much as you can—photochemical smog. Breathing exercises can sometimes help, look into yoga and programs for people with asthma.

The healthier you are the less you will be bothered by your emphysema. So take good care of yourself, healthy diet and exercise in moderation, all that stuff you were going to get around to some day . . . Your some day is now!

Never substitute any folk remedy for your doctor's recommendation. Always discuss any folk remedy you would like to try with your doctor before doing any experimentation.

Remedies with 🫖 *are made using an infusion. Those with* 🍵 *are made using a decoction. Instructions for both methods are on pages 4 - 7. Variations and other procedures are contained in the text following the description of that remedy.*

Acupuncture

Acupuncturists claim to be able to relieve the symptoms of emphysema. They help sufferers breathe more easily and improve the circulation of blood through the lungs. Consult a qualified practitioner for acupuncture treatment.

Chiropractor

Some breathing difficulties are believed to be the result of slight spinal problems which according to chiropractic teaching can alter nerve impulses to the lungs. Chiropractors claim to be able to treat emphysema and ease difficult breathing.

Elecampane *(Inula helenium)*
also called Scabwort, Horseheal

India's traditional Ayurvedic physicians have used this herb for nearly 2,000 years. They make a cold infusion of the root and warm the resulting liquid before drinking to treat emphysema.

1. 1 root, cut into small pieces
2. Soak (overnight or for 8 to 10 hours) in 750 ml (3 cups) cold water
3. Strain, discarding solids and heat
4. Drink hot, 1 cup, three times a day

Eucalyptus *(Eucalyptus globus)*

Throughout their 40,000 year history, Australian Aborigines have used eucalyptus for a range of ailments. European settlers took to this useful healing plant and have since made eucalyptus a popular healing plant all over the world, especially for any illness that affects breathing. The fresh, resinous scent of eucalyptus has a cleansing and invigorating effect on the body and spirit.

1. A handful of leaves

2. A basin of boiling water

3. Cover head with a towel and inhale the vapours

Acupuncture

A connection between the body organs and the surface of the body is the underlying principle of acupuncture. There are fourteen meridians—twelve main meridians and a front and back meridian. The meridians are invisible lines on the surface of the body. Acupuncture points lie along the meridians. According to traditional Chinese medicine, the body's life force or Qi[1] (Chi) circulates along the meridians and it is the disruption of Qi (Chi), the circulating life, force that is both the cause and symptom of disease.

Traditional acupuncturists use needles of varying bore and sharpness to stimulate acupuncture points. Other

continued over page

---

[1]   *pronounced 'chee'*

Acupuncture
continued from previous page

variables include the amount of movement, length of time the needle is left in place, the depth to which the needle is inserted and the number of treatments.

Despite initial scepticism in the west, more and more traditional medical practitioners are using acupuncture as a complement to their conventional medical practices.

The key to understanding acupuncture and other traditional Chinese medical practices is Qi (Chi). Unfortunately Qi (Chi) is a difficult concept for most westerners. According to traditional Chinese beliefs, health is a state of balance and harmony with the internal and external environment. When the balance is disturbed, disease can follow.

The traditional beliefs about balance and harmony, expressed in the system of Yin and Yang, are better known (though not necessarily better understood) in the west. Yin and Yang represent conflicting influences, simplistically described with comparisons like— cold/hot, sweet/sour, male/female. In Chinese philosophy it is the balance of these influences that is important. Anything that promotes an imbalance can cause disease. The flow of Qi (Chi) from the internal organs and along the meridians helps to maintain balance. An imbalance or interruption in Qi (Chi) is a sign of disease. Bringing Qi (Chi) back into harmonious balance is the way health is restored.

continued over page

Acupuncture
continued from previous page

The importance of Qi (Chi) is not unique to the practice of acupuncture. It is central to all traditional Chinese medical teaching. The ultimate aim of every discipline in traditional Chinese medicine is to restore the flow of Qi (Chi) to harmony and balance.

Even herbal remedies have their basis in Qi (Chi). So while western herbalists look to chemical components in medicinal plants and herbal remedies and their corresponding use in conventional pharmaceutical preparations to validate their beliefs in the healing power of herbs, Chinese herbalists look to a plant's ability to influence Qi (Chi).

Watercress *(Nasturtium officinale and N. microphyllum x officinale)*

This Chinese remedy uses watercress to relieve breathlessness, mix watercress juice with carrot and parsley juice for a refreshing remedy. Use a juice extractor to make your watercress, carrot and parsley juice.

Ylang-Ylang *(Cananga odorata also called Canangium odoratum)*

A good body massage with ylang-ylang oil (1-2 drops of essential oil diluted with 10 millilitres of good quality vegetable or nut oil) makes a soothing and wonderfully fragrant traditional treatment for difficult breathing.

A juicy bit of gossip

If you want to get the most out of folk remedies that recommend fruit, vegetable or herb juices, you'll want to invest in a juice extractor, or juicer. Once you do, you'll be amazed at the variety of juices you can make at home. Making your own juice is easy and fun. You'll also be surprised at how tasty the remedies can be — if you combine juices.

Carrot makes the perfect base for vegetable juice. You'll be amazed just how sweet carrot juice is, and how well it blends with other vegetable juices.

Ginger, garlic, watercress, cucumber and alfalfa are just some of the 'juices' used in the folk remedies in this book. What could be easier than getting your healing dose of juice in a glass of yummy fruit or vegetable juice? Once you get a taste of fresh, natural fruit and vegetable juices you will never go back to processed juices again.

If you are like most people you'll soon be hooked, experimenting with different combinations and craving the savoury tang of carrot, cucumber, celery, tomato and basil juice, or the luscious sweetness of apple, pineapple and ginger juice, fresh from the juicer.

Woundwort (Stachys palustris)
and Wood Betony (Stachys officinalis)

In the Middle Ages an infusion of equal parts of these two herbs was drunk to ease breathlessness.

Eye Redness

If you burn the candle at both ends your eyes will pay the price. Itchy, red, irritated eyes will give you away every time. Don't cry though, relief is on the way. Try one of these soothing folk remedies and don't stop until you can see the whites of your eyes.

Indigo *(Indigofera tinctoria)*

Tibeto-Lamaist healers use intricate diagnostic methods to establish the nature of a disease. Their healing system is founded on the teachings of the fifth century physician Pien-Chueh. Their recommended treatment is a decoction of indigo, used as an eye wash to soothe red eyes.

Eyebright *(Euphrasia officinalis)*

Scottish Highlanders use eyebright to make a soothing milk infusion to treat sore, red eyes. Use milk instead of water to make this infusion. True traditionalists wear a kilt while applying the solution to the eye with a feather, but it probably will work just as well if you wear your street clothes and apply the liquid with an eye dropper.

Remedies with ☕ are made using an infusion. Those with 🍲 are made using a decoction. Instructions for both methods are on pages 4 - 7. Variations and other procedures are contained in the text following the description of that remedy.

Greater Celandine (Chelidonium majus)

Both Dioscorides and Gerard praised greater celandine for its ability to soothe eye ailments. Two thousand years ago the Roman physician, Pliny said that the juice of celandine was used by swallows to give sight to their young. This remedy, another milk infusion, soothes eye redness and may give you a bird's eye view of the world. Use milk instead of water to make this infusion.

Egg White

In Turkey folk healers break an egg and apply the last few drops of the raw egg white to sore, red eyes, three times a day.

Lovage (Levisticum officinale)

This remedy was introduced by the seventeenth century English physician and herbalist Nicholas Culpeper. It uses an extraction of lovage leaves, 1 or two drops of which were applied to red, irritated eyes.

Chickweed (Stellaria media)

Here's another remedy made popular by Nicholas Culpeper. This one uses the juice extracted from chickweed leaves to treat red eyes. Use the liquid in a compress on sore eyes

Barberry *(Berberis vulgaris)*

A hundred years ago American folk healers began using barberry to relieve red eyes. They soften the root bark (the outer covering of the root) and use the liquid that is squeezed from the softened root to make this soothing compress for red, irritated eyes.

1. Soften the plant material by repeatedly pouring boiling water over it
2. Squeeze the softened root and collect the liquid that results
3. Use the liquid in a compress on sore eyes

Eye Strain

Eye strain is another one of those modern (usually self-inflicted) ailments. Eye strain is caused by the same sorts of things that strain other muscles. But because we don't think of the muscles in our eyes, eye strain sometimes takes us by surprise. Any time you spend long periods doing the same thing (staring at a computer monitor, playing a computer game, reading at close quarters, even watching television) your eyes will protest. Rather than ache, your eyes are creative and institute a go-slow or work-to-rule ban.

Before you try one of the following folk remedies to ease your eyes back to work, pay attention to how it feels. Struggle to focus on the newspaper. Stretch your arms to get the book just that little bit further from your eyes. Shift positions to shine more light on the menu.

Don't you feel guilty for all the times you made fun of your parents. Now you know how they feel. Stop making fun of Mum when she searches for her reading glasses. Don't laugh at Dad as he stretches and strains to read the paper. Remember it will happen to you too—it's just a matter of time and now that you know what it's going to be like . . . it's not so funny is it?

Remedies with ☕ *are made using an infusion. Those with* 🍲 *are made using a decoction. Instructions for both methods are on pages 4 - 7. Variations and other procedures are contained in the text following the description of that remedy.*

Hawkweed *(Hieracium pilosella, also known as Mouse-ear)*

The seventeenth century English physician and herbalist, Nicholas Culpeper, recommended people suffering from eye-strain drink an infusion of hawkweed.

Some old-fashioned remedies that are found in the folk-remedies of many cultures

Fennel [1] *(Foeniculum officinale)*

Tibeto-Lamaist healers use a decoction of fennel as a wash to treat eye strain.

Peppermint [2] *(Mentha piperita)*
or Spearmint [3] *(Mentha spicata)*

Those dark circles under your eyes are another result of eye strain. If you re tired of looking like a panda, try applying the juice from freshly crushed mint leaves to the darkened skin.

---

[1] avoid during pregnancy

[2] avoid during pregnancy and if breast feeding do not give in any form to very young babies

[3] avoid during pregnancy and if breast feeding do not give in any form to very young babies

Bitter Almond [1] *(Prunus dulcis var. amara)*
Apricot *(Prunus armeniaca)*
or Coconut Oils *(Cocos nucifera)*

If your suffer from eye strain you are guaranteed to spend some time squinting. If you squint you're the delicate skin around your eyes will wrinkle. If the skin is dry the wrinkles will be worse. To lubricate dry skin use 1 or 2 drops of any of these oils diluted with 10 millilitres of good quality vegetable or nut oil. Gently massage the diluted oil into the delicate skin around your eyes.

BATES METHOD

In 1900 American ophthalmologist Dr William H Bates developed these seven exercises to remedy eye strain.

Shifting

Move your gaze constantly from one point of interest to another. As the eyes become more relaxed, the movement becomes smaller, helping your sight to become clearer.

Blinking

Get into the habit of blinking regularly, once or twice every ten seconds, to clean and lubricate the eyes.

Palming

Sit comfortably at a table with your back and neck straight and head level. Rest your elbows on a cushion

continued over page

---

[1]   Bitter almonds are not for eating, not only because of their bitter, unpleasant taste but because the kernels and crude oil of bitter almonds contain prussic acid, HCN (also known as hydrogen cyanide). Bitter almonds are grown primarily for their oil while sweet almonds are grown for their edible nuts.

BATES METHOD
from previous page

on the table and close your eyes. Then, without touching your eyes cover them with your cupped palms. Think of something pleasant. Do this exercise for ten minutes at least, twice a day.

Remembering
While doing the palming exercise, see if without straining to recall an object or experience you can 'see' the item or experience in detail, including colours. According to Dr Bates, remembering things in the mind's eye helps you to see them more clearly in reality.

Near and far focusing
Take a pencil in each hand. Hold them in front of your face, one about 7.5 cm (3 inches) away, the other at arm's length, keeping your arms close together. Focus on one pencil, then blink and focus on the other. Repeat several times whenever an opportunity arises.

Splashing
First thing every morning, splash your eyes 20 times with warm water and then 20 times with cold water to stimulate circulation. Reverse the process last thing at night. Be sure to keep your eyes closed when doing this exercise.

Swinging
Standing with your feet apart, gently swing from side to side, letting your point of focus swing along with your body's movement. Be aware of the visual movement as this relaxes your eyes and helps them to become more flexible. Repeat whenever an opportunity arises.

Fatigue

Fatigue is the price you pay for burning the candle at both ends. Unfortunately, in the nineties, doing too much in too little time has become a way of life. Taking good care of yourself—and that includes eating a healthy, balanced diet—will help you stay energised. But unless you regularly pause and renew yourself mentally and physically all that care will come to nought. One day you will wake-up and feel like you're running on empty.

When that happens try one of these folk remedies to rejuvenate your mind body and spirit.

Basil[1] *(Ocimum basilicum)*

Basil, or as it is known in India 'tulsi', has been used as a sacred, religious herb for nearly 2,500 years (since early Vedic times). Test its healing reputation for yourself and try a massage with 1 -2 drops of basil diluted with 10 millilitres of good quality vegetable or nut oil. It will help relieve muscle fatigue and invigorate a sagging spirit.

Remedies with 🫖 *are made using an infusion. Those with* 🍵 *are made using a decoction. Instructions for both methods are on pages 4 - 7. Variations and other procedures are contained in the text following the description of that remedy.*

---

[1]   *do not use essential oil in any form during pregnancy*

When basil made its way to ancient Greece it earned the name 'basilicum' after basileus, meaning king. Basil was considered a royal herb and was believed to be the source of high energy. Basil the Great used the herb that shares his name to refresh his armies. Try drinking this refreshing basil infusion whether you do battle at the office or on the home front.

Chamomile[1] *(Chamaemelum nobile, Roman, or C. recutita, German)*

Chamomile baths have been used to sooth fatigue since the time of the ancient Egyptians. If you want to follow the practice of ancient Egyptian beauties add a bag of chamomile heads and leaves to your hot bath to ease pain and fatigue.

If you'd rather follow English beauties sip a cup of soothing chamomile tea while your steeping in your chamomile scented bath.

Rosemary *(Rosmarinus officinalis)*

This remedy from the ancient Egyptians uses invigorating rosemary oil to bring you back to life. Use rosemary oil (dilute 1-2 drops of rosemary oil with 10 millilitres of good quality vegetable or nut oil) and massage the head and upper body to energise and aid recovery from mental exhaustion.

Northern Kurrajong *(Brachychiton diversifolius)*

Australian Aborigines chew the inner bark of this plant to overcome fatigue and relieve thirst.

---

[1]   avoid excessive doses and the oil in any amount during pregnancy

Trail Mix, Chocolate, Bee Pollen and Baked Beans

For chronic fatigue Vermont folk healers recommend getting at least 8 hours of uninterrupted sleep every night. Well, if you could do that you wouldn't be fatigued now would you? Luckily they also suggest eating trail mix (a oat, grain, nut and dried fruit mixture similar to muesli), chocolate, bee pollen (up to 100 grams/3 oz a day) and baked beans sprinkled with vinegar.

Parsnip *(Pastinaca sativa)*

Parsnips, steamed or baked for lunch or dinner, once a day or every other day, is a fatigue fighter from the good old days.

Massage

Massage may be the oldest therapeutic treatment—it has after all been practised therapeutically in the Middle and Far East since at least 3000 BC—but it is undoubtedly the most enjoyable therapy known.

If you are tired from over exertion rather than from any medical condition, a brisk, general massage is a tonic for the mind, body and spirit. For a quick pick-me-up at the end of a long day a friend will do. But for best results treat yourself to a professional massage from a qualified massage therapist.

Acupressure

If you are just too pooped to pop, try this DIY acupressure technique to revive sagging spirits. Apply pressure at a point three thumbs width from under (behind) the kneecap, in the hollow on the outer edge of this skin. Press inward. Alternatively apply pressure to the centre of the palm at the point where the middle finger rests when the hand is folded inwards. For best results consult a trained therapist.

Always running on empty?

If you wake-up bone tired after three late nights in a row, if you're weary from working seven days a week for weeks on end, or if you're exhausted from being a full-time Super-Mum or Super-Dad, you shouldn't be surprised. If you've been under a mental or physical strain it's normal to feel tired, and a few days R and R will do you the world of good.

But what if you have been taking good care of yourself, getting a good night's sleep, eating three balanced meals, doing all the right stuff, and you still wake up feeling like you've just gone 10 rounds with Jeff Fenech?[1]

If, no matter what you do, you always feel tired, you may be suffering from something other than normal fatigue. Any chronic illness can put a drain on your energy reserves. If you are more tired than usual, it may be a sign that your illness is getting worse. And extreme, unrelenting fatigue can be a sign of diseases like glandular fever (mononucleosis), Chronic Fatigue Syndrome, and some forms of thyroid disease.

So, if in spite of your best efforts, you are always exhausted, consult your doctor for a thorough check-up.

[1]   an Australian boxing champion

Aromatherapy

If you are physically exhausted try using a stimulating essential oil, like black pepper, lemon, lemongrass or rosemary oil. Put a few drops on a tissue or handkerchief and inhale the invigorating volatile oil. Or put six to ten drops into your bath water and relax in the warm bath for at least ten minutes.

If you are mentally exhausted use sage, savoury or rosemary oils in the same way.

Acupuncture

Acupuncture should only be done by a trained practitioner but it's getting easier and easier to find acupuncturists. So, if you want to try acupuncture finding a qualified practitioner shouldn't be a problem. In traditional Chinese medicine fatigue is often traced to a dysfunction of the internal organs and acupuncture treatment is directed at those organs.

Korokio *(Corokia buddleioidea)*

The Maori used a decoction of korokio as a general tonic.

Try this remedy and you may find yourself recovering from fatigue with a short rest at Her Majesty's pleasure!

Marijuana *(Cannabis sativa)*

In ancient times, the Arabian physicians Avicenna and Serapian used cannabis for a variety of ailments. The Persians extracted juice from a fresh plant and took a few drops to relax and overcome fatigue. The remedy was said to be especially useful for fatigue from over-walking.

The Persians did a lot of walking so we can probably take their word for the efficacy of this remedy. Persia (today most associated with the modern nation of Iran) was an ancient kingdom in south west Asia. Early Persians were nomadic. They migrated through the Caucasus (a mountain range between the Caspian and Black Seas in the former Soviet Union) to what is now the Iranian plateau. A long journey in anybody's book.

Fever

Feed a cold-starve a fever or is it starve a cold and feed a fever? It's which ever makes you feel better. A fever is not a disease but a sign of your immune system in high gear. It is usually a signal that your immune system is mounting an attack against a bacterial or viral invader. In adults, in small doses, for short periods of time, a fever is nothing to worry about.

If you can stand it, let a fever run its course, it's caused by your body fighting infection. It's just one weapon your body uses to fight bacterial and viral invaders. Some doctors think that the fever actually helps your body get well quicker. That's why so many folk remedies for fever and common ailments that cause fevers rely on a herb to stimulate your body to produce a little extra heat. If the fever makes you too uncomfortable and you don't want to ride it out, try one of the following folk remedies to turn the heat down.

What's normal? Most people's temperature is around 36.7-37.2°C (98-99°F). From 37.2 to 37.8°C (99 to 100°F) is a low-grade fever. If your temperature is above 37.8°C (100°F) you well and truly have a fever.

Remedies with ☕ are made using an infusion. Those with ♨ are made using a decoction. Instructions for both methods are on pages 4 - 7. Variations and other procedures are contained in the text following the description of that remedy.

When is a fever dangerous?

Never ignore a fever:

● in young children, especially in infants under 4 years old

● above 40.6°C (105°F) in any one of any age if it does not go down within a few hours of standard treatment

● above 41.1°C (106°F) in any one of any age

● accompanied by a stiff neck or any fever that lasts more than five days

● in an adult with a chronic illness.

In these situations a fever can be dangerous, even deadly, and you should consult your doctor immediately.

Bayberry *(Myrica cerifera) also known as Wax Myrtle*

The Native American Choctaw tribe drank a decoction of bayberry to reduce a fever.

Boneset *(Eupatorium perfoliatum) also know as Feverwort*

Two thousand years ago, the Greek physician Dioscorides recommended an infusion of boneset to treat intermittent, relapsing and chronic fevers. Native North Americans also used boneset, the leaves this time, for its ability to induce sweating, a longstanding folk remedy for fever.

Kanono *(Coprosma australis)*

Drinking an infusion of kanono leaves was the traditional Maori way to lower a fever.

Sick or Sorry?

It's not much of a choice, but often that's the choice our ancestors faced.

The trend today is to suspect science and technology and trust nature. But mother nature is not always a loving parent . . . some of the most potent poisons come to us direct from nature's bounty.

Through the ages people have mistakenly seen the violent response to particular medicinal plants as proof of the plant's efficacy. The following is a classic example.

Ignatia *(Strychnos ignatii) also known as Saint Ignatius Bean*

Over two hundred years ago, people in the Philippines treated fever with this plant's seeds. Whether it worked or not is open to debate. If the fever goes down because the patient died, does it still count as an effective remedy? The unlucky patient would probably think not.

If you're thinking that this plant's scientific name seems vaguely familiar, you should know that all members of the genus to which this plant belongs—Strychnos—contain a nerve poison. And that's where the familiarity comes from, the nerve poison is called strychnine!

Anise *(Pimpinella anisum)*

Egyptian folk healers have used a decoction of anise roots to reduce fevers for at least 3,500 years. Nineteenth century

American folk healers also recommended drinking a decoction of anise root.

Chamomile [1] *(Chamaemelum nobile, Roman, or C. recutita, German)*

This remedy comes to us from Nicholas Culpeper, one of the great English herbalists. He recommended drinking an infusion of chamomile leaves. If the fever was accompanied by body aches and pains he recommended rubbing the soles of the feet to promote sweating and bring down the fever.

Here are more remedies from English physician and herbalist, Nicholas Culpeper.

Bugloss *(Echium vulgare) also known as Viper's Bugloss*

If you don't like an infusion of chamomile, maybe you would prefer this recommendation from Culpeper's arsenal, drinking an infusion of bugloss.

Butterbur *(Petasites hybridus)*

If neither bugloss nor chamomile is to your liking? Drinking a decoction of butterbur was another of Culpeper's recommendations to bring down a fever.

Coltsfoot [2] *(Tussilago farfara)*

Or how about coltsfoot? Drinking an infusion of coltsfoot is another of Culpeper's anti-fever treatments.

---

[1]   avoid excessive doses and the oil in any amount during pregnancy

[2]   restricted herb in Australia and New Zealand, due to presence of alkaloid pyrrolizidine, which has been shown to cause liver damage in rats

Willow [1] *(Salix alba)*

Herbalists and folk healers have been telling people to drink a decoction of willow bark to reduce fever, inflammation and pain for thousands of years. Modern herbalists recommend an infusion of powdered willow bark. Even western medical practitioners recommend willow bark, at least indirectly. But they recommend using the synthetic form of salicylic acid. And rather than having you drink a decoction of willow bark they will have you take it in tablet, capsule or soluble form, and they'll call it aspirin.

Take two decoctions of willow bark and call me in the morning

The next time you run into someone who doesn't believe that herbal remedies can be effective, ask them if they have ever used a western 'drug' that has its origin in folk wisdom and herbal medicine. If they say no, ask them what they use instead of aspirin! The bark of white willow has a long history of medicinal use. Traditional Chinese medical practitioners began using it for pain relief about 500 years before the birth of Christ. During the first century AD, in ancient Greece, Dioscorides used willow bark for pain and inflammation.

Nicholas Culpeper recommended willow, bark, leaves and seeds for almost everything, up to and including suppressing sexual desire. When European colonists

continued over page

---

[1]   *Treat willow as you would aspirin, do not take if you are pregnant and do not give to children under two or to children suffering with a cold, flu or chicken pox*

continued from previous page

went to North America they brought willow trees with them and continued to use a decoction of willow bark medicinally. Observant folk healers would have seen the Native Americans using the local willow varieties for the same purposes.

In the 1820s European chemists began experimenting with willow bark. Eventually the active ingredient—salicin—was identified. Scientists began searching the plant kingdom for other plants that produce salicin, and by the mid 1900s it was universally accepted that salicin and its precursor, salicylic acid, effectively reduced fever, pain and inflammation, though exactly how these chemicals work remains a mystery.

While salicin and salicylic acid work, when purified and concentrated they are too potent to use safely. So researchers developed a synthetic form of salicylic acid —acetylsalicylic acid or as it is more commonly known today—aspirin.[1]

Bergamot *(Monarda didyma, M. fistulosa, M. citriodora and M. punctata)*

For centuries folk healers in West African coastal countries have used juice extracted from bergamot peel or rind in their fever remedy. They rub the juice on the forehead, chest and limbs to reduce a fever.

---

[1] *If you want to know more about aspirin and find out why some researchers are calling it the wonder drug of the nineties read The Aspirin Handbook, by Joe Graedon and Tom Ferguson, M.D., published in Australia and New Zealand by Bookman Press, Melbourne Victoria.*

Gypsum *(Crystalline Hydrated Calcium Sulfate CaSO₄·2H₂0*

Tibeto-Lamaist healers use an intricate diagnostic system to establish the nature of disease. The traditional system originated with Pien-Chueh, a fifth century BC physician. The system is so complex that training a traditional practitioner in this discipline takes nearly 20 years. Luckily you don't have to study for 20 years to benefit from their knowledge. All you have to know is that they recommend taking 2.5 grams (½ teaspoon) of powered gypsum to reduce a fever.

Cinnamon [1] *(Cinnamomum zeylanicum in the west, C. cassia in China, C Cassia from the bark = rou gui or from twigs gui zhi)*

Ancient Chinese and Indian healers recommended drinking powdered cinnamon mixed with a little cold water to reduce fever.

French folk healers also use cinnamon in their fever remedy, but go the ancient's one better. Not satisfied with a simple decoction of cinnamon and cloves this remedy looks just the thing to drive a fever away, it's not for drivers though. If you are at home for the evening give it a try, the whiskey will warm you, right down to the tips of your toes.

1. 1 small stick of cinnamon plus a few cloves in a saucepan

2. Add 2 cups water and bring to a slow boil

3. Simmer 3 minutes

4. Remove from heat

5. add 10 ml (2 teaspoons) lemon juice
     30 ml (1 ounce) dark honey
     30 ml (1 ounce) good quality whiskey

6. Stir well, cover and let stand for 20 minutes

7. Drink, 125 ml (½ cup) at a time spread over 3 or 4 hours

---

[1]   *avoid in pregnancy*

White Cypress Pine *(Callitris glaucophylla)*

Australian Aborigines frequently used smoke in their medicinal practices. This traditional fever remedy starts with burning white cypress pine branches in a small hole in the ground to make a strong fire, with plenty of smoke. When suffering with a fever you stood in the smoke taking in the healing warmth of the fire and inhaling the aromatic smoke. Then you jumped in the sack for a good, long sleep.

Eucalyptus *(Eucalyptus globus)*

Australian Aboriginal folk healers also recommended drinking an infusion of eucalyptus leaves to break a fever.

1. Break a few leaves and steep in 250 millilitres (1 cup) water for 10 minutes
2. Drink as needed

Catnip *(Nepeta cataria)*

Folk healers in the US state of Pennsylvania recommend drinking an infusion of catnip to relieve a fever.

Cocoa *(Theobroma cacao)*

For centuries Mexicans have used cocoa to treat fevers. They made a drink rather like the way we now make coffee, but they use dried ground, cocoa beans instead of roasted coffee beans.

10 grams (2 teaspoons) ground cocoa beans

250 millilitres (1 cup) hot water or hot milk

Drink as needed

Cocoa made this way will be bitter, so if you really want to enjoy your cocoa remedy, you will probably want to add a little honey

Coffee *(Coffea arabica, C. liberica, C. robusta)*

While their southern cousins in Mexico used cocoa to treat fever, North American folk healers recommended fever sufferers drink an infusion of coffee beans.

20 grams (1 tablespoon) of ground coffee beans
1 cup boiling water
Drink 3 cups a day

Dandelion *(Taraxacum officinale)*
also known as pu gong ying

Dandelion's modern reputation as a garden pest would shock our ancestors. To them dandelion was a valuable healing plant. This drink, a combination of a decoction of dandelion root and an infusion of dandelion leaves, comes from North America where it is a longstanding fever remedy.

Decoction
1 litre (1 quart) water
50 grams (2 ½ tablespoons) dried, dandelion root, cut in to small pieces
1. Simmer 12 minutes
2. Remove from heat
3. Add to decoction
4. 15 grams (3 teaspoons) dried, finely chopped dandelion leaves
5. Steep 20 minutes
6. Strain and sweeten with 1 teaspoon pure maple syrup
7. Drink 1 cup every 5 hours until fever breaks

Biochemic Tissue Salts

If you're into Biochemics use Ferrum Phosphate—if the fever is accompanied by a rapid pulse, flushed face, chills and vomiting of undigested food. Use Kali Phos—if the fever is associated with a nervous condition and general weakness.

Ginger [1] *(Zingiber officinalis)*

Long before Europeans arrived on the North America continent healers of the Native American Rappahannock tribe drank an infusion of wild ginger leaves to reduce fever.

Chinese physicians also use ginger in their fever remedy, though they favour ginger root. When you are suffering from a fever a traditional Chinese physician will tell you to add a little ground, dried, ginger-root to everything you eat and drink.

Borage *(Borago officinalis) also known as Bee Bread*

Borage, with its cucumber-like fragrance, has a look and taste similar to comfrey. Drinking an infusion of borage leaves, flowers and stems is a popular fever remedy. High fevers or those that last a long time can be dehydrating. Borage leaves contain potassium, calcium and mineral salts so the infusion can also help correct any electrolyte imbalance caused by a fever.

Horseradish *(Amoracia rusticana)*

Horseradish is an old household remedy for fever. In south eastern Europe they collect horseradish roots and store them

---

[1]   *use sparingly during pregnancy*

in sand so they can have horseradish on hand throughout the year. You can use fresh or dried horseradish root to make this potent infusion. ☕

Foot Massage

Ancient Egyptian healers recommended rubbing lotus into the soles of a feverish Pharaohs' feet.

Tamarind *(Tamarindus indica)*

In the Middle East they drink an infusion of tamarind to treat fever. Steep several hours, dilute the concentrated infusion with an equal volume of water before drinking. ☕

Sponge Bath

A lukewarm sponge bath, concentrating on the hands, head and feet, is a simple, old-fashioned remedy for fever.

Cabbage *(Brassica oleracea)*

In case you haven't noticed, a cabbage patch is a necessity in a folk healer's garden. A cabbage leaf placed on your forehead is soothing and helps to lower your temperature. If you children baulk at wearing a cabbage leaf headband, or laugh uncontrollably whenever you sport a cabbage leaf on your burning brow, try the modern version of the ancient remedy, a damp facecloth or flannel applied to the forehead.

Peach Syrup *(Prunus persica)*

This remedy, a favourite of some Native American tribes, is a syrup made from a decoction of peach kernels and bark. It is used to treat a variety of illnesses like colds, bronchitis almost anything that could cause a fever.

1. Pound: peach bark 170 grams (⅔ cup)
2. Split: peach kernels, 170 grams (⅔ cup)
3. Add: 500 millilitres (2 cups each apple cider vinegar and pure distilled water
4. Steep: 5 days in a warm place, shake several times each day
5. Simmer: Gently until the volume is reduced by ½
6. Add: 125 millilitres (½ cup) brandy or whisky as a preservative
7. Use: 20 ml (1 tablespoon) every 3-4 hours
8. Store: after the liquid has cooled store in a well-sealed bottle or jar, discard unused portion after 1 month

Gentian *(Gentiana marcrophylla) also known as gin jiao*

India's traditional Ayurvedic physicians use a decoction of gentian root to treat fevers.

5 grams (1 teaspoon) dried, ground gentian root
3 cups of water
1. Boil 30 minutes
2. Drink 5 ml (1 teaspoon) 3 or 4 times a day before meals

Cottage cheese

Here's a way to use up the last little bit of cottage cheese in the refrigerator, use it to make a cooling compress!

1. Mix cottage cheese, milk and a few drops of vinegar, stir until the mixture thickens
2. Spread onto a cotton or linen cloth and apply to the forehead

A bitter end

Angostura is the primary ingredient in the popular flavouring agent, Angostura Bitters. The bitterness comes from the angostura. The concoction, an alcoholic extraction, also contains cinnamon, coves, mace, nutmeg, etc to make it palatable.

Angostura isn't the only alcohol infused herbal drink, though it's one of the most familiar. Campari, Benedictine and Chartreuse are also alcoholic herbal infusions. Less well known are the after-dinner 'digestive' liqueurs popular in Italy, Germany and Hungary. Familiar medicinal plants used to flavour 'digestives' include gentian, cinchona and angelica.

3. Wrap the whole mess with a towel and leave it on for a half hour or so

4. Repeat as necessary

Angostura (Galiepa officinalis)

Named after an old Venezuelan town, but made in Trinidad, this herb was introduced to the rest of the world in 1788, by Dr Ewer who recommended drinking a decoction of the plant's roots to treat fevers.

30 grams (1 ounce) bark

1 cup water

1. Bring to the boil

2. Strain, discarding solids

3. Allow to cool, then take 20 millilitres (1 tablespoon) doses

Flatulence

Flatulence is the polite name for a problem that isn't discussed in polite company. It's not discussed, but it is talked about. Flatulence—or as it is more commonly called wind—is the subject of more jokes than any other bodily function. Nothing, it seems, is funnier than someone with wind, unless of course that someone is you.

Wind is most commonly caused by what you eat. Some people are lactose intolerant. Milk or cheese really puts the wind up them. Fizzy drinks and spicy foods are other people's downfall. Then there's cabbage, broccoli, Brussels sprouts and cauliflower, fibre, beans and pulses—all well known wind producers. Some people get wind just from breathing!

How do you keep from being the butt of all those wind jokes? Whatever you do, don't cut out the food that's good for you just because of a little wind. Instead, build your tolerance for fruit, fibre and cruciferous vegetables—the good they can do for your health is worth the effort. Once your digestive system gets used to processing these foods you should be okay. Anytime you find the wind picking up, try one of the following remedies.

Remedies with 🫖 *are made using an infusion. Those with* ☕ *are made using a decoction. Instructions for both methods are on pages 4 - 7. Variations and other procedures are contained in the text following the description of that remedy.*

Allspice *(Pimenta diocia)*
also known as Jamica Pepper, Pimento

In Costa Rica drinking an infusion of allspice has been used for centuries to treat wind.

Anise *(Pimpinella anisum)*

Ancient Chinese, Egyptian and Greek physicians all recommended anise to relieve wind. Try chewing a pinch of anise seeds to relive wind and sweeten your breath.

Cardamom *(Elettaria cardamomum)*

For centuries, drinking an infusion of crushed cardamom seeds has been the Indian remedy for wind.

Bergamot *(Monarda didyma, M. fistulosa, M. citriodora and M. punctata)*

Ever since Columbus brought a bergamot tree back from the Canary Islands Italians have sipped the juice extracted from bergamot peel and rind to relieve wind.

Asafoetida *(Ferula assa-foetida)*
also known as Devil's Dung

This plant grows in the Indus Valley and in the mountains of Hindu Kush. It was used by the local healers nearly two thousand years ago as a remedy for wind. The gum-resin of the plant is taken in very small doses either mixed with lukewarm water or in powdered form, sprayed on food. Only use it in very small doses or you'll know exactly why this potent herb's other name is 'devil's dung'.

Cinnamon [1] *(Cinnamomum zeylanicum in the west, C. cassia in China, C Cassia from the bark = rou gui or from twigs gui zhi)*

America's nineteenth century herbalists recommended drinking an infusion of cinnamon to relieve wind.

Catnip *(Nepeta cataria)*

During the Middle Ages European folk healers took to this herb as a remedy for wind. Drinking an infusion of catnip was the recommendation.

Fennel [2] *(Foeniculum officinale)*

Nearly 2000 years ago the Greek physician Dioscorides recommended drinking an infusion of crushed fennel seeds to relieve wind.

Rosemary *(Rosmarinus officinalis)*

The ancient Romans used rosemary oil to ease wind. A good massage on the lower chest, abdomen and pelvic area with 1 - 2 drops of rosemary oil (diluted with 10 millilitres of good quality vegetable or nut oil) was their soothing and fragrant recommendation.

Dill *(Anethum graveolens)*

Seventeenth century English herbalist, Nicholas Culpeper, wrote that dill was 'the gallant expeller of wind'. He recommended chewing a little dill seed, about 2.5 grams (½ teaspoon) twice a day to relieve wind.

---

[1]   avoid in pregnancy
[2]   avoid during pregnancy

Galangal *(Alpinia officinarum) also known as Catarrh Root*

For centuries traditional Chinese healers have advised their patients to drink an infusion of galangal roots to treat wind.

These old-fashioned remedies for wind are so common in so many cultures they are might as well be called universal wind remedies.

Carbonated Liquids

Sip warm, old-fashioned colourless lemonade or plain soda water to relieve wind.

Barley Water

If you want to try this old-fashioned remedy for wind, look in Grandma's cookbook for a recipe for barley water, made with barley and fruit juice.

Goat's Milk

Or try drinking goat's milk, it has a reputation for easing persistent wind.

Massage - especially good for infants

First relax the child's muscles with a warm hot water bottle at the base of the child's lower back or abdomen.

Lie the child in front of you, on his or her back. Lift the child's legs, bending them at the knees, then release.

Gently massage the child's abdomen in downward strokes from below the rib cage to the pelvis, hand over hand. Do this six times.

Continue massaging the abdomen, moving your hands in a clockwise direction, around the abdomen.

Grasp the child's ankles, straighten legs, pulling them towards you, then slowly bend the legs at the knees by pushing the child's legs towards their abdomen, so that knees touch the chest. Hold for 10 -30 seconds while child breathes slowly. Do this five times, turn child on their left side and place a warm (not hot) hot-water bottle on their tummy.

Aromatherapy

To treat wind blend 1-2 drops of basil, sage, peppermint and myrrh oils in 40 millilitres of good quality vegetable or nut oil. Massage the oil into the skin of the abdomen, always moving your hands in a clockwise direction. If you want the real thing though, treat yourself to a professional massage and aromatherapy by a trained practitioner.

Naturopathy

If you are troubled with chronic wind consult a registered naturopath for a complete program of diet, compresses, massage and exercises.

Flu

The flu, an infectious viral disease that spreads like wildfire has been around for a long time and that won't change for a long time, if ever. Like most viruses the flu virus is constantly changing. If you catch the flu this year you'll be past by next year and maybe the next. By the third or fourth year the flu virus will have changed enough and you'll be susceptible to infection again.

Don't confuse a flu with a bad cold. While both are caused by a virus, they are different diseases. With a cold, even a bad one, you feel less than your best, but you're not incapacitated. With the flu, your head throbs, your muscles ache, your temperature rises suddenly, and you're drained of energy. A cough, runny nose and a sore throat almost always accompany the flu to complete the dreary picture. With a cold you start feeling better almost before you know you're sick and you're back to normal after a few days. With the flu you may not be convinced that you'll ever get better or that getting better is worth the effort. It can take weeks to fully recover from the flu.

Remedies with 🫖 are made using an infusion. Those with 🍲 are made using a decoction. Instructions for both methods are on pages 4 - 7. Variations and other procedures are contained in the text following the description of that remedy.

Don't be a martyr when it comes to the flu, stay home and stay in bed. Let your body marshall all its resources in its fight against the flu. Drink plenty of liquids and use whatever pain reliever works best for you. But never give aspirin to anyone under 2 years of age.

Don't underestimate the flu, it was and still is a killer. People who suffer from chronic illnesses (especially respiratory and cardiovascular conditions) and anyone over 65 should have a flu shot every year. Even if the shot doesn't prevent you from catching the flu, it will reduce the severity of the disease. Once you start, keep up with the shots, because you won't be developing natural immunity to the evolving flu virus. When the next new flu virus appears it could have you down for the count. Don't get a flu shot if you are allergic to eggs though. The flu vaccine is grown in eggs, if you are allergic you could have a violent reaction to the shot.

Bayberry (Myrica cerifera) also known as Wax Myrtle

During the early nineteenth century Samuel Thomson an American herbalist in the New England area of the US popularised drinking an infusion of bayberry as a flu remedy and praised it for the ability to produce heat within the body.

Celery (Apium graveolens)

This remedy is almost as old as the flu itself—it comes to us from India's ancient Ayurvedic physicians. They recommended drinking an infusion of freshly crushed celery seed to treat flu like symptoms.

Cinnamon [1] *(Cinnamomum zeylanicum in the west, C. cassia in China, C Cassia from the bark = rou gui or from twigs gui zhi)*

In the twelfth century the German abbess and herbalist, Hildegard of Bingen, recommended drinking an infusion of cinnamon to treat the flu. 🫖

Cinnamon [2] *(Cinnamomum zeylanicum in the west, C. cassia in China, C Cassia from the bark = rou gui or from twigs gui zhi)*
Clove *(Syzgium aromaticum)*
and Lemon *(Citrus limon or C. medica, var. limonum)*

This old French folk remedy is even tastier than Hildegard of Bingen's cinnamon remedy but it's not for teetotallers. With their characteristic style, French folk healers recommend drinking an infusion of cinnamon and cloves to which you added lemon juice, honey, and the secret ingredient—whiskey to give the flu the knock out punch.

1. Take a small stick of cinnamon and a few cloves
2. Pour 500 millilitres (2 cups) of water, over the cinnamon and cloves
3. Bring to a slow boil and allow to simmer 3 minutes
4. Remove from heat
5. Add 10 millilitres (2 teaspoons) lemon juice
6. 45 millilitres (1 ½ tablespoons) dark honey
7. 60 millilitres (2 tablespoons) whiskey
8. Stir well, cover and let it stand for 20 minutes
9. Drink half a cup at a time every 3 or 4 hours

---

[1]   avoid in pregnancy
[2]   avoid during pregnancy

Coffee *(Coffea arabica, C. liberica, C. robusta)*

American folk healers must have been a practical lot. They recommend a flu remedy that is nothing more involved than drinking a cup of coffee, something that was sure to be in every family's pantry. If you need a recipe:

30 grams (1 tablespoon) ground coffee beans
250 millilitres (1 cup) boiling water
1. Steep 10 minutes and strain
2. Drink 3 cups a day

Catnip *(Nepeta cataria)*

This flu remedy, a simple infusion of catnip, was a popular drink throughout Europe during the Middle Ages.

Red River Gum *(Eucalyptus camaldulensis)*

More than forty thousand years of Aboriginal tradition has given this remedy a prominent place in the all time herbal hall of fame. A few crushed leaves in boiling water creates a healing steam that can help you breathe more easily. Eucalyptus oil rubbed into the chest works the same way, while eucalyptus oil rubbed into the joints helps to ease aches and pains. Best of all, fresh, invigorating eucalyptus soothes and strengthens the spirit.

Stringybark *(Eucalyptus tetrodonta)*

For centuries, this species of eucalyptus was the preferred flu treatment for the people of Papaua New Guinea. They got double duty out of the remedy too, chewing on the leaves and drinking a decoction of fresh, young leaves.

Coltsfoot [1] *(Tussilago farfara)*

Coltsfoot has been in every traditional Chinese medicine chest for the last 200 years.Drinking an infusion of coltsfoot is the standard recommendation when you are suffering from the flu.

Garlic [2] *(Allium sativum)*

Garlic has been used medicinally for ages. Modern science has proved garlic to have anti-oxidant, antiseptic and anti-viral properties, it helps you get over the flu and it's good for your all around health. Eat a clove of garlic three times a day.

Friar's Balsam

The fuzzy headed feeling that accompanies the flu is almost as bad as the aches and pains. Inhaling Friar's Balsam (tincture of benzoin) can help clear your head. Apply a few drops to your handkerchief and inhale the fumes.

Horseradish *(Amoracia rusticana)*

This head-clearing remedy—drinking an infusion of horse-radish—comes from the cultures of south eastern Europe. In the good old days they had to collect horseradish roots in winter and store them in sand to make sure that they always had stock on hand. You can grow your own or buy fresh or

---

[1]   restricted herb in Australia and New Zealand, due to presence of alkaloid pyrrolizidine, which has been shown to cause liver damage in rats

[2]   avoid during pregnancy and if breast feeding

dried horseradish at the health food store, greengrocer or the corner supermarket.

Pukatea *(Laurelia novae-zelandiae)*

Drinking an infusion of pukatea bark is a traditional Maori way to soothe sore throats from colds and flu.

Special Diet

Folk healers in Israel prescribe strict bed rest, home made chicken soup, lemon soda, aspirin, copious amounts of fruit juice, and beef tea. Follow the recipe below to make your own beef tea. Ask your Mum for her recipe for chicken soup. Better yet, call your Mum and ask her nicely to make some of her special recipe. You know that there's nothing quite like it.

Beef Tea

1. Remove all the fat from a piece of round or rump roast
2. Put into 600 millilitres (1 pint) cold water
3. Soak 2 hours
4. Simmer 3 hours, do not boil
5. Add cold water from time to time to keep the volume constant
6. Put the roast in to a colander, and use a weighted pot to press all the juices out of the roast
7. Add this juice to the cooking liquid
8. Strain and drink as needed throughout the day

Raspberry [1] *(Rubus idaeus)* Jam and Tea

A hot cup of strong sweet tea is a wonder drug. You only need to watch an old movie to see the miraculous way a cup of tea is used to revive a person in distress. Folk healers on Guadalcanal, the largest of the Solomon Islands, may have been the first to codify the healing powers of a strong, sweet-cuppa. They tell flu sufferers to drink a cup of hot tea—with a teaspoon of raspberry jam added—six or more times a day.

---

[1]   *avoid high doses during pregnancy*

Food Poisoning

You'd have to be pretty sick to give any of these remedies for food poisoning a try. They are good examples of the old saying, ". . . the cure is worse than the disease!" If food poisoning— with its vomiting, diarrhoea, cramps, and fever—isn't bad enough, you'll find that often as not a folk healer will recommend using remedies that make some of the least favourite symptoms of food poisoning worse.

Many folk healers take the view that getting the offending food out of your system is the only way to go. Western medical practitioners agree—almost.

Your doctor would probably tell you that it's better to ride it out than to medicate it into submission. Your body really does need to get rid of the offending organisms to regain complete health. So eviction is better than suppression. That's why they tell you to use commercial anti-diarrhoeal medications as a last resort.

No matter what else you do, make sure you drink plenty of liquids when you're suffering from food poisoning. You'll need to replace the fluids your losing (in both directions). Apple

---

Remedies with ☕ *are made using an infusion. Those with* 🍵 *are made using a decoction. Instructions for both methods are on pages 4 - 7. Variations and other procedures are contained in the text following the description of that remedy.*

juice, water and bouillon are all good fluid replacements and they won't tax your digestive system.

Food poisoning is almost always self-inflicted and you usually know that you've been had with the first bite. One bite is all it takes, sometimes not even that. Most organisms that cause food poisoning are powerful enough to do their damage even in microscopic doses.

Preventing food poisoning is better than suffering with it. Know how to store food properly—what needs to be refrigerated, how to keep food warm (or cold) safely, how long food can be stored, and such. Have proper, insulated containers for taking food on a picnic, to the beach or to the footy so you can keep hot food hot and cold food cold. Finally, remember if it smells off, it probably is!

Mustard *(Brassica nigia)* and Salt *(Sodium Chloride)*

Not many people could stand this remedy, after all throwing up is one of the worst things about food poisoning. But if you need to get what's in your stomach out, and you want to get it out fast, drinking a strong solution of either salt or mustard will do the trick. A castor oil chaser will help to soothe your throat and line your stomach after the vomiting.

Fennel [1] *(Foeniculum officinale),* Horseradish *(Amoracia rusticana)* and Apple Cider

If mustard or salt water is not your thing, try stewed fennel, horseradish leaves and apple cider vinegar, all simmered

---

[1] *avoid during pregnancy*

Food poison versus chemical poison

While conventional medical practitioners will often recommend you riding out a bout of food poisoning, they rarely promote vomiting as a medicinal activity. About the only time that you'll find a doctor recommending vomiting is cases of chemical poisoning. Chemical poisoning is not the same as food poisoning. Even in cases of chemical poisoning using an emetic (a substances that makes you vomit) is only recommended in specific circumstances against certain poisons.

For some poisons re-exposing the mouth and throat to the chemical is more dangerous than leaving it to be digested in the stomach. For others letting your body digest the chemical is the more dangerous course.

With so many chemicals in a modern home (in household cleaning, automobile and garden products) it is impossible for a lay-person to know how to treat every type of poisoning. Keep chemicals well out of the reach of inquisitive children. Always overestimate their determination to get into forbidden areas. Keep the phone number for Poison Information handy. Keep it with your other emergency phone numbers. If you can store numbers on your phone, use the memory function to store emergency numbers like the Poison Information phone number. That way you won't have to search for it in an emergency.

together for about 10 minutes. This vile concoction has been used for centuries to clear a sour stomach.

Olive *(Olea europaea)*

Two tablespoons of olive oil is a most common, old-fashioned emergency remedy.

Purgative

—that's a polite way of saying something that makes you vomit. Believe it or not while you might associate vomiting with being sick, it sometimes is recommended to help you get better fast. Vomiting was often the only way our ancestors had to get a noxious substance out of their system.

Kôwhai *(Sophora tetraptera)*

The Maori used a decoction of kôwhai bark as a purgative and to treat the contagious skin disease, scabies. But the bark had to be from a tree growing on a hillside and from a root pointing toward the sun.

Honey and Vinegar

New England folk healers recommend drinking honey and vinegar for mild cases of food poisoning.

Dry Mustard and Egg White

In Uganda, traditional folk healers feed the sufferer dry mustard, egg whites and water while they chant, "Katui Nui Bomba".

What to do if?

Food poisoning and its accompanying cramps, nausea, vomiting and diarrhoea won't hang around forever. But the very young, elderly and chronically ill are more at risk from fever, vomiting and diarrhoea, whatever the cause. Don't delay getting them to the doctor.

Three days of vomiting and diarrhoea after eating improperly stored chicken is bad enough but some organisms that cause food poisoning are notoriously lethal. Clostridium botulinum, the microbe that causes botulism, produces one of the most potent toxins known. Poisonous mushrooms and toxic shell fish are also real killers. Any of the following symptoms are potentially deadly in anyone of any age, lookout for them and don't delay getting proper medical if they appear.

When these symptoms accompany food poisoning they spell danger:

- Severe diarrhoea or bloody stools
- Difficulty swallowing, breathing, tingling or numbness or paralysis especially after eating wild mushrooms or suspicious shell fish
- High fever
- Abdominal pain
- Vomiting so severe that you can not keep down any liquids of any kind

Foot Odour

Would you turn down a free trip to Japan because you're too embarrassed to take off your shoes in public? Does your partner make you take off your shoes and wash your feet in the garage? Do you blush and check your feet any time someone wrinkles their nose and asks "What's that dreadful smell?"

Then my friend you have a problem, but help is on the way. A few precautionary measures, a folk remedy or two and you'll be smelling like a rose. Well at least you'll no longer be accused of using your feet as a chemical weapon.

People that have problems with foot odour usually have overactive feet. Their feet work hard and sweat hard too. That's where the odour problem begins, and that's where your war on foot odour begins. Wash your feet well and often. You'll get the jump on odour before it takes hold. Then use foot powder, to help soak up any excess perspiration. Sprinkle a little talcum powder in your shoes too, for extra protection. Finally, even if no one sees them, even if they don't look dirty, change your socks often (several times a day if necessary).

Remedies with ☕ are made using an infusion. Those with ♨ are made using a decoction. Instructions for both methods are on pages 4 - 7. Variations and other procedures are contained in the text following the description of that remedy.

Sweat can build up in fabric. Socks that look clean can smell foul after just a few hours in the presence of sweaty feet.

After you have implemented these preventative measures try one of these folk remedies and enjoy the sweet smell of your success.

Willow [1] *(Salix alba)*

In England folk healers make an infusion of powdered white-willow bark, add a pinch of borax and use the mixture as an odour killing foot bath.

Cypress *(Cupressur sempervirens)*

In France folk healers banish foot odour with a few drops of cypress oil in the bath. For an extra boost, some say to add a few drops of sunflower oil to the cypress oil as you add it to your bath. Massage your feet with a little sunflower oil before bathing.

Yoghurt and Vinegar

Mix 1/4 pint (150 ml) of yoghurt and 1 teaspoon of vinegar, brush the mixture over your feet, rub in well and leave on for five minutes, rinse and dry your feet thoroughly.

Oak *(Quercus robur)*
and Pot Marigold [2] *(Calendula officinalis)*

The Romany people, who are sometimes called Gypsies, have a lot of experience with hard working feet. For centuries they

---

[1]   Treat willow as you would aspirin, do not take if you are pregnant and do not give to children under two or to children suffering with a cold, flu or chicken pox.

[2]   Do not confuse with French Marigold, Tagetes patula

have chosen the wandering life, traipsing over the countryside and in modern times the streets and pavements of cities as well.

Their folk healers recommend washing your feet with a decoction of oak bark in which you infuse a handful of marigold blossoms. Extra steeping makes the resulting liquid concentrated enough to fight the strongest foot odour. After the liquid has reduced by half, remove from heat and allow to cool. Add a handful of marigold blossoms and steep for 13 hours. Strain through gauze and use as necessary.

Lavender [1] *(Lavandula angustifolia)*
or Lemongrass *(Cymbopogon citratus)*

A few drops of either lavender or lemongrass oil added to your footbath is antiseptic and deodorising.

Alum

You can make your own an old-fashioned antiperspirant for a fraction of the price of commercial products. Use 5 grams (1 teaspoon) powdered alum and 600 ml (1 pint) warm water. Add it to the water in your footbath for to help reduce sweating.

Foot Massage

Massage clean feet with a mixture of 120 millilitres (6 tablespoons) of witch hazel and 20 millilitres (1 tablespoon) glycerine.

---

[1]   *avoid high doses during pregnancy*

Forgetfulness

Here's a quiz to test your memory

Do you:

    a) lose your glasses, even when you wear them on a chain around your neck?

    b) end each day with a string tied on every finger to remind you of all the things you thought of throughout the day?

    c) turn and run when you see someone you know at the shops because you're afraid you won't remember their name?

    d) what was the question?

If you answered d, it's too late for you. If you answered a, b or c you still have hope.

Everyone forgets something sometime, even Albert Einstein was so preoccupied with his new theories he forgot to wear socks. Preoccupation is often the cause of forgetfulness. If you're thinking about the stocktaking sale when you park your car you are likely to forget where you parked. One way

---

Remedies with ☕ are made using an infusion. Those with ♨ are made using a decoction. Instructions for both methods are on pages 4 - 7. Variations and other procedures are contained in the text following the description of that remedy.

to get around this type of forgetfulness is to tell yourself what you are doing when you do it. It will help you end the panic that comes when you can't remember if you turned the iron off before you left the house. When you turn off the iron, say to yourself "It's Monday (or what ever day it is) and I am turning the iron off". By telling yourself what you are doing you are more likely to remember doing it. Saying the day of the week helps you to be sure that it was today not yesterday or last week that you are remembering. While this technique sounds silly, it makes sense.

But this technique only works if you forget whether or not you did something like turn the iron off. It doesn't help if you can't remember to turn it off at all.

You are more likely to forget when you are under stress, because one thing drives out the other. Your brain does this to protect you. It's trying to keep the most important things up-front, where you can get at them. Whatever you have forgotten is still there, but stored up the back, out of the way.

That's why relaxing is a good way to refresh your memory. If you don't believe it, think of the times you've spent a day, trying to remember someone's name, the title of a movie or the words to a song. Just when you've given up and are falling asleep, in that split second between being awake and asleep you'll remember what has been bugging you all day. You know it will.

But remembering tonight that you were supposed to pick-up your mother-in-law at the airport yesterday won't help you save your marriage today. There are however all sorts of books from which you can learn memory improvement techniques, different tricks for different things, like speeches, dates, numbers and names. The following folk remedies will be a welcome addition to your memory enhancing arsenal.

Sage [1] *(Salvia officinalis)*

Sage grows wild in southern Europe, especially in the countryside of Croatia and Dalmatia. During the Middle Ages it was a popular medicinal plant and gained a reputation as being good for the head and brain. It was said to quicken the senses and memory. Follow the lead of Dalmatian and Croatian folk healers and use sage in your cooking. It goes so well with lamb and game meats, it will be easy to remember to take this medicine.

Autogenic Training

Developed in the 1920s by German psychiatrist Johannes Schultz, Autogenic Training is a form of programmed relaxation that combines elements of Zen, yoga and what modern self-help psychology calls visualisation.

When you use Autogenic training to solve a problem you will work with a therapist who will develop six specific statements and a special visualisation to use with each statement. As you focus on each statement you also focus in turn on the arms, heartbeat, breathing, abdomen and forehead A final, recall statement returns you to a fully alert state.

Autogenic training is most effective when combined with other visualisation practices or hypnotherapy. Autogenic exercises should only be developed and practiced with the guidance of a trained Autogenic practitioner.

---

[1]   *avoid therapeutic doses in pregnancy. Small amounts used in cooking are quite safe.*

Hypnotherapy

Hypnosis can be used to correct the psychological causes of forgetfulness. Ask your doctor to recommend a qualified hypnotherapist if you feel that hypnosis would aid the development or recovery of your memory.

Basil [1] *(Ocimum basilicum),*
Rosemary *(Rosmarinus officinalis)*
or Sage [2] *(Salvia officinalis)*

These three oils are important in aromatherapy. Rosemary oil is used to stimulate the pineal gland, which stimulates the crown chakra which helps you remember. Basil oil is used to promote clear thinking and clarify the intellect. Sage is used to strengthen the senses and memory. Consult a qualified aromatherapist (who should also be a qualified therapeutic masseur or masseuse) for best results.

---

[1]   *do not use essential oil in any form during pregnancy*

[2]   *avoid therapeutic doses in pregnancy. Small amounts used in cooking are quite safe.*

Frostbite

Frostbite? In Australia? You've got to be kidding! No, not really. You don't have to winter in the Antarctic to get frostbite. You don't even have to take yourself off to the snowfields in Tasmania, Victoria or New South Wales. It doesn't even have to be below freezing. You just have to be out and exposed to the right (or should that be wrong) conditions for frostbite to bite you.

The right combination of wind speed, temperature and humidity can turn a cold winter's day into frostbite weather thanks to what is called the 'wind chill factor'. You don't need a calculator to get a rough estimate of the wind chill factor, use this rule of thumb instead. The wind makes the effective temperature lower than what you read on the thermometer. If you lower the temperature on the thermometer two degrees for each kilometre per hour of wind speed you will have a rough, but conservative estimate of wind chill. If you do a lot of bushwalking, or snow skiing you should invest in a thermometer that includes a wind chill chart. There are small ones designed to be worn clipped to your jacket. It only needs to save you from frostbite once to make it worth whatever it costs.

Remedies with ☕ are made using an infusion. Those with ⬱ are made using a decoction. Instructions for both methods are on pages 4 - 7. Variations and other procedures are contained in the text following the description of that remedy.

What should you do if you get caught with your guard down?

If it's windy getting out of the wind is the next best thing to getting out of the cold. If it is very cold and you are stuck in an unsheltered spot, curl yourself into a ball. It will help you to conserve your body heat and you won't have to worry about hypothermia—which can kill—on top of the frostbite.

You need to attend to frostbitten skin. You need to rewarm the skin and underlying tissues safely to minimise damage. Now is not the time to experiment with folk remedies. Now is the time to put your faith in thermodynamics—the study of how energy, in the form of heat in this case, is transferred from one thing to another.

If you act fast when the first signs of frostbite appear (the skin will be numb and white) you may not suffer any lasting damage, just minor peeling and blistering. If you ignore it you may have to have the damaged tissue removed, that means losing anything from a piece of skin to a whole finger, toe, foot, leg, hand or arm!

Don't act blindly. Forget old wives tales. Don't rub frostbitten skin with snow, it doesn't help it does more damage. Forget out-of-date information about slow, gentle thawing. Modern advice says thaw as quickly as you can without burning the skin. Don't use dry radiant heat, like a fire or heat lamp, that's guaranteed to burn frostbitten skin. Do use warm water—about body temperature (normal warm body temperature not frostbitten body temperature). Don't allow frozen tissue to thaw and re-freeze.

Stick it up your jumper!

In the early stages of frostbite try this warm-up technique, it's gentle and easy.

You can do it for yourself and you can do it while walking, an important consideration when you're bushwalking because frostbite often strikes when you are away from base camp.

It only works on fingers and hands, unless you are a contortionist and can twist yourself in strange positions. The remedy? Stick your hand under your jumper or jacket, right into your armpit, it's the warmest spot on your body.

With severe frostbite the skin will be white, numb and frozen solid. When it starts to defrost it will probably blister, swell and turn blue or purple. This is when frostbite is most dangerous. Severe frostbite needs immediate professional care to avoid permanent damage and amputation. If you have to wait for medical attention do what you can. Start the thawing process, but only if you are sure you can keep the tissue from re-freezing. Re-freezing is more dangerous than leaving it frozen. If you have to walk back to civilisation leave your shoe or boot on, all night if needs be. If you take off your shoe or boot your foot will swell and blister. You'll never get your boot back on!

When you get home and the doctor has pronounced your tissues on the mend, that's the time to try some of the following folk remedies.

Southernwood (Artemisia abrotanum)

In Europe an infusion of southernwood is used to make a soothing, antiseptic compress for frostbitten skin. Apply warm, using a cotton towel. 🫖

Onion (Allium cepa)
Turnip (Brassica rapa)
and Lard

Folk healers in Pennsylvania scrape a turnip into a teacup of lard, and put it on the back of a warm stove letting it 'cook' for 24 hours. Then they strain the liquid lard and remove the turnip pieces. They allow the lard to cool and use the resulting 'ointment' every night to hasten healing of frostbitten skin.

Rabbit Fat

The Maori are adaptable and inventive, as their remedy for frostbite shows. They use the fat from rabbits—introduced by New Zealand's European settlers—to soothe and heal frostbitten skin.

Gunpowder and Lard

Another Maori remedy for frostbite skin is an ointment made from gunpowder and lard, mixed together and smeared on frostbitten skin.

Mullein (Verbascum thapsus)

This plant gets its other name, Adam's Flannel, from its soft, velvety leaves. In England, folk healers crush and grind fresh mullein leaves in olive oil. Then they store the leaves and oil in a closed bottle, in a warm place, for several days. The resulting ointment, infused with mullein is used to soothe and aid healing of frostbitten skin.

Autogenic Training

People experienced in autogenic practices claim to be able to use it to protect themselves from severe cold. Unless you're wintering in the Antarctic it's probably not worth the effort (if you're an Aussie) to learn Autogenic techniques for the odd occasion when you may face frostbite weather. Our cousins across the Tasman are another story. Though it is better to avoid frostbite than to expose yourself to it, even if you can protect yourself from it. If you are interested in this aspect of autogenic training, you should learn the practice from a qualified therapist. It's not for do-it-yourselfers.

Naturopathy

A naturopath will prepare a program of diet, baths and exercises to help heal frostbitten skin. Consult a registered practitioner for treatment.

Genital Herpes

While the virus that causes genital herpes is different from the one that causes a cold sore, the difference is small. The real-life difference between the two viruses is that one is associated with sexual transmission. No-one thinks any differently about a person that has a cold sore on his or her lip. Since genital herpes is—for all practical purposes—nothing more or less than a cold sore on or around the genitals it only makes sense to treat it the same way. The stigma that has sometimes been associated to genital herpes is more a reflection on a person's views about sex than the actual seriousness of infection with genital herpes.

Like a cold sore, genital herpes is caused by a virus that spends most of its time in hiding, but never really leaves your body once it gets invited in. The blister-like sore of genital herpes is just like a cold sore. You can get either sore in either area. The only way to tell the difference is through genetic testing of the virus.

Genital herpes is spread through contact with an active sore. The virus is transmitted from active sores to your skin—and like the cold sore virus once it takes up residence it's there for

---

Remedies with ☕ are made using an infusion. Those with ☕ are made using a decoction. Instructions for both methods are on pages 4 - 7. Variations and other procedures are contained in the text following the description of that remedy.

the duration. That means once you've got it, you've got it for good. That's the bad news, but it's not as bad as it sounds at first. While your first outbreak may be severe enough to cause a fever, very painful sores and for some people flu like symptoms, you may never have another outbreak. Lots of people don't. Or you may have infrequent outbreaks—when you are ill, under stress, or living life in the fast lane. Some people though have frequent outbreaks. If you do, you may be able to get a prescription for acylovir, an anti-viral drug that can reduce the frequency of outbreaks.

Take good care of yourself, eat well and keep a positive frame of mind and genital herpes is liable to be less of an intrusion in your life than other chronic ailments. Women with genital herpes should tell their gynaecologist. There is some evidence of an increased risk of cervical cancer in women with genital herpes, so your gynaecologist may want to re-evaluate your pap smear schedule. It's even more important for a pregnant women to tell her obstetrician, mid-wife—or other birthing professional—that she has genital herpes. If the woman has an active sore at the time of birth the newborn can be infected with genital herpes. That doesn't mean that if you have genital herpes you can't have a normal, healthy delivery of your baby. It just means your condition will have to be monitored during your pregnancy and different precautions may be necessary during the delivery to protect your baby from infection.

Blackberry (Rubus ulmifolius)

More than three hundred years ago the English physician and herbalist Nicholas Culpeper recommended using fresh or

What else do you need to know about genital herpes?

Learn how to recognise an impending outbreak and active sores.

This isn't as silly as it sounds. Unlike a cold sore, which is impossible to miss, a genital herpes sores can be in an out-of-the-way spot. As well, herpes sores can sometimes exist in the genital area with very mild, physical symptoms.

Abstain from sex during an outbreak.

Genital contact is out when the herpes virus is out of hiding. So abstain from genital sex, it's the responsible thing to do. Just to be on the safe-side you should use a condom even when sores are absent, unless you are in a monogamous relationship, just in case any stray viruses are present. Since you should use a condom in any non-monogamous relationship anyway, this isn't a big deal.

---

dried blackberry leaves and branches to make an ointment that would soothe sores in the genital area.

30 grams (1 ounce) green plant material cut into small pieces or 10 grams (2 teaspoons) dried, powdered herb

1. Mix with 500 grams (1 pound) hog lard
2. Heat the lard until liquid and mix the herb well into the liquid lard
3. Strain while the lard is liquid to remove any herb particles
4. Pour into a glass jar to cool, do not close the jar until the lard is fully cool

Purple Coneflower [1] *(Echinacea augustifolia)*

A decoction of purple coneflower root is a traditional Native American remedy for skin conditions.

Morning Glory *(Ipomoea pes-caprae)*

In the Bahamas local practitioners recommend herpes suffers use an infusion made from morning glory flowers and leaves to soothe and promote healing of herpes sores. Bathe herpes sores with the infusion twice a day for a week or until the sores are completely healed.

Tapioca *(Manihot esculenta)*

Venezuelan folk healers use tapioca to treat herpes sores. They recommend applying a paste of cool tapioca to active sores. Tapioca is made from the long, thick, tuberous root of the manioc or cassava plant.

Turmeric *(Curcuma longa)* *and Lime* *(Citrus aurantifolia)*

In India a traditional remedy for herpes sores is made from powdered turmeric, mixed with lime juice and a little water. Mix the Turmeric powder with the juice squeezed from half a lime and enough water to make a smooth paste. Apply to sores.

---

[1] restricted herb in Australia and New Zealand due to presence of alkaloid, shown to cause liver damage in rats

Have heaps of fun and reap the benefit in better health

According to researchers in the US having fun helps you fight off disease. What's even better, pleasant experiences have more of an effect on your immune system than bad experiences do.

This is especially good news for herpes sufferers and others with chronic or long time conditions that are exacerbated by stress.

It seems that when something good happens it boosts your immune system and the effect lasts a few days. When something bad happens it has a negative effect on your immune system—but it only lasts one day.

So doing pleasant, enjoyable things is just as important as avoiding stress is to your overall health.

So, what are you waiting for, go ahead and giggle, it's good for you!

Gingivitis

When your dentist tells you you're losing your grip, it's not a foray into amateur psychology. It's a warning that your gums are starting to show signs of gum disease. If you think that once you get through your childhood with a minimum number of fillings you will be through with caring for your teeth, think again. Every tooth in your head can be perfectly healthy, with nary a filling in sight, and you can still lose each and every one of your teeth to gum disease. Gingivitis is a catch-all term usually used to describe the first stages of gum disease—red, swollen gums that bleed easily. Gum disease is the primary cause of adult dental problems.

Your mouth, like the rest of your body isn't your exclusive domain. It's home to a whole host of bacteria, both good and bad. The bacteria that cause plaque are normal residents of your mouth. Keep the plaque in check, no worries. When it gets too comfy along the gum line the bacteria that causes plaque can't resist going wild, breeding like crazy and in the process, irritating your gums. Irritated gums are not able to hold on to your teeth the way they should. Your irritated gums recede, and this further loosens their grip on your teeth.

Remedies with 🫖 *are made using an infusion. Those with* 🍲 *are made using a decoction. Instructions for both methods are on pages 4 - 7. Variations and other procedures are contained in the text following the description of that remedy.*

Eventually your dentist is telling you that you are losing your grip.

It doesn't have to be this way, take good care of your gums and they will keep a tight hold on your teeth.

Tips for tip-top gums

Next time you visit the dentist, ask for a brush-up. After your teeth have been cleaned ask for a demonstration of brushing and flossing techniques. Things have probably changed a lot since your first lesson.

After you take the trouble to learn the newest and best techniques for brushing and flossing, use them! Twice a day, every day at a minimum! Three times a day is even better—after every meal or snack better still. But be a realist. Don't give up if you can only get to it twice a day, every little bit helps.

And buy an extra toothbrush, and rotate the two, use one in the morning , the other at night, so each gets the chance to dry between use.

Purple Coneflower [1] *(Echinacea augustifolia)*

For gum problems the Native Americans of the plains area of what is now the U.S. made a mouthwash from a decoction of echinacea root.

---

[1]   *restricted herb in Australia and New Zealand due to presence of alkaloid, shown to cause liver damage in rats*

Plantain *(Musca paradisiaca)*

Rub the juice extracted from plantain leaves on your gums, it's been recommended by folk healers for it's ability to soothe sore gums since 1588.

Old-fashioned remedies

Tincture of Myrrh

Put a few drops of tincture of myrrh in warm water, then swish it around your mouth. It's supposed to soothe and harden gums.

Black Molasses, Honey, Garlic

Rub any of these on your gums, they have a reputation for healing and toughening gums.

Sea Salt and Hydrogen Peroxide *(H_2O_2)*

Mix 5 grams (1 teaspoon) sea salt with 10 ml (2 teaspoons) hydrogen peroxide in 20 ml (1 tablespoon) water to make a mouthwash for sore gums.

Rhatany *(Krameria triandra)*

Peruvian folk healers recommend drinking a decoction of this native shrub for gum and tooth problems.

If you would rather buy than make your Peruvian tooth tonic, you'll find rhatany in some herbal toothpastes and powders (available in health food and natural medicine stores).

Bicarbonate of Soda, Salt and Hydrogen Peroxide

Folk healers in America's New England states tell you to toss your toothpaste and mouthwash into the rubbish bin. Instead, they say, brush with a paste of baking soda and salt dissolved in a little water. Then rinse with a diluted solution of hydrogen peroxide (5 ml H_2O_2 in 20 ml hot water).

While they were at it those folk healers in New England would tell you to change your diet:

In: Liver, salmon, fish, chicken, celery, carrots, broccoli, asparagus, beans, potatoes, turnips, blueberries, raspberries, strawberries, apples, oranges, yoghurt, low-fat milk, natural cheese, whole grain products, oats and peanuts

Out: Sugar, lollies[1], sweets (cakes, slices, sweet biscuits[2]), sultanas[3], dates, dried apricots, carbonated beverages, beer and wine.

Indigo (Indigofera tinctoria)

Indigo has been used medicinally since the Middle Ages. Drinking a decoction of indigo root was said to be just the thing to soothe and heal irritated gums. If you try this remedy do it on the weekend, it's liable to turn the inside of your mouth dark, dark blue.

---

[1] candy in the U.S.
[2] cookies in the U.S.
[3] raisins in the US.!.

Gout

Gout? You've got to be joking! Pull the other one! Only cigar chomping, high-living, big wig, cartoon characters get gout. Wrong! Gout is no joke. It's a real and very painful type of arthritis. Gout is caused by excess uric acid in your blood. When uric acid levels get too high the uric acid crystallises and the crystals deposit in your joints. In the cartoons it's always the big toe that aches, but in real-life gout can strike any joint.

It's normal to have some uric acid in your blood. Uric acid is a natural by-product in the metabolism of many foods. When you have too much uric acid in your blood—either because you eat a lot of high purine foods or because your body can't excrete the uric acid fast enough—the uric acid crystallises, the crystals deposit in the joints and cause the excruciating pain.

Remedies with 🫖 *are made using an infusion. Those with* 🍲 *are made using a decoction. Instructions for both methods are on pages 4 - 7. Variations and other procedures are contained in the text following the description of that remedy.*

High purine foods, what to avoid

● Fish (especially sardines, anchovies, shellfish, mackerel)
● Meat and poultry (especially offal)
● Some vegetables and grains (lentils, mushrooms, oatmeal, dry peas, asparagus, cauliflower)
● Alcohol (okay, it's not food, but it does contribute to gout)

If you avoid or reduce your consumption of high purine foods and drinks and increase the amount of water you drink you should reduce, if not eliminate, your bouts with gout.

Celery *(Apium graveolens)*

The ancient Greeks used celery for healing, India's traditional Ayurvedic healers still do. The medieval German abbess and herbalist, Hildegard of Bingen, thought celery seeds were the best remedy for gout. She recommended drinking an infusion of celery seeds to soothe the pain of gout.

Clove *(Syzgium aromaticum)*

If the celery seed infusion didn't work Hildegard might have recommended another of her favourite remedies for gout, an infusion of clove.

Blackberry *(Rubus ulmifolius)*

Folk healers sometimes call blackberry goutberry, so it's no surprise that it is also recommended as a remedy for this painful condition. Drink an infusion made from the bark, leaves, root or fruit. Use any leftover liquid as a soothing wash or compress for sore joints, apply with a clean, cotton cloth.

Agrimony *(Agrimonia eupatoria, also known as Church Steeples)*

English physicians and herbalists have been telling gout sufferers to drink an infusion of dried agrimony since about 1700.

Biochemic Tissue Salts

Nat Phos *(sodium phosphate)* is the recommendation for active gout, with Nat Sul *(sodium sulphate)* once a day to help eliminate toxins.

French Beans *(Phaseolus vulgaris)*
also called Haricot Beans or Haricot Verte

Use a juicer to make some green bean juice—a popular French remedy for gout. Drink 150 ml (5 oz) a day. Mix it with carrot or apple juice because the strong, green-flavour of the bean juice is not pleasant on its own.

Elecampane *(Inula helenium)*
also called Scabwort or Horseheal

The Greek physician, Galen (130 - 200 AD) who is sometimes called the founder of experimental physiology, recommended drinking a decoction of elecampane root to soothe painful joints.

Wall Germander [1] *(Teucrium chamaedrys)*

In medieval times wall germander was used to make a popular remedy for gout. They broke the herb off at the root, crushed the stem, leaves and flowers and applied the crushed herb to a painful joint.

Lily-of-the-valley *(Convallaria majalis)*
also called Lady's Tears

The English herbalist Gerard developed a unique way of treating gout using lily-of-the-valley. He filled a glass bottle with lily-of-the-valley flowers and placed the bottle in an ant's nest. He left the flower-filled bottle in the nest for a couple of days. Then he removed it from the nest, removed the flowers and applied the flowers directly to a painful joint. The flowers probably picked up formic acid from the ants and this may have helped heat the joint and soothe the pain of gout.

Blackcurrant *(Rubes nigra)*

In the eighteenth and nineteenth centuries blackcurrant leaves were used to make a poultice to soothe painful, gouty joints.

1. Take a handful of fresh blackcurrant leaves
2. Steep in boiling water until soft
3. Mash the leaves and apply while still warm to the painful joint
4. Hold the poultice in place with a cloth or bandage, repeat as needed

---

[1]   *use sparingly*

White Deadnettle *(Laminum album)*

For centuries, the young fresh leaves of white deadnettle were used to make a poultice to soothe gouty joints.

1. A handful of white deadnettle leaves
2. Steep in boiling water until soft
3. Mash the leaves into a pulp, apply warm to the painful joint
4. Hold in place with a cloth or bandage, repeat as needed

Holly *(Ilex aquifolium)*

In Paraguay they extract the juice from holly leaves and apply it to painful, gouty joints. Be very careful with holly, the berries are extremely toxic and should never be used in any medicinal application.

Garlic [121] *(Allium sativum)*
and Cherry *(Prunus avium)*

Not together! Folk healers in the former Soviet Union tell gout sufferers to avoid alcohol, liver and sweetbreads, eat a clove of raw garlic twice a day and drink a glass of cherry juice morning and night.

Only for the bold (or the lonely)

If you're game, give this Tibetan remedy a go . . . mix rancid milk, butter and cow dung, apply the mixture to the painful, gouty joint. You probably shouldn't go out in public wearing this one!

---

[1]   *avoid during pregnancy and if breast feeding*

Navelwort *(Umbilicus rupestris)*

In the Middle Ages, French folk healers recommended applying navelwort's small, juicy leaves to painful joints.

Goutwort *(Aegopodium podagraria)*
also known as Goutweed, Ground Elder

In the seventeenth century a poultice made from the leaves and root of this plant became popular as treatment for gout.

1. Boil leaves, roots and stems of a whole goutwort plant in 1 litre (1 quart) water
2. Boil 20 - 30 minutes
3. Strain, discarding liquid
4. Apply warm softened plant material to the painful joint

You can also drink an infusion of goutwort leaves

Mustard *(Brassica nigra)*

Gout is another remedy that seemed to respond to Grandma's favourite, the mustard plaster.

1. Grind mustard seeds with a little water
2. Coat the skin of the affected area with petroleum jelly (this prevents the mustard from blistering or irritating the skin)
3. Apply the paste to the sore area, holding it in place with gauze and adhesive tape. This plaster can be kept on for several hours, for best results leave on overnight

Haemorrhoids

Ask your best friend why haemorrhoids are embarrassing and you're liable to be told "Don't ask me! I don't have them!" in a loud and strident voice. It's hard to tell whether humorous advertisements for haemorrhoid treatments help or hurt the public image of this common ailment. Although if you suffer from haemorrhoids you know they're no laughing matter. Humour may help people relax and talk about this common ailment. Some studies say that up to 80% of all adults will suffer from haemorrhoids at some time in their life.

So what is a haemorrhoid? Nothing more exotic than a swollen vein in your anus. You're more likely to suffer from haemorrhoids if your parents did, but heredity isn't the whole story. Diet and toilet habits also contribute to your risk of developing haemorrhoids.

Healthy eating—lots of fibre and lots of water—is just plain good for you. This sort of diet also helps to keep your bowel movements soft and easier to move through your digestive system. This means that each bowel movement is easier on your haemorrhoids and better for the overall condition of your intestines.

Remedies with ☕ *are made using an infusion. Those with* 🍵 *are made using a decoction. Instructions for both methods are on pages 4 - 7. Variations and other procedures are contained in the text following the description of that remedy.*

Take your haemorrhoids for a walk

One old-fashioned remedy that still makes sense today is to walk. Walk frequently, every day if possible. Walking is an wonderful way to get your daily exercise. It's good for almost every part of your body. Anyone can do it, anywhere. When it comes to haemorrhoids, walking helps to move your food through your bowels, which makes it easier for you to have a bowel movement, which is easier on your haemorrhoids, etc. etc.

Not all old-fashioned remedies are so sensible though, as if haemorrhoids aren't enough of a problem, some folk healers recommend using a raw clove of garlic as a suppository. Now that would give your friends something to laugh about.

Aloe [1] *(Aloe vera)*

Two thousand years ago the Greek physician Dioscorides wrote about using aloe gel to soothe and heal painful skin conditions. Haemorrhoids obviously qualify in the pain department. Grow your own aloe plant and apply the gel from a freshly broken leaf directly on the haemorrhoid.

Pot Marigold [2] *(Calendula officinalis)*

In the nineteenth century drinking an infusion of pot marigold was a popular English remedy for bleeding haemorrhoids.

---

[1]   *consuming large quantities can cause vomiting, avoid in pregnancy*
[2]   *do not confuse with French marigold, Tagetes patula*

Cypress *(Cupressur sempervirens)*

Dilute 1-2 drops of cypress oil with 10 millilitres of good quality vegetable or nut oil and apply to the haemorrhoids.

Pour cold water on haemorrhoids!

It's simple and painless. Some folk healers say it helps to prevent haemorrhoids. Even if it doesn't prevent haemorrhoids, it's sure to wake you with a start!

Bathe your anus with cold water every morning.

Figwort *(Scrophularia nodosa)*

Since the Middle Ages this decoction of figwort has been a popular, double-duty haemorrhoid remedy. Strain the decoction, saving liquid and solids. Drink the strained liquid, 1 cup, three time a day and use the softened solids against the inflamed haemorrhoid.

Coriander *(Coriandrum sativum)*

If you suffer from haemorrhoids, a traditional Chinese medical practitioner might tell you to increase the amount of coriander you eat. Sprinkle a little on your food and take your medicine while you add a little spice to your life.

Horsechestnut *(Aesculus hippocastanum)*

India's traditional physicians tell haemorrhoid sufferers to drink an infusion of horsechestnut. Save a little bit of the liquid and use as a soothing wash for the haemorrhoid.

Horse Feathers!

If you don't like the taste of the horsechestnut infusion, give this old fashioned remedy a try, it can't hurt (unless you sit on it).

Carry a horsechestnut in your pocket, folk healers believe that as the horsechestnut hardens your haemorrhoid will shrink.

Pilewort [1] *(Ranunculus ficaria)*

A decoction of pilewort is a longstanding folk remedy—how else do you think it got its name. The liquid is used in a warm compress to soothe and shrink swollen, painful haemorrhoid veins.

Alum *(hydrated aluminium potassium sulfate)* *and lard*

Some folk healers recommend applying this ointment to haemorrhoids.

Alum 5 grams (1 teaspoon) alum
Mixed with 40 grams (2 tablespoons) pure lard
Apply as necessary

Navelwort *(Umbilicus rupestris)*

During the Middle Ages the French used navelwort leaves to sooth the pain of haemorrhoids. Their recommended treat-

---

[124] *caution, do not take internally*

ment? Apply moist navelwort leaves directly to the haemorrhoids.

Archangel *(Lamium album)*
also known as Blind Nettle, White Dead Nettle

In Germany and France nettle juice is an old favourite for
treating haemorrhoid pain. Take 20 ml (1 tablespoon) three
times a day.

Horse-eye *(Mucunu urens)*

For over 200 years the people of Venezuela have used an
alcohol infusion of horse-eye beans to make an ointment with
which they treated haemorrhoids.

1. Dry and grind a handful of beans
2. Soak the powder in alcohol (1 part powdered beans to
   5 parts alcohol, by weight)
3. Soak 24 hours then strain through a very fine sieve
4. Apply directly to the haemorrhoids

Hangover

If only you could remember how bad your last hangover felt, on your way to getting your next one. That's the problem. When you wake up with wobbly knees, a fuzzy head and an upset tummy you swear you'll never over-indulge again. But if you're like most people, the memory of the hangover fades with time—and with the number of drinks you have. Unless you have a will of steel, sooner or later you are going to end-up hiding from the sun, swearing at chirping birds, and searching the house for something, anything that will let you feel like a member of the human race again.

If you want to avoid a hangover, there is really only one folk remedy for you. Don't over indulge. Do drink slowly and have some food in your stomach when you start drinking and throughout the evening. The food helps to slow your body's absorption of alcohol from your digestive system.

If you want to get rid of a hangover there is only one guaranteed, tried and true method. It's called time. The simple fact is that your body needs time—time to get the alcohol, and the by-products your body produces as it digests the alcohol, out of your system.

Remedies with ☕ are made using an infusion. Those with ♨ are made using a decoction. Instructions for both methods are on pages 4 - 7. Variations and other procedures are contained in the text following the description of that remedy.

"But isn't there anything I can do RIGHT NOW?" you shout trying to make yourself heard over the sound of the jackhammer in your head.

There are lots of home remedies for hangovers. If you favour one, give it a go. Most can't make you feel any worse. And one of them might help dull the stabbing pain in your eye, soothe the queasiness in your stomach or send the shakes bye-bye. If you say this magic spell while you are recovering from your hangover you may be one of the lucky ones. You may never spend another day as one of the living dead.

Carefully now repeat after me:

". . . I will not over-indulge, I will learn to say no, I will not over-indulge, I will learn to say no . . . ."

If you don't already have a favourite remedy of your own try one of these.

Prairie Oyster

Don't confuse a prairie oyster with a mountain oyster—a raw sheep or bull's testicle—though a lot of people would say that drinking a prairie oyster—a raw egg with Worcestershire sauce—is equally off-putting

Honey

Gulp a tablespoonful of honey. For really stubborn hangovers melt 60 millilitres (twelve teaspoons) of honey in a little warm water, and drink that.

If a headache is the price you pay for over indulging . . .

Kawakawa *(Macropiper excelsum)*

The Maori chewed kawakawa leaves to soothe headache pain. Self-inflected or not, a headache is a headache.

The hair of the dog that bit you

Probably the best known hangover remedy, the hair of the dog that bit you is another way of saying to dose yourself with the same poison that got you into this state. This is a favourite hangover remedy, but be warned, it's also a very dangerous remedy. For it to be effective you must remember it's the hair of the dog that bit you, not its whole bloody pelt!

The next three remedies all belong to the 'hair of the dog that bit you', school of thought, and as such, have probably caused as many hangovers as they are claimed to have cured.

Bloody Mary

Tomato juice with a dash of Worcestershire sauce, a jigger of vodka (or gin) and ice

Screwdriver

Orange juice, a jigger of vodka (or gin) and ice.

Beer

A favourite on a hot summer's day— an icy cold glass of beer.

The next two are claimed to help right a topsy-turvey tummy.

Stodgy Food

Eat yoghurt, porridge or drink a vanilla milk shake or a pineapple spider[1].

Tummy Fresheners

Try a few drops of peppermint cordial.

Many people find they are terribly thirsty after a night on the turps

Cold Water

This one, a favourite of French folk healers, has made the rounds of most university campuses. It's simple, and cheep and best of all it's good for you whether you've over-indulged or not. The hard part is having enough of your wits about you when you retire for the night to take advantage of the remedy. That's when you are supposed to take a few minutes to drink a couple of glasses of cold water—before you go to climb into bed. The water is supposed to prevent a hangover, but probably will only moderate its strength.

Vegie Juice

Any healthy, fresh vegie juice will do you a world of good. But celery juice—with a dash of soda water, and a drop of Tabasco sauce—is supposed to be the best vegie juice for toppling tipplers.

---

[1]   ice-cream soda in the US.

Finally, the Romany people of Hungary have a reputation for living the travelling life to the fullest. Their recommendation, one of the following:

- Nibble raw cabbage dipped in vinegar
- Eat a bowel of chicken broth with rice
  or
- Drink lemon juice and baking soda in a half glass of water.

Headache

Stabbing, throbbing, pounding headaches; blinding, stinging, piercing, headaches; tension headaches; referred pain headaches; migraine headaches; cluster headaches; sinus headaches; and "Not tonight Honey, I've got a headache," headaches. If you're an average member of the human race you've had at least one headache in the past year. If you're less lucky you've had more than one. And if you're just plain jinxed you may suffer from chronic headaches.

For most of us a headache is an occasional discomfort. You usually know what caused it and what to do to keep from getting another one in the near future. If you suffer from chronic headaches you're forgiven for thinking that the only thing you need to know about them is that sooner or later you'll get another one.

Chronic tension headaches are bad enough, but the two monsters on the headache scene—migraines and cluster headaches—are pure torture. More women than men suffer from migraines, vice versa for cluster headaches. The symptoms of migraine and cluster headaches can be crippling. Wait, you

---

Remedies with 🫖 *are made using an infusion. Those with* ☕ *are made using a decoction. Instructions for both methods are on pages 4 - 7. Variations and other procedures are contained in the text following the description of that remedy.*

haven't heard the worst news. Few people suffer just one,
these devils keep coming back . . . and back . . . and back.

Is your headache more than a pain in the . . . head?

Okay, admit it. When you were a teenager at school you thought your headaches were caused by some exotic, tragic and yet somehow glamorous disease. When you found out they were caused from wearing your beanie too tight you gave up on becoming famous in upper Whoop-Whoop and studied for your leaving certificate. But somewhere deep in your subconscious is a little seed of doubt. You just know you life story would make a ripper tele-movie.

When should you be concerned about your headaches?

- If you suddenly start having chronic headaches
- If the pattern of your chronic headaches changes (location, frequency, duration or intensity)
- If your headaches are accompanied by dizziness, nausea, memory loss or blurred vision

If you experience any of these symptoms you should consult your doctor so that he or she can rule out any serious medical condition.

Banana (Musa [1])

This migraine remedy from the West Indian island nation of Trinidad and Tobago is weird. But migraine sufferers will go to any length to make a migraine go away. Folk healers in Trinidad and Tobago make an ointment of ripe banana peel, vinegar and whole-meal (whole-wheat) flour. They spread the mixture on a hot, moist cloth, fold and roll the cloth and apply the whole thing to the forehead and back of the neck.

Tea (Camellia sinensis var. sinensis, China Tea; C. Sinensis var. assanica, Assam Tea)

This traditional Chinese remedy is much easier than the previous remedy, and it is supposed to be just as effective against any sort of headache: drink a cup of double strength tea.

Coffee (Coffea arabica, C. liberica, C. robusta)

If you prefer coffee to tea, follow the American folk healers recommendation and drink a cup of double strength coffee when you feel a headache coming on.

Warm Showers

A warm shower is always a pleasure. Some folk healers recommend directing the shower spray onto your spine and the nape of your neck, it's supposed to help ease headache pain.

---

[1] because all cultivated bananas are sterile hybrids, they do not have exact species names.

Chamomile [1] *(Chamaemelum nobile, Roman, or C. recutita, German)*

Way back when, in the olden days, Discorides—the Greek physician—and Pliny—the Roman naturalist—told people suffering from a headache to drink an infusion of chamomile.

Lemon *(Citrus limon or C. medica, var. limonum)*

If none of the preceding remedies takes your fancy, how do you feel about lemon peel? According to American folk healers a bit of lemon peel and a handkerchief is all you need to make a great headache remedy. Apparently you peel a lemon and place the peel in a handkerchief (pith side against the handkerchief) and place the handkerchief on your forehead. You leave it there until:

● you feel a burning sensation

● your headache goes away

● someone embarrasses you by asking why you have a piece of lemon peel wrapped in a hankie on your forehead, whichever comes first!

● Or—if you prefer—try salted lemon juice or salted cut lemons applied to your temple.

Boneset *(Eupatorium perfoliatum) also know as Feverwort*

In the seventeenth and eighteenth centuries, feverfew was a popular remedy for headaches. Sufferers were told to chew one or two fresh boneset leaves. If they couldn't stand the bitter taste of the boneset leaves, they drank an infusion of boneset.

---

[1]   *avoid excessive doses and the oil in any amount during pregnancy*

Fennel [1] *(Foeniculum officinale)*

French folk healers recommend drinking fennel juice if you suffer from migraines or dizziness.

Recommend this and you'll be in hot water!

According to Indonesian belief all a woman suffering from a migraine needs to do is get busy! Washing the dishes or the clothes—by hand of course—is said to be a miracle cure for a headache. Hands up if you think this remedy was devised by married male folk healers.

According to traditional belief, a little lemon juice is added to the water and the combination of hot water and lemon juice transfers the blood from the woman's head to her hands and thus relieves the headache. Of course you don't want too much blood in the little woman's head, it might get her thinking.

Now, women, be honest. Don't you think that if your partner did the dishes and clothes while you soaked your hands in warm water and had a soothing massage with lemon or other suitable fragrant oil, your headache would disappear that much faster?

Coltsfoot [2] *(Tussilago farfara)*

India's traditional Ayurvedic physician tell you to have a snuff of powdered coltsfoot if you are suffering from a headache.

---

[1]   *avoid during pregnancy*
[2]   *restricted herb in Australia and New Zealand, due to presence of alkaloid pyrrolizidine, which has been shown to cause liver damage in rats*

Basil [1] *(Ocimum basilicum)*

If you don't feel up to a nose full of coltsfoot try a massage with basil oil to get you feeling up to snuff. That's what India's traditional Ayurvedic recommend for headache relief. Use the basil oil to massage your forehead and behind your ears but don't forget to dilute the basil oil, 1-2 drops of basil oil with 10 millilitres of good quality vegetable or nut oil before you apply it to your skin. If you're looking for a tastier remedy, chew basil leaves.

Give this one a miss if you have children—you'll never live it down!

If you have a headache in Vermont the folk healers there will tell you to wet a brown paper bag with vinegar, sprinkle it generously with black pepper, and apply it to your head.

Rosemary *(Rosmarinus officinalis)*

Remember your last household repair crisis? Multiply the headache you had then by about a million to imagine the headaches that went along with the building of the pyramids. The ancient Egyptian folk remedy for headaches must have worked, the pyramids got built didn't they? Ancient Egyptian healers recommended a massage with rosemary oil. to end headache pain. If you want to try this yourself, the massage should concentrate on the area that aches. And don't forget to dilute the 1-2 drops of the rosemary oil with 10 millilitres of good quality vegetable or nut oil before using it on your skin.

---

[1]   *do not use essential oil in any form during pregnancy*

Does your headache make you feel like a stunned mullet?

Jamaican Dogwood *(Piscidia erythrina)*

The bark of this plant contains the powerful narcotic, piscidin and should only used under the supervision of a trained herbalist. It can be used to treat migraine, but is most commonly used by West Indian fishermen—to stupefy fish, thereby making the fish easier to catch.

Kawakawa *(Macropiper excelsum)*

The Maori chewed kawakawa leaves to soothe headache pain.

Metrosideros *(Metrosideros albiflora)*

Drinking an infusion of metrosideros bark is a traditional way for New Zealanders to reduce pain.

Old-fashioned remedies from here, there and everywhere

Aromatherapy

Scented leaves can help clear the cobwebs from your mind. Take a few scented leaves from your favourite garden plants. Crush the leaves between your fingers and inhale deeply taking in their rich natural fragrance.

Rose *(Rosa canina)*

Add a few drops of soothing, romantic rose oil to your warm bath and experience bliss.

Lavender [1] *(Lavandula angustifolia)*

Put 3 drops of lavender oil on a sugar cube and allow the cube to dissolve slowly in your mouth.

Potato *(Solanum tuberosum)*

Roast or steam a potato and eat it au naturel—the potato not you—without salt, butter or cheese.

Children don't get headaches - they give them!

But what Mum or Dad can stand to see a child in pain? Here are a couple of headache remedies especially for children.

For pain in the front or the sides of the head, apply a cold wet towel the child's forehead or to the top and sides of their head. Re-apply when the towel becomes warm.

For tension headaches in the back of and deep inside the head try a warm towel applied to the back of the head and neck. Re-apply when the towel cools.

Pot Marigold [2] *(Calendula officinalis)*

Pour a cup of boiling water on a handful of marigold flowers and leaves. When it's cold, use the liquid in a compress, apply it to your eyes and forehead.

---

[1]   *avoid high doses during pregnancy*
[2]   *do not confuse with French marigold, Tagetes patula*

Heartburn

It may be a day of complete fire ban, but no one told your digestive system. You've just downed a three course meal at your favourite grease emporium and you're paying the price.

The burning sensation known as heartburn is caused by stomach acids bubbling up and out of your stomach and irritating your oesophagus. Over-eating and over-indulging in rich fatty-foods are primary causes. Spicy food, chocolate, coffee—and other caffeinated drinks—and lying down after a meal can also turn up the heat on heartburn.

Potato *(Solanum tuberosum)*

Use a juicer to extract the juice from a potato. Dilute the potato juice with warm water: one part juice to 2 or 3 parts water. Drink this juice before breakfast, lunch and at night before going to sleep. Prepare each dose fresh.

Milk

Some folk healers recommend sipping fresh milk for temporary relief of heartburn.

Remedies with 🫖 *are made using an infusion. Those with* ☕ *are made using a decoction. Instructions for both methods are on pages 4 - 7. Variations and other procedures are contained in the text following the description of that remedy.*

Don't panic, but do pay attention

Stomach acid is strong and concentrated. When it comes in contact with the unprotected surface of your oesophagus the pain can be so intense that you think you are having a heart attack.

When your doctor tells you it's only heartburn you're liable to be so happy that changing your diet will see a small price to pay. You mentally kick up your heals, and think "I'm not dying, I'm not dying!"

Enjoy the reprieve. But don't make the mistake of dismissing all heartburn-like pain. It could be a fatal mistake. While most heartburn is just that, heartburn and nothing to worry about—ulcers and heart attacks can cause similar symptoms.

If you notice:
- unusually painful or frequent attacks
- blood in your stool
- vomiting, with blood
- frequent attacks without obvious reason (like a change in your diet)

- breathing difficulties, especially shortness of breath
- dizziness

See your doctor, it may not be heartburn at all.

Oat *(Avena sativa)*

Dry, uncooked oats, have a reputation for temporarily relieving heartburn. Be sure to chew well or the oats can swell in your stomach and play havoc with your digestion.

Grapefruit *(Citrus paradisi)*

Dried grapefruit peel is an American folk remedy for heartburn.

1. Peel a grapefruit and grate the peel
2. Dry thoroughly and store
3. Suck or chew 5 grams (1 teaspoon) of the dried peal whenever you suffer heartburn

Date *(Phoenix dactylifera)*

The Arabs made good use of the date, one of the few fruits to thrive in the desert. Arab folk healers recommend eating dates that have been soaked in hot water for 5 - 10 minutes and drinking the soaking water as a 'chaser'.

Catnip *(Nepeta cataria)*

During the Middle Ages, drinking an infusion of catnip was popular throughout Europe as a remedy for a wide range of ailments, including heartburn.

Liquorice *(Glycyrrhiza glabra)*

Ancient Chinese, Greek and Egyptian folk healers all used liquorice as a remedy for heartburn. Be sure to use true liquorice as some lollies are made with artificial liquorice flavouring. Eat 5 grams (1 teaspoon) liquorice as needed.

Milk and Soda Water

Folk healers from the New England states of America recommend drinking a glass of equal parts milk and soda water.

Comfrey [1] *(Symphytum officinale) also known as Knitbone*

For centuries, the Romany people, who are sometimes called Gypsies, have used comfrey powder to treat heartburn.

The Romany technique for administering the remedy is novel. You place a pinch of powdered comfrey root on your tongue. Hold it there for a few minutes—allowing your saliva to accumulate—then swallow!

Kiwi Fruit *(Actinidia sinensis)*
also called Chinese Gooseberry

Thank you. Thank you. Thank you New Zealand. You took the obscure Chinese gooseberry and turned it into Kiwi fruit—one of the most popular fruits in the world. Its delicious taste—sometimes described as a cross between watermelon and strawberry—is divine. And some folk healers think Kiwi fruit's enzymes—like papain and bromelain—can help relieve heartburn. So the next time you bite into a succulent fresh piece of Kiwi fruit for desert don't feel guilty. Don't explain. Just smile, and take your medicine.

Charcoal

Your ancestors had to use ashes from their hearth for this remedy, you just have to go to the health food store or pharmacy and buy some activated charcoal, mix it with a little water and drink it.

---

[1] *restricted herb in Australia and New Zealand due to presence of alkaloid, shown to cause liver damage in rats*

Some old-fashioned quickies, folk remedies you can take whenever heartburn flares

● Take 5 grams (1 teaspoon) bicarbonate of soda in glass of hot water

● Drink lots of plain water

● Eat a bowl of porridge

● If you can find it try drinking goat's milk

Heart Problems

What two words are more frightening than 'Tax Audit'? You guessed it, 'Heart Attack', and rightly so. One heart in good working order is vital for a long and healthy life.

Cardiovascular disease is the most common cause of death in Australiaand New Zealand. Coronary heart disease and stroke together cause about 32% and 10% of all deaths respectively. Over the past 10 years improved treatment and prevention programs have focused on reducing the incidence of and mortality from cardiovascular disease.

These programs recognise the role genetics plays in determining your probability of developing cardiovascular disease. But research shows that there are things you can do that may reduce your chance of suffering a heart attack. So, even if you can't choose your ancestors, you can choose the way you live your life. And the choices you make may help to minimise your risk of developing heart disease.

Your first step toward better health—whether or not you have been diagnosed with cardiovascular disease—is to start following the National Heart Foundation's diet and exercise recommendations.

Remedies with 🫖 are made using an infusion. Those with 🍲 are made using a decoction. Instructions for both methods are on pages 4 - 7. Variations and other procedures are contained in the text following the description of that remedy.

If your doctor does diagnose heart disease—work with him or her to develop a program to improve your overall health.

Never substitute a folk remedy for your doctor's recommendation and never add a folk remedy to your routine with out discussing it with your doctor first. But you may find the following folk remedies, used by folk healers in the past, interesting.

Spring Adonis *(Adonis vernalis)*

Folk healers in the former soviet Union recommend drinking an infusion of spring adonis to strengthen the heart.

Chickweed *(Stellaria media)*

To strengthen the heart the Swiss eat chickweed.

Butterbur *(Petasites hybridus)*

Over 300 years ago, English physician and herbalist, Nicholas Culpeper, recommended drinking a decoction of butterbur to strengthen the heart.

Lily-of-the-valley *(Convallaria majalis)*
also called lady's tears

Drinking a decoction of Lily-of-the-valley roots was a favourite with healers in England and the former Soviet Union.

Hawthorn Berries *(Crataegus oxycantha,*
C. monogyna, C. pinnatifida) called shan zha in China

In Ireland hawthorn berries are used in traditional folk remedies. Drinking an alcohol infusion of ripe hawthorn berries is
the recommendation to strengthen the heart.

Dandelion *(Taraxacum officinale)*
also known as pu gong ying

Another European folk healer's favourite, dandelion which
has been recommended for high-blood pressure and heart
complaints. Drinking an infusion of dandelion roots to which
you add a sprinkling of freshly picked dandelion leaves is the
recommendation for heart problems.

Garlic [1] *(Allium sativum)*

It seems like garlic has been used as a remedy for every
ailment known to humankind, and that includes heart complaints. One of the first to proclaim garlic's heart strengthen-
ing abilities was the Greek physician Dioscorides. He
recommended drinking the following potent garlic infusion.
Steep six cloves or garlic in 250 millilitres (1 cup) cool water
for six hours. Then drink.

Yerba Mate *(Ilex paraguensis) also known as Paraguay Tea*

In the mountains of Paraguay, where the air is thin and
oxygen deprivation is a daily danger, mate is an all purpose
tonic. Drinking an infusion of mate gets the nod for treating
heart complaints.

---

[1] *avoid during pregnancy and if breast feeding*

Hiccups

When a comedian hiccups at all the wrong times or a cartoon character hiccups uncontrollably, everyone laughs and laughs. When you start hiccupping at noon and are still at it at midnight it's not so funny. You keep thinking that you have it under control. Then hic .... another hiccup escapes and you are back at square one. The thing about hiccups is that they are involuntary. So trying not to hiccup is futile. Hiccups are caused by involuntary spasms in your diaphragm—a power-ful muscle that separates your chest from your abdomen—which are followed by an equally involuntary closing of your upper windpipe (larynx).

Most hiccups last a few seconds, others a few minutes, but sometimes the Wicked Hiccup Witch puts a curse on you and your hiccups last for hours. One poor soul in America had the hiccups for SIXTY FIVE YEARS! Now that was some curse! Anything longer than a couple of minutes is embarrassing, irritating, exasperating, exhausting and painful.

Most hiccups will be gone almost before you realise you have them. But ... hic ... if you ... hic ... find ... hic . .. yourself with ... hic ... a ... hic ... bad ... hic ... case ... hic ... of

---

Remedies with 🫖 *are made using an infusion. Those with* 🍵 *are made using a decoction. Instructions for both methods are on pages 4 - 7. Variations and other procedures are contained in the text following the description of that remedy.*

... hic ... hic ... hic ... cups you may .... hic ... want to .. . hic ... try one of these rem ... hic ... edies a try ... hic ...

Anise *(Pimpinella anisum)*

John Gerard was a busy chap, he was a herbalist and surgeon; the superintendent of Lord Burghley's gardens; and Chief Secretary of State to Queen Elizabeth I. Do you imagine that while discussing matters of state with Her Majesty he would have been so bold as to share his remedy for hiccups—chewing a pinch of anise seeds?

Blue Cohosh *(Caulophyllum thalictrodes)*

To treat hiccups Native Americans drank a decoction of blue cohosh root.

Dill *(Anethum graveolens)*

To banish hiccups, seventeenth century English herbalist, Nicholas Culpeper, recommended chewing a pinch of dried dill seeds and following the dill seeds with a drink of water.

Valerian *(Valerian officinalis)*,
Blackberry *(Rubus ulmifolius)*,
Chamomile [1] *(Chamaemelum nobile, Roman, or C. recutita, German)*
and Fennel [2] *(Foeniculum officinale)*

For centuries the Romany people, who are sometimes called Gypsies, have treated hiccups with this elaborate potion, a

---

[1] *avoid excessive doses and the oil in any amount during pregnancy*
[2] *avoid during pregnancy*

mild decoction of valerian root, blackberry and peppermint leaves, chamomile blossoms and fennel seeds.

1. Use a handful each, valerian root, blackberry and peppermint leaves, chamomile blossoms and fennel seeds.
2. Cut the valerian root into small pieces
3. Crush blackberry leaves and peppermint leaves
4. Add to 600 millilitres (1 pint) water and bring to the boil
5. Steep 15 minutes, strain carefully
6. Drink 1 cup, lukewarm drink 3 times a day

Sugar

This remedy also comes from the Romany people, the Hungarian clans this time. Their healers tell people who want to get rid of hiccups to eat 20 grams (1 tablespoon) of sugar.

Basil [1] *(Ocimum basilicum)*

In India basil is called "tulsi" and has a reputation as an anti-spasmodic. A massage with basil oil is the recommended anti-hiccup treatment. Be sure to dilute the basil oil (1 -2 drops of basil oil in 10 millilitres of good quality vegetable or nut oil) and let its refreshing, aromatic, scent take over.

Water

A folk healer in Senegal would tell you to drink ten sips of water while holding your nose. Then, just when you least expect it your Senegalese folk healer would startle you, usually with a war whoop.

---

[1]   *do not use essential oil in any form during pregnancy*

You've probably know at least one person that swears by one of the following old-fashioned remedies. Some are pure DIY, others require a helping hand from a trusted friend.

● Breathe in deeply and hold your breath while slowly counting to ten

● Take a small breathe in, hold for four seconds, take a second breathe in and hold for another four seconds. Repeat again if you can before letting your breathe out and breathing normally

● Gargle for a couple of minutes with hot or cold water

● Drink a glass of water slowly, from the side of the glass farthest from you (prepare for dribbles)

● Have someone give you a sudden slap on the back

● Have someone drop something cold down the back of your neck, door keys and ice cubes are said to do the trick.

Impotence

Okay, it happened—on second thought make that, it didn't happen. OKAY. You don't want to talk about it. But is that the way adults deal with a problem? I don't think so. And impotence is nothing if not an adult problem. It's also something you don't think about until it strikes you. Not talking about it isn't going to help, because you wont be able to get it out of your mind until you deal with it.

Contrary to popular myth normal adult men are not sex machines, perpetually ready to perform. In the real world most men will find themselves in this situation at least once in their life. So give yourself (and your partner) a little credit. You are not just a sex toy. An occasional no-show doesn't say anything more about your masculinity than a bad round of golf. It just means you are human. A one-off experience is most likely caused by stress, tiredness or over-indulgence in alcohol—or other recreational drug.

Chronic problems are another story. Years ago the medical profession thought that impotence was almost always caused by psychological problems. Now they know that almost half of the men that suffer with chronic impotence have some

---

Remedies with ☕ are made using an infusion. Those with ☕ are made using a decoction. Instructions for both methods are on pages 4 - 7. Variations and other procedures are contained in the text following the description of that remedy.

physical or structural problem. That means that something can be done about it. But not unless you talk about it—at least to your doctor.

Oysters, champagne and chocolate all have a reputation as aphrodisiacs, but what do folk healers recommend?

Lemon Balm *(Melissa officinalis)*
also known as Sweet Balm and Bee Herb

History tells us that Bombastus Paracelsus, a sixteenth century Swiss physician and alchemist learned about melissa while working as a chemist in the Tyrol mineral mines. He called lemon balm the 'elixir of life' and often recommended drinking an infusion of lemon balm to his patients that sought help with sexual performance difficulties. It's even rumoured that he treated European kings and princes, whose over-indulgent lifestyle put a cramp in their amorous ambitions. Sadly (or fortunately) there are no surviving copies of Women's Weekly or New Idea to confirm these rumours.

Blackberry *(Rubus ulmifolius)*

In ancient China healers told men suffering with impotence to eat unripe blackberries.

Fenugreek [1] *(Trigonella foenum-graecum)*

Another recommendation from healers in ancient China, drinking a decoction of fenugreek.

---

[1]   *avoid during pregnancy*

Ginkgo (Ginkgo bilobe) also known as Maidenhair Tree

India's traditional Ayurvedic physicians treat impotence with a specially prepared dose of ginkgo.

Ylang-Ylang (Cananga odorata
also called Canangium odoratum)

This fragrant essential oil is a favourite with perfumers for its exotic, sensual appeal. It's no surprise then that it has a reputation as an aphrodisiac. It's said to be most effective when impotence or frigidity has an emotional basis.

Cannabis and free love . . . a match made in heaven?

It's no coincidence that "Make love not war", "If it feels good do it" and the "Summer of love" went hand in hand with cannabis . . . pot . . . marijuana . . . weed.

The hippies of the 60s and 70s were by no means the first to associate marijuana and amorous ambitions.

Two hundred years ago a German folk healer—known simply as Zuru—told men in need of extra sexual stimulation to chew cannabis seeds and leaves to solve performance problems they might experience.

Incontinence

Incontinence makes people uncomfortable, in more ways than one. That means that many men and women are suffering needlessly. It's normal to feel embarrassed the first time you experience an involuntary loss of urine. But don't let that embarrassment keep you from getting help. It's not the end of the world. Your doctor will most likely be able to help reduce—even eliminate—accidents in the future. In women, a displaced uterus (usually caused during childbirth) can cause incontinence. In men, an enlarged or inflamed prostate gland can be the cause. These conditions require medical evaluation and treatment.

What can you do to help yourself? Avoid diuretics like alcohol, caffeine, grapefruit juice and watermelon. Don't over do it on fluids. Be sure to drink plenty of water during the day, but pace yourself. If you have more difficulty holding your urine at night, set a cut-off time early in the evening, perhaps no fluids after 5:00 pm.

Recognise that your bladder is ageing along with the rest of you. You probably can't run as far as you did when you were twenty. Why should your bladder be exempt from the effects

---

Remedies with 🫖 *are made using an infusion. Those with* ♨ *are made using a decoction. Instructions for both methods are on pages 4 - 7. Variations and other procedures are contained in the text following the description of that remedy.*

of time? Solving incontinence may be no more complicated than adjusting your mental time frame. Anything within a 3–6 hour time range between trips to the toilet is normal.

If you find yourself going every hour or so, you may just have developed a bad habit. Try gradually working your way up to 3 hours between trips to the toilet. Or, you may find that you are waiting too long and your sphincter muscles just can't cope with an overfull bladder.

Talk to your doctor about Kegel exercises

Developed by Dr Arnold Kegel in the late 1940s, these exercises were designed to help women overcome stress incontinence—often experienced by women during and after pregnancy. But it turns out that these exercises can help either sex prevent, reduce or eliminate some forms of incontinence.

The exercises deliver an extra benefit to women and their partners—enhanced sexual response from the toned and strengthened uro-genital muscles.

Ask your doctor for more information about Kegel exercises.

Blackberry (Rubus ulmifolius)

Healers in ancient China told people suffering from incontinence to eat unripe blackberries.

Parsley (Petroselinum crispum)

Healers in ancient Rome had incontinence sufferers eat parsley leaves and drink a decoction made from crushed parsley seeds and chopped parsley roots.

Cranberry (Vaccinium macrocarpon)

Early last century, cranberry juice became popular as a remedy for all urinary problems. It's acidic and low in ash, so cranberry juice boosts your bladder's health and makes the local environment unhealthy for common disease causing bacteria.

Acupressure

This ancient therapeutic massage practice has been used in China and Japan for well over 3000 years. Like many eastern practices acupressure is based on improving the body's own healing powers, increasing vitality and preventing illness rather than killing specific disease causing organisms. Consult a registered practitioner for treatment.

Ingrown Nails

An ingrown nail is a little problem that can cause a great deal of discomfort. Improper nail care and poorly fitting shoes are usually the cause of ingrown nails. A less common cause is damaging the nail bed—by stubbing your toe or dropping something heavy on it.

After you treat your ingrown nail, try to figure out why it developed. That way you may be able to avoid getting another one. You only need to worry if you have a chronic problem with ingrown nails. If that's the case you may want to see a podiatrist or chiropodist to see if corrective measures are needed.

If your ingrown nail breaks the skin, watch out for signs of infection—red puffy skin; white or yellow discharge; or a dark line that appears to originate from the site of the break in the skin. If you notice any of these symptoms see your doctor, you may need a course of antibiotics to wipe out the infection.

Magnetis Polus Ausralis

This homoeopathic remedy should be purchased from a practicing homoeopath.

Remedies with ☕ are made using an infusion. Those with 🍲 are made using a decoction. Instructions for both methods are on pages 4 - 7. Variations and other procedures are contained in the text following the description of that remedy.

Filing

Folk practitioners in the US state of Vermont would tell you to cut a V shaped groove in the middle of your toenail. It's supposed to encourage the nail to grow upwards rather than downwards into your tender skin.

Butter

Traditional Kenyan healers apply fresh butter to the toe, bandage it then brush it with a cow's tail twice daily.

Papaya *(Carica papaya)*

Healers in Hawaii wrap the affected toe in papaya leaves.

Insomnia

Mary and Bill are both exhausted. Mary can't fall asleep. Bill falls asleep as soon as his head hits the pillow but wakes after an hour and can't get back to sleep. Both Mary and Bill are suffering from insomnia. Like most insomniacs their inability to sleep is made worse by their belief that everyone else in the world is enjoying a good night's sleep, while they struggle through another sleepless night. In fact, insomnia is very common—according to some researchers up-to one-third of the population suffers from occasional insomnia. Statistics aren't very comforting when you're tossing and turning in bed at night, trying to fall asleep. But then, the only thing that really comforts an insomniac is a good night's sleep.

Before you start worrying make sure that you really are suffering from insomnia. Some people worry needlessly. They don't have insomnia at all, they just need less sleep than the 'Eight Hour Rule' says is normal. The only thing that you should consider normal, is how many hours YOU need to operate efficiently. Some people get by on five hours sleep, others need ten, and men tend to need less sleep than women.

Remedies with ☕ are made using an infusion. Those with 🍵 are made using a decoction. Instructions for both methods are on pages 4 - 7. Variations and other procedures are contained in the text following the description of that remedy.

Lemon Balm *(Melissa officinalis)*
also known as Sweet Balm and Bee Herb

In 1020 the Persian doctor, Avicanna wrote, "Balm driveth away all troublesome cares and thoughts arising from melancholy". During the Middle Ages herbalists throughout Europe prescribed lemon balm for insomnia, by the sixteenth and seventeenth centuries balm was so popular it had a reputation as a cure-all. 🫖

Hops *(Humulus lupulus)*

Stuffing your pillow with dried hops is an ancient remedy for insomnia that is still recommended by aromatherapists and folk healers.

Catnip *(Nepeta cataria)*

Early American folk healers in the state of Pennsylvania told insomniacs to drink an infusion of soothing catnip. 🫖

Jamaican Dogwood *(Piscidia erythrina)*

The bark of this plant contains the powerful narcotic, piscidin and should only be used under the supervision of a trained herbalist. It has been used to treat insomnia but is more commonly used by fishermen in the West Indies. They use it to stupefy fish—it makes the fish easier to catch.

Celery *(Apium graveolens)*

The ancient Greeks treated insomnia with an infusion of celery seed. They also drank celery wine to relax after strenuous exercise.

Lavender [1] *(Lavandula angustifolia)*

Lavender has been a favourite of aromatherapists since the time of the ancient Egyptians. A massage with 1–2 drops lavender oil—diluted with 10 millilitres good quality vegetable or nut oil—soothes the mind, body and spirit, preparing you for a good night's sleep.

Honey

This sweet and sour remedy comes to us from traditional Slavic folk beliefs. According to tradition the darker the honey, the quicker you will be in dreamland.

1. Mix 40 millilitres (2 tablespoons) honey with 60 millilitres (¼ cup) each lemon and orange juice
2. Add 100 millilitres (3 ounces) warm water, stir and drink it

Rose *(Rosa canina)*

According to English physician and herbalist, Nicholas Culpeper, a mixture of lettuce juice and rose oil applied to the forehead and temples will cure insomnia caused by a headache. Be sure to dilute 1–2 drops of rose oil with 10 millilitres of good quality vegetable or nut oil before using it on your skin.

Ylang-Ylang *(Cananga odorata)*
also called Canangium odoratum

According to aromatherapists a whole body massage with ylang-ylang oil is your ticket for the slumberland express. Dilute 1-2 drops of ylang-ylang oil with 10 millilitres of good quality vegetable or nut oil before you use it on your skin.

---

[1] *avoid high doses during pregnancy*

Hot Tea with Banana Liqueur

Folk healers in England tell insomniacs to sleep 'head to the north, feet to the south', and drink a cup of hot tea with banana liqueur just before going to bed.

Squawvine *(Mitchella repens)*

Drinking an infusion of squawvine was the Native American Menominee tribe's treatment for insomnia.

Tarragon *(Artemesia dracunculus)*

The French folk remedy for insomnia is to drink an infusion of fragrant tarragon.

Massage

What could be more soothing than a massage before bedtime. You'll get best results from a professional massage therapist. But unless your partner happens to be a masseur or masseuse this may not be the most practical remedy. Rest assured that a sympathetic partner can do wonders with a little guidance.

The following old-fashioned remedies and old-wive's tales have been around forever. If one works for you, go for it!

- Try either a cold bath or a warm bath before retiring
- A warm footbath is comforting and is supposed to promote sleep by causing blood to rush from your head to your feet
- Follow your footbath with a gentle massage using a light vegetable oil

● Turn the bed so that the head faces true north, with the foot of the bed raised slightly

---

Insomnia or foot odour, you call that a choice?

In some parts of Italy villagers sleep with garlic cloves between their toes or rub their feet with garlic oil before going to bed. It's said to ensure a good night's sleep. This remedy probably is most effective if your inability to sleep is due to an over-amorous partner.

Irritable Bowel Syndrome

Diarrhoea, constipation and abdominal pain—that's a trifecta no one wants. Unfortunately, if you suffer from irritable bowel syndrome (IBS, also called spastic colon) you've got a good chance of suffering one—or all—of these symptoms. IBS is caused by different things in different people. Certain foods, drinks and even stressful occasions—things that may not phase other people—irritate your digestive system.

Try to identify the foods, beverages and stresses that cause your flare-ups; caffeine, fat, dairy products, and spicy or gas producing foods—like beans, broccoli and cauliflower—are some of the most common causes of IBS.

Alfalfa *(Medicago sativa) also known as Lucerne*

For centuries traditional Chinese medical practitioners have used alfalfa sprouts to soothe digestive upsets. Eat sprouts on your salads and sandwiches, it's an easy, tasty way to take your medicine.

Remedies with ☕ *are made using an infusion. Those with* 🍲 *are made using a decoction. Instructions for both methods are on pages 4 - 7. Variations and other procedures are contained in the text following the description of that remedy.*

Clove *(Syzgium aromaticum)*

Chewing cloves and eating food spiced with cloves is another digestive treatment handed down from Chinese traditional medical practitioners.

India's traditional Ayurvedic healers also recommend cloves for digestive problems, and have done for the past 2000 years. Eating food spiced with cloves and drinking an infusion of powdered cloves is their recommendation.

Ginger [1] *(Zingiber officinalis)*

Here's another long standing Ayurvedic method for dealing with digestive complaints. Add ground ginger root to all your food.

Sesame *(Sesamum indicum or S.orientale)*

If you don't like cloves or ginger, try a massage with sesame oil. Generations of traditional Indian Ayurvedic healers have recommended it as a way to soothe irritating intestinal complaints.

Basil [2] *(Ocimum basilicum)*

If you go to a Malaysian folk healer when you are suffering from irritating intestinal ailments or internal parasites you're likely to be told to take 2.5 grams (½ teaspoon) basil oil—down the hatch.

---

[1]   use sparingly during pregnancy

[2]   do not use essential oil in any form during pregnancy

Chamomile [1] *(Chamaemelum nobile, Roman, or C. recutita, German)*

Drink an infusion of chamomile. That's the Spanish folk healer's recommendation. 🫖

Caraway *(Carum carvi)*

Caraway seeds have a long history in Egyptian folk medicine. They have been used in remedies for digestive problems for at least 3000 years. You can either use caraway seeds on your food or try an infusion of powdered caraway. 🫖

Chaparral *(Larrea divaricata L. tridentata)*
also known as Creosote Bush

In the seventeenth century European settlers saw Native American tribes using chaparral for a range of ailments, including digestive problems. An infusion of chaparral leaves and twigs is the traditional Native American way to soothe digestive problems. 🫖

Cinnamon [2] *(Cinnamomum zeylanicum in the west, C. cassia in China, C Cassia from the bark = rou gui or from twigs gui zhi)*

When the biblical Hebrews had digestive problems they used cinnamon, either powdered and sprinkled on food or drank suspended in water.

---

[1]   *avoid accessive doses and the oil in any amount during pregnancy*
[2]   *avoid in pregnancy*

A remedy that cuts the mustard . . . *and how!*

Mustard *(Brassica nigra)*

In ancient Rome, mustard seeds were used to make a tonic for people suffering digestive problems. They were careful with the remedy, which releases allyl isothiocyanate from the seeds, albeit in small doses. Allyl isothiocyanate, the primary active ingredient in mustard seeds and oil, is toxic and a strong irritant. It makes up 99% of mustard oil—considered one of the most toxic of all essential oils. The ancient Romans didn't need to know that it was allyl isothiocyanate, all they need to know was that a little was okay, a little more was a disaster.

They made the tonic using a pinch of ground mustard seed mixed with a very large volume of water or vinegar. This was further diluted with an equal volume of water before drinking.

Castor *(Ricinus communis)*

Until the middle of this century, castor oil was the digestive tonic of choice for folk healers in the Middle East. Castor oil wasn't just a favourite in the Middle East either, ask your parents or grandparents to tell you about the 'bad-old-days' when a spoonful of castor oil was a weekly ritual in most people's homes. Back then, if you were lucky, your Mum mixed the castor oil with an equal volume of fruit juice. By all reports this trick didn't fool anyone. It didn't even make the castor oil taste better, it just ruined the taste of fruit juice.

Dandelion (Taraxacum officinale)
also known as pu gong ying

While you hack away in your garden, cursing the latest invasion of your prescious lawn by the dandelion from hell, think of Belgium, where for the past hundred years they have grown dandelion as a commercial crop. The leaves are featured in salads and the root is dried, roasted and ground to use medicinally For digestive problems Belgian folk healers recommend drinking an infusion of powdered dandelion root.

Coriander (Coriandrum sativum)

Powdered coriander sprinkled on food was used to treat digestive complaints in ancient Greek, Egyptian and Indian cultures. Anytime you use powdered coriander in a recipe you are following in their footsteps.

Dill (Anethum graveolens)

Dill was the favourite digestive aid in ancient Rome. Garlands of dill were hung in dining halls to prevent stomach upsets. Just in case the garlands didn't work, dill seeds were available so that over-indulgent guests could chew the seeds when digestive problems threatened to cut into their feasting time.

Fennel [1] (Foeniculum officinale)

Over in the new world, the Puritans chewed on fennel seeds to soothe digestive ailments.

---

[1]   *avoid during pregnancy*

Gentian (Gentiana lutea) also known as gin jiao

Sixth century Arab physicians learned about gentian from the Greeks. Through their vast trading empire the Arabs were responsible for introducing gentian to the Chinese. Traditional Chinese medical practitioners still recommend a decoction of dried, powdered gentian root to soothe digestive disorders. Drink 5 millilitres (1 teaspoon) before every meal.

Ginkgo (Ginkgo bilobe) also known as Maidenhair Tree

When they suffered from digestive problems the ancient Japanese ate roasted ginkgo seeds.

Sage [1] (Salvia officinalis)

Drinking an infusion of sage leaves is a common European folk remedy for gastric upsets.

Savory (Satureja hortensis, Summer Savory; S. montana, Winter Savory)

Drinking an infusion of savory to relieve digestive problems was popular with the ancient Greeks and Romans; the early Saxons; the Britons during the Middle Ages; and the early American settlers.

Papaya (Carica papaya)

Papaya contains enzymes that can help you digest the food you eat. That's probably why papaya is so popular with folk healers—it couldn't be it's luscious taste, could it? They often

---

[1]   avoid therapeutic doses in pregnancy. Small amounts used in cooking are quite safe.

recommend eating green papaya and drinking papaya juice for digestive problems. It's so popular with IBS sufferers because it tastes so good.

Old-fashioned Folk Remedies

Charcoal

Eating charcoal is a very old-fashioned remedy for bowel problems. Whatever you do, don't eat a piece of burnt wood from your fireplace. You can buy charcoal biscuits and tablets from health food stores.

Mustard *(Brassica nigra)*

A traditional remedy for digestive complaints in many rural areas of the world is to nibble a wild mustard leaf.

Jet Lag

You know what a pain it is every time Day Light Saving Time starts and ends? You go around grumbling as you reset your watch and the clocks in your house. Then for a few days you're a little unsettled, not sure if you're Arthur or Martha. That's because it's not quite so easy to reset your internal, biological clock. This problem, magnified many times over is why you feel disoriented when you travel across time zones.

Guess what? Folk remedies for jet lag are pretty thin on the ground. What do you expect? Air transport is a recent complication in human lives. Wilbur and Orville only got their powered flying machine off the ground in Kitty Hawke in 1903. Our ancestors never had to worry about such nonsense. In fact, universal time and synchronised time zones didn't even exist until railroad operators found it too impractical and inconvenient to deal with 'local' time—or more accurately local times. You see, until then each locality set their own time and no one cared whether adjacent towns' times were synchronised.

In the nineties, however jet-lag is a common problem, especially for those of us living in Australia and New Zealand.

Remedies with 🫖 are made using an infusion. Those with 🍲 are made using a decoction. Instructions for both methods are on pages 4 - 7. Variations and other procedures are contained in the text following the description of that remedy.

When we leave home it's hard not to travel to another time zone. Whether you are travelling on business or pleasure, if you feel as if you're about to meet yourself coming in the other direction, you won't be able to put your best foot forward— you'll be too nervous about stepping on your own toe!

Most modern healers (folk or otherwise) agree that avoiding alcohol, getting a little exercise and adjusting your sleeping patterns to approximate the timing at your destination are good practices for minimising the effect of jet lag. The jury is still out on the use of stimulants. But many folk healers believe that a mild stimulant like caffeine—or it's relative theophylline, found in tea—is an effective way to relieve the symptoms of jet-lag.

So, it's:
"A cup of Joe, thanks"
"A cup of hot chocolate, please"
"A cuppa, ta"
"Gimme a coke"
or
"Mate, por favor"

Coffee *(Coffea arabica, C. liberica, C. robusta)*

No recipe here, you won't be making your own, you'll have to make due with whatever the airline is offering.

Cola *(Cola nitida) sometimes written Kola*

If you take your own cola herb you may be able to make some cola tea but if that's too much trouble for you just drink a coke, cola is one of the ingredients in the top-secret, hush-hush recipe.

Yerba Mate (Ilex paraguensis) also known as Paraguay Tea

It's BYO mate, mate. If you want to drink this South American tea you'll have to bring it, unless you're flying a South American airline, then you just might be in luck.

Tea (Camellia sinensis var. sinensis, China Tea; C. Sinensis var. assanica, Assam Tea)

One thing's for sure, you'll be able to get a nice hot cuppa on the flight.

Cocoa (Theobroma cacao)

A cup of hot chocolate is especially nice if you need a little soothing but also want a hint of stimulant in your hot beverage. There's something about hot chocolate that makes you feel all warm and cosy.

Kidney Stones

Don't fool around with kidney stones. Seek medical attention immediately. It's not likely you'll need to be given this advice twice. When the stone is in your kidney you probably wont have any symptoms. But when it moves into your urinary tract you will have a first hand experience of PAIN.

No one will have to convince you to go to the doctor, though you may be asked to stop screaming long enough to be admitted to the hospital.

A kidney stone is a minuscule crystal of salt and minerals. It's magically transformed to the size of Uluru when it hits your urinary tract.

The good news is that nowadays you probably won't need major surgery to get rid of the thing. New treatments include laser, shock wave and ultrasound. Ultrasound works by vibrating the crystal structure at just the right frequency to break the stone into smaller bits that can easily (relatively speaking that is) pass through your urinary tract.

Remedies with ☕ are made using an infusion. Those with ♨ are made using a decoction. Instructions for both methods are on pages 4 - 7. Variations and other procedures are contained in the text following the description of that remedy.

These four remedies all come to us from the English physician and herbalist, Nicholas Culpeper.

Blackberry *(Rubus ulmifolius)*

Drink a decoction of blackberry root.

Birch *(Betula verrucosa)*

Drinking the juice extracted from young, fresh birch leaves was recommended for either kidney or bladder complaints.

Bird's Foot Trefoil *(Lotus corniculatus)*

Drinking an infusion of birds foot trefoil was another of Culpeper's suggestions for people suffering with kidney complaints.

Butcher's Broom *(Ruscus aculeatus)*

Finally, if none of the previous recommendations take your fancy, try drinking a decoction of butcher's broom.

Buchu *(Barosma betulina)*

This plant belongs to the same family as orange, lemon and rue. It was a popular herbal remedy with indigenous South Africans. An infusion of buchu makes a minty drink that is said to help dissolve kidney stones.

In 1847 Henry Helmbold introduced the US to buchu. He must have been an evangelist for buchu because he became known as Helmbold the Buchu King. His royal decree for people suffering with kidney complaints was to drink an infusion of buchu leaves.

Burdock *(Arctium lappa)*

During the Middle Ages, "Drink an infusion of burdock," was the European folk healer's recommendation for people suffering with kidney complaints. 🫖

Chervil *(Anthriscus cerfolium)*

Last century, Spanish folk healers used chervil to treat people suffering from kidney complaints. The remedy wasn't terrible, in fact it's tasty, sprinkle raw chervil leaves, on bread and enjoy the flavour as you eat your medicine. Yum!

Chamomile [1] *(Chamaemelum nobile, Roman, or C. recutita, German)*

India's traditional Ayurvedic physicians recommend drinking an infusion of chamomile to people suffering from kidney complaints. This was also the recommendation of ancient Egyptian healers—a tradition that modern day Egyptian folk healers still follow. 🫖

Parsley *(Petroselinum crispum)*

In ancient Greece eating parsley was the way to go if you were suffering with kidney ailments.

Celery *(Apium graveolens)*

Two thousand years ago celery was already being used as a medicinal plant. Eating celery and drinking celery juice were common recommendations for kidney ailments. If you want to give this one a go, eat fresh green celery stalks and leaves and sip a glass of celery juice with a little honey.

---

[1]   avoid excessive doses and the oil in any amount during pregnancy

Golden rod (Solidago virga aurea)

Drinking a decoction of golden rod was the recommendation of European herbalist Arnoldus de Villa Nora.

Elder [1] (Sambucus nigra)

Drink a decoction of crushed elder bark if you want to treat your kidney stones the Romany way.

Parsnip (Pastinaca sativa)

Eighteenth century religious reformer, John Wesley, told people to eat steamed or baked parsnips for lunch or dinner every day and to drink the water in which the vegetables were cooked to treat your kidney stones and gallstones. Whether he received this wisdom from heavenly or earthly sources was not recorded.

Radish, White (Raphanus sativus) also known as Daikon

This remedy is well known in England but it's only for masochists. Drink radish juice every day 250 -500 millilitres (1 -2 cups) daily for 2 - 3 weeks. Decrease weekly until you are drinking 125 millilitres (½ cup) 3 times weekly and continue for a month. If you're a glutton for punishment you can repeat the treatment.

---

[1]   *do not use during pregnancy*

Some old-fashioned remedies from here, there and who knows where

Beet *(Beta vulgaris)*

Eat beet tops and beet root daily.

Corn *(Zea mays)*

Drink an infusion of sweet corn silk, some people think it helps to soothe irritations in the urinary tract.

Glycerine

Take 1 tablespoon of glycerine on an empty stomach.

Unique Romany culture follows through to folk remedies

This multi-part remedy from the Romany people of Hungary features:

Onion *(Allium cepa)*
Parsley *(Petroselinum crispum)*
and Asparagus *(Asparagus officinalis)*
and Gin!

It's a doozey of a remedy and it's a sure bet that anyone using it would be over 0.05 first thing in the morning. It must have been a rollicking good time on the road if the driver of your horse-drawn cart was suffering from kidney stones.

1. Drink the juice from a red onion twice a day
2. Eat raw asparagus
3. Stew a bunch of parsley in 600 millilitres (1 pint) water until liquid is reduced by half
4. Cool
5. Add a glass of gin to the stewed parsley and drink the whole dang thing every morning

Menopause

No surprises here! Folk remedies for menopausal symptoms are based on the mistaken belief that the symptoms are caused by mental or psychological weakness. Of course modern science has shown that the symptoms are caused by changing hormonal levels as your ovaries start to close-up shop. All those symptoms, from hot flushes to chills, to sleeping problems and yes, even stress and nervousness are caused by fluctuations in hormonal levels. But this information hasn't made its way into the consciousness of every member of the community. Not yet at least, but things are changing. They really are!

But when uninformed people start giving you advice like, 'relax', 'ignore it' and 'it's all in your mind' they can drive you crazy. When you think about it though, most of these people will be men. So how did they get to be experts?

It's when you're being bombarded with these self-appointed experts' helpful advice that the following folk remedies will come in handy, whether you're in need of a soothing interlude because of the sometimes stressful experience of menopause

Remedies with ☕ are made using an infusion. Those with ♨ are made using a decoction. Instructions for both methods are on pages 4 - 7. Variations and other procedures are contained in the text following the description of that remedy.

or the sometimes stressful task of dealing with experts who really don't have a clue.

One final warning. Many women look forward to the menopause and liberation from the constant worry about birth control. Well girls... it ain't over 'til it's over. If you don't want to be 60+ at your youngest's university graduation you'll need to be vigilant with whatever birth control method you are using, all the way through the menopause. Don't stop until your doctor has confirmed that you are finished ovulating. On the other hand many women who have had children in their forties say that having a child at that age keeps them young!

Black Haw *(Viburnum prunifolium)*

Well before Columbus arrived in the new world, Native American women were drinking a decoction of black haw to relive menopausal symptoms. Later, American healers in the Eclectic movement took up the practice as well.

Cypress *(Cupressur sempervirens)*

A gentle massage with cypress oil (dilute 1-2 drops of cypress oil with 10 millilitres of good quality vegetable or nut oil) has a reputation for developing a tranquil state of mind.

Barberry *(Berberis vulgaris)*

French folk healers recommend you drink an infusion of barberry when suffering menopausal symptoms.

Quinine [1] *(Cinchona spp.)* and Gin

In India, gurus prescribe drinking hot gin with quinine. Another way to get your quinine and gin is by sipping a tall, ice-cold gin and tonic! It might not be approved by Indian gurus, but it's soothing just the same. Note: this remedy is not suitable for pregnant women who may have begun, but not completed the menopause.

Lady's Mantle [2] *(Alchemilla vulgaris)*

Drink an infusion of lady's mantle. That's the European folk healer's recommendation for overcoming menopausal symptoms.

Some old-fashioned remedies

Sage [3] *(Salvia officinalis)*

Drinking an alcoholic infusion of sage is an old-fashioned remedy that many folk healers use, but the origin of the remedy is lost in time. It's simple to make but takes a while to get to the finished product.

100 grams (4 oz) of sage leaves

1 bottle of organic wine

1. Put the sage leaves into the wine and let steep for 2 weeks
2. After two weeks add a dash of honey, shake well and leave it to steep for 24 hours
3. Strain well, drink 150 millilitres (5 ounces) before lunch and dinner

---

[1]   the bark of many species fo cinchhona produces quinine along with other important alkaloids.

[2]   avoid during pregnancy

[3]   avoid therapeutic doses in pregnancy. Small amounts used in cooking are quite safe.

Lemon Balm *(Melissa officinalis)*
also known as Sweet Balm and Bee Herb

Lemon balm seems to be the old-fashioned cure all for menopausal symptoms. First drink an infusion of lemon balm. Then put a handful of lemon balm leaves under your pillow. Then get some lemon balm oil and put it into your bath. Follow these recommendations and according to some folk healers, a calm and peaceful state of mind is just around the corner.

Mugwort *(Artemisia vulgaris)*

A clue to this old-fashioned remedy's origins lies in the plant's scientific name. It's associated with Artemis, the Greek goddess of chastity, the moon and the hunt. Drinking an infusion of mugwort is supposed to help relieve hurt and weariness. Mugwort is a relative of the notorious Artemisia absinthium—wormwood—the herbal flavouring used in the banned liqueur, absinthe.

Aromatherapy

Aromatherapists use the essential oils of sage, cypress and geranium to soothe menopausal symptoms. An aromatherapist may recommend using a mixture of the oils in an inhalant. You can also scent the air using an 'oil burner'. It's like an incense burner, but it uses low, indirect heat to volatilise the oils.

The oils can also be used in your bath or—when diluted—as massage oils. Always dilute essential oils in the ratio 1-2 drops essential oil to 10 millilitres of good quality vegetable or nut oil. A sympathetic partner is the easiest way to get a massage, but for best results consult a qualified aromatherapist.

Menstrual Cramps

Menstrual cramps are caused by the same chemicals that trigger the normal sloughing of tissue and fluid each menstrual cycle. The discovery that menstrual cramps had a biological cause was a welcome one. But no one is sure why some women never suffer with cramps, while others dread each cycle and the regular experience of painful, debilitating cramps. A good old-fashioned hot-water bottle held against your tummy is one of the best all around soothers for abdominal cramps of any sort.

Lemon Balm *(Melissa officinalis)*
also known as Sweet Balm and Bee Herb

Drink an infusion of lemon balm, that was the North American folk healer's treatment for menstrual cramps.

Black Cohosh *(Cimicifuga racemosa)*

For centuries the Algonquian Indians used black cohosh for all sorts of 'women's problems', including menstrual cramps. The name, cohosh comes from the Algonquian word for rough,

---

Remedies with *are made using an infusion. Those with* *are made using a decoction. Instructions for both methods are on pages 4 - 7. Variations and other procedures are contained in the text following the description of that remedy.*

a reference to the plant's roots. Drinking a decoction of black cohosh roots was the recommended course of action for menstrual cramps.

Catnip *(Nepeta cataria)*

In Europe, catnip has been used medicinally for at least 2000 years. In pre-Elizabethan England drinking an infusion of dried catnip was a popular remedy for menstrual cramps.

German folk healers also tell you to drink an infusion of chamomile to relieve menstrual cramps.

Coffee *(Coffea arabica, C. liberica, C. robusta)*

America's nineteenth century herbalists told women to drink a cup of coffee to soothe the pain of menstrual cramps.

Ginger [1] *(Zingiber officinalis)*

Ginger is a popular medicinal plant in traditional Chinese medicine. For menstrual cramps the recommendation is to drink an infusion of powdered ginger root.

Evening Primrose *(Oenothera biennis)*

While not a folk remedy, an extract from the seeds of evening primrose—gamma linolenic acid—is being studied for its ability to regulate the production of prostaglandins and the premenstrual symptoms that prostaglandins cause. Look for evening primrose capsules in your local health food store or pharmacy.

---

[1]   *use sparingly during pregnancy.*

Motion Sickness

There's no nice way to say it, if you suffer from motion sickness you're not going to get asked to join the car-pool or join the gang on their bus trip to Alice Springs.

That you know it's coming before it happens, is cold comfort. It's better to know you are going to vomit before it actually happens, but since you usually can't do anything to stop it, thinking about it only makes it worse. In the scope of human problems motion sickness is really pretty trivial, more of an inconvenience than a problem. But as inconveniences go, motion sickness gets a place in the top ten. After all unless you are antisocial, the day is going to come when you are going to want to hop in the car, jump on a plane, catch the train or board a ship. So be prepared.

Before you commit to a long trip, try one of these folk remedies on a short trip.

Bon voyage!

Remedies with 🫖 *are made using an infusion. Those with* 🍲 *are made using a decoction. Instructions for both methods are on pages 4 - 7. Variations and other procedures are contained in the text following the description of that remedy.*

Some oldies-but-goodies . . .

- Suck a slice of lemon, or a slice of ginger root
- Travel lying down, with your head low in a comfortable position

Nicotinum

This is a homoeopathic remedy. It's available from registered homoeopaths. A dosage of 30c taken every 2 or 3 hours is the usual recommendation for overcoming sea-sickness.

Ginger [1] *(Zingiber officinalis)*

Hawaiian folk healers recommend drinking an infusion of ginger root—slice and crush the ginger root before making your infusion. Chinese traditional healers recommend chewing ginger to prevent sea-sickness.

In ancient India, ginger was used for a whole range of ailments. A massage with ginger oil was the recommended remedy for overcoming motion sickness. Dilute 1-2 drops of ginger oil with 10 millilitres of good quality vegetable or nut oil before using.

Galangal *(Alpinia officinarum) also known as Catarrh root*

In ancient China physicians used galangal to treat travellers that became sick while taking a sea journey. Drinking an infusion of powdered galangal root was the recommended treatment. ☕

---

[1]   *use sparingly during pregnancy.*

Peppermint [1] *(Mentha piperita)*

A massage with peppermint oil is the traditional French way to relieve the symptoms of motion sickness. Always dilute 1-2 drops of the essential oil with 10 millilitres of good quality vegetable or nut oil before using it on your skin.

Try one of these massage remedies for children suffering from motion sickness:

● Press at the base of the second, third and fourth toe, in turn. Then repeat on the other foot. Hold the pressure on the underside of the toe for thirty to sixty seconds.

● Place your index finger inside the bottom of the child's ear and your thumb behind the child's ear. Then pull, simultaneously so that the hollows of each ear moves outward. Do this for one or two minutes or until sickness eases.

● Press across on the bottom of the child's left foot—from the middle of the foot up to the ball of the foot. Press into any tender points and maintain the pressure for ten to thirty seconds.

Soda Crackers, Lemon and a Copper Penny

Hawaiian healers advise eating soda crackers, sucking a lemon, and applying a copper penny to the navel—though where anyone can find a copper penny now days is a mystery in itself!

---

[1]   avoid during pregnancy and if breast feeding do not give in any form to very young babies

Acupressure

Apply pressure at a point three fingers width above your wrist—along the central line formed by the middle finger. Apply the pressure towards the centre of the wrist. Look for wrist bands—available from natural pharmacies, health food stores, and some airports. These are said to perform the same function.

Muscle Cramps

It's your own fault. That's right, if you regularly suffer with muscle cramps you are probably doing something wrong. Maybe you don't stretch enough before exercising, or maybe you don't replenish the salt your body looses when you sweat a lot, or maybe you spend your days impersonating a slug, sitting around in the same position for hours and hours.

Self inflicted pain is nothing to be proud of, but that doesn't mean that folk healers will ignore you. It just means that you won't get any sympathy for your suffering.

Cramp bark *(Viburnum opulus)*
also known as High Cranberry Bush

With a name like this you'd expect it to be used to treat cramps, and you'd be right. Drinking a decoction of the plant's bark is recommended for either muscle cramps or period pain.

Honey

In ancient Egypt the treatment for cramps was honey, 10 ml (2 teaspoons)—or the ancient Egyptian equivalent—honey at each meal was thought to do the trick.

Remedies with 🫖 *are made using an infusion. Those with* 🍲 *are made using a decoction. Instructions for both methods are on pages 4 - 7. Variations and other procedures are contained in the text following the description of that remedy.*

Don't let night cramps, cramp your sleeping style

As if being woken up in the middle of the night with a cramp in your leg isn't bad enough. You may find yourself sleeping alone if you don't do something about it.

Your partner won't be suffering the pain of the cramp. But your nighttime antics, hopping around, hooting and gasping with pain, is equally disruptive to his or her sleep.

It may sound strange, but the cramps that strike in the dead of the night can be caused by muscle fatigue. When everything is working properly your muscles contract and relax as you move in your sleep. When your muscles contract, but don't get around to relaxing, you may wake-up with a start, and find yourself right smack in the middle of cramp city,

The best way to prevent this sort of nighttime cramp is to make it easy for your body to move. You want to avoid anything that restricts your movement—heavy bed cloths, a too tightly made up bed, tight fitting pyjamas or a too cold bedroom.

If you are often troubled with night cramps, and none of the above mechanical fixes help, your cramps may be caused by a calcium deficiency. But check with your doctor before adding a calcium supplement to your diet.

Ginger [1] *(Zingiber officinalis)*

Drinking an infusion of ginger is the traditional Indian treatment for cramps. Use slivers of fresh or powdered dried ginger to make the infusion.

Heat exhaustion is not cool!

When Australia turns up the heat it doesn't do it by halves. Every year someone has a near miss (or worse). Someone gets stranded or lost on an outback track without the information, equipment or training necessary for survival in our unforgiving environment.

Even if you never get further from Melbourne than Geelong you can still suffer from heat exhaustion. When heat exhaustion is not treated properly, the next step— heat stroke—can be deadly.

Few people drink as much water as they should. In the heat this is a big mistake. Plain, cool water is the best way to avoid becoming dehydrated. Though if you are an athlete it may not be possible to drink enough water to replace the electrolytes you lose during heavy exercise. In that case you may want to drink an electrolyte replacement drink like Lucozade or Staminade.

---

[1]   *using sparingly during pregnancy*

Muscle Pain

It doesn't matter if the ache comes from a too vigorous start to a new exercise regime or a long-term fitness habit. When your muscles ache, you are going to have to take it easy so your muscles have time to heal.

Soreness and stiffness are signs that you have done some damage to the muscle tissues. What you need to understand is that every time you exercise you do some damage to your muscles. So relax. While you're at it—relaxing that is, you can also try giving one of these folk remedies time to work.

Fenugreek [1] *(Trigonella foenum-graecum)*

In ancient China healers used fenugreek to treat muscular aches and pains. Modern day Chinese herbalists still recommend drinking a decoction of fenugreek seeds to their patients suffering with muscle pain.

Remedies with ☕ are made using an infusion. Those with 🍲 are made using a decoction. Instructions for both methods are on pages 4 - 7. Variations and other procedures are contained in the text following the description of that remedy.

---

[1]   avoid during pregnancy

Mandarin or Tangerine
(Citrus reticulata var. deliciosa)

More than a thousand years ago Moroccans started using shredded tangerine peel to make this decoction, a drink that they believed would help sore muscles heal.

1. Shred the peel from 3 tangerines
2. Bring to the boil in 1 litre (1 quart) water
3. Steep 1 hour
4. Strain, discarding solids
5. Drink 1 cup, lukewarm every 5 hours
6. Add a little honey if you like

Lavender [1] *(Lavandula angustifolia)*

A gentle massage using lavender oil is the aromatherapist's recommendation to clients suffering from muscle pain. Concentrate your massage on the sore muscles and don't forget to dilute 1 - 2 drops of the lavender oil with 10 millilitres of good quality vegetable or nut oil before using on your skin.

Clary Sage Oil *(Salvia sclarea)*

Another recommendation from the realm of aromatherapy is to use clary sage oil to massage the sore muscles. Clary sage oil has a reputation for toning muscle tissue and relieving muscle cramps. Remember to dilute 1 - 2 drops of the clary sage oil with 10 millilitres of good quality vegetable or nut oil before using.

---

[1]   *avoid high doses during pregnancy*

Eucalyptus *(Eucalyptus globus)*

Australian Aborigines used many native plants for medicinal and spiritual practices, though none took the fancy of European settlers like eucalypts did. One of the most common and most enduring uses of eucalypt oil is to soothe sore muscles. Remember to dilute 1 - 2 drops of eucalypt oil with 10 millilitres of good quality vegetable or nut oil before using.

Lemongrass *(Cymbopogon citratus)*

Australian Aborigines have been using native lemongrasses to soothe muscle pain for thousands of years. The traditional method is to prepare a decoction of crushed green leaves to be drunk and used as a wash or warm compress on the sore muscles.

Lemon *(Citrus limon or C. medica, var. limonum)*

This massage with lemon oil comes to us from American folk healers, it's one of their favourite remedies for sore muscles. Don't forget to dilute 1 - 2 drops of lemon oil with 10 millilitres of good quality vegetable or nut oil before using.

Ginger [1] *(Zingiber officinalis)*

You'll need to be really suffering to go to this much trouble, but this traditional Japanese remedy for muscle pain is still popular today. It must do something!

1. Bring 4 litres (1 gallon) water to the boil in a large enamel pot with lid
2. While the water is coming to the boil wash and grate a large ginger root

---

[1]   *use sparingly during pregnancy*

3. Do not peel the ginger

4. When grating the ginger turn it clockwise so that the tough inner fibres open up

5. Place the grated ginger on to a piece of muslin, drawing the corners of the fabric up to hold the ginger and secure this 'bag' with a piece of string

6. Turn the heat down under the boiling water

7. Squeeze any ginger juice from the bag into the boiling water then drop the bag into the pot

8. Simmer 7 minutes

9. After 7 minutes use a spoon to press the bundle of ginger against the side of the pot releasing as much ginger as possible into the water

10. Remove the pot from the heat and use the liquid warm as a compress on the sore muscles

11. Use the compress for about 40 minutes and repeat every 4 - 6 hours until the soreness is gone

St John's Wort (Hypericum perforatum)

This Romany remedy requires patience and a little foresight. It takes 20 days to prepare!

1. Fill a 1 litre (1 quart) clear-glass bottle with St John's wort blossoms

2. Pour olive oil over the blossoms filling the bottle

3. Seal the bottle and place it in full sun for one cycle of the moon (20 days) After 20 days strain and transfer the strained oil to an amber glass container for storage

4. Use a piece of cotton wool to apply the oil to painful muscles

5. Do not expose skin treated with this oil to the sun, it is a photo-sensitiser

Nappy Rash

Ah, the joys of parenthood. If you are a new parent you can be sure of one thing. Sooner or later your child will suffer from nappy rash. It's caused by baby's sensitive skin coming in contact with a harsh chemical environment. That environment is created by the decomposition of the baby's urine. The decomposition starts as soon as the urine leaves the baby's body and comes into contact with the nappy and the air.

That doesn't mean that you have neglected your baby. Some babies' skin is more sensitive than others. Some babies produce more potent or concentrated urine. Some babies are sensitive to different foods and develop nappy rash when their diet changes.

Most nappy rash clears within a day or two of extra, tender-loving- care. Sometimes nappy rash is more persistent. Then you may have to be more rigorous in your treatment. If you are using cloth nappies try an extra rinse to be sure all the chemicals from the washing powder are rinsed from the fabric. You may even want to try a vinegar rinse. It's supposed to neutralise the high pH that can develop in the washed cloth fibre and bring the fabric's pH closer to that of the baby's skin.

Remedies with ☕ *are made using an infusion. Those with* ☕ *are made using a decoction. Instructions for both methods are on pages 4 - 7. Variations and other procedures are contained in the text following the description of that remedy.*

Grandma's remedy

Ever practical, Grandma would have gotten rid of nappy rash by getting rid of the nappy. It makes sense, too! This is one of the best ways to banish nappy rash from your baby's bum. A bare bottom exposed to fresh air and indirect sunlight will soon be—what else—as smooth as a baby's behind! Lie a very young baby on thick, absorbent cotton-towelling, a couple of layers thick. Let the fresh air and indirect sunlight do its magic. Never put a baby in the direct sunlight.

As your baby gets older—and the volume of urine produced gets larger—this solution is no longer practical, but you can still get some benefit from this all natural remedy by leaving the bub, sans nappy for a few minutes after each changing. This is an excellent practice as it can help prevent nappy rash from developing in the first place. If nappy rash does develop, it will help the irritated skin heal.

Wash irritated skin with fresh cool water or a solution of very dilute vinegar—40 millilitres (2 tablespoons) vinegar to 1 litre (1 quart) water—and use soft, cloth nappies to dry irritated skin. You may want to try one of Grandma's other favourites, a little calendula cream or slippery elm powder on stubborn cases.

Some remedies from here and there and who knows where...

• use bicarbonate of soda, cornflour or arrowroot powder on irritated skin

• try pawpaw ointment, but only if the rash is dry, the ointment is greasy and can further irritate a moist rash

● or try castor oil cream

● increase the amount of fluids to dilute the urine and lessen the irritation

● as a last resort, try yoghurt, it is supposed to be effective against rashes caused by yeast like infections.

It maybe something your baby ate, even if the rash is on the baby's bum!

If nappy rash appears out of the blue, it may be due to a change in the child's diet. Try eliminating any new foods and see if the rash goes away. Remember though that most nappy rash will go away in a day or two, whether you do anything about it or not.

Turmeric (Curcuma longa)

In Samoa mothers use powdered turmeric to treat nappy rash. They just sprinkle some powdered turmeric on to their hands and rub it into the baby's irritated skin. If baby's skin is very irritated they mix the powder with a little coconut oil to make it easier to apply.

Nausea

Nausea, the name says it all really. Just saying nausea is enough to make some people feel a little nauseous. Nausea is a very personal topic. It's not the kind of experience you want to share with anyone—as either the share-er or the share-ee. All sorts of things, from scents to sights can trigger that unmistakable queasy feeling. Another reason that nausea has a reputation for being such a personal subject is that what you call a sweet scent your best friend might call a stench.

Better than worrying about how to get rid of nausea, avoid getting it in the first place, that's the most reliable course of action. We all have a few things that we know will set our stomachs churning, tossing and turning—you get the picture.

Know what tips your tummy topsy-turvey and avoid looking, touching, tasting or smelling it. That way your battle is half won.

Because nausea is such a personal experience, finding an effective remedy is also a very individual choice. Try remedies until you find one that works for you then stick with it, no matter what anyone else says. After all, you are the one who is going to be sick if the remedy doesn't work.

Remedies with 🫖 *are made using an infusion. Those with* ☕ *are made using a decoction. Instructions for both methods are on pages 4 - 7. Variations and other procedures are contained in the text following the description of that remedy.*

Cinnamon [1] *(Cinnamomum zeylanicum in the west, C. cassia in China, C Cassia from the bark = rou gui or from twigs gui zhi)*

America's nineteenth century herbalists recommended drinking an infusion of ground cinnamon to relieve nausea.

Catnip *(Nepeta cataria)*

According to traditional Pennsylvanian folk healers, drinking an infusion of catnip is just the thing to relieve nausea.

Lime *(Citrus aurantifolia)*

This Samoan remedy has been around as long as anyone can remember. Drink a few millilitres of fresh lime juice, it's supposed to be a wonder-cure for stopping nausea and vomiting.

Galangal *(Alpinia officinarum) also known as Catarrh Root*

Drinking an infusion of galangal is the ancient Chinese way to relieve nausea.

Ginger [2] *(Zingiber officinalis)*

It's not surprising that this old-fashioned English remedy is popular with young and old alike. Drinking a glass of ginger ale is so popular most people think of it as a treat rather than a treatment!

---

[1]   *avoid in pregnancy*
[2]   *use sparingly during pregnancy*

Bergamot *(Monarda didyma, M. fistulosa, M. citriodora and M. punctata)*

Drinking an infusion of bergamot leaves and flowers is another old-fashioned remedy for nausea. Bergamot's scientific name honours the sixteenth century Spanish physician, Dr. Nicolas Monardes who no doubt used bergamot in many herbal preparations.

Chamomile [1] *(Chamaemelum nobile, Roman, or C. recutita, German)*
Blueberry *(Vaccinium corymbosum)*
and Oak *(Quercus robur)*

You can almost feel the lure of the gypsy life when you make this old Romany remedy, a drink made with chamomile blossoms, blueberries and a bit of powdered oak bark.

Stock mixture
A handful of chamomile blossoms
25 dried blueberries
20 grams (1 tablespoon) powdered English oak bark

Nausea remedy
1. Take 20 grams (1 tablespoon) of the stock mixture
2. Add to 250 millilitres (1 cup) water and bring to the boil
3. Simmer for 3 minutes
4. Steep 15 minutes
5. Strain, drink lukewarm 1 cup 3 times a day

---

[1] *avoid excessive doses and the oil in any amount during pregnancy*

For Children

Nausea in children presents a special problem. Many remedies—conventional and herbal—are not suitable for children. One exception is rice water, the strained water from cooked rice. It's easy to digest and is supposed to help settle an upset tummy.

Give older children a lolly or the hard pit[1] from a piece of dried fruit to suck on for 30 minutes or so. As the nausea retreats you can gradually switch to giving the child some chipped ice to suck, then clear liquids to drink and finally to bland, solid foods to eat.

Acupressure

To western minds using massage to settle the stomach sounds odd. But in China and Japan no one would think twice if you said you went for acupressure to remedy a bout of nausea. Here are two DIY methods you can try:

Method 1

First, find the crease on your inner wrist. Then measure the width of three fingers along your arm—towards your shoulder—and press downward on this spot.

Method 2

First, locate the spot that falls midway between your sternum (breast bone) and your naval and equidistant from your hip bones. Then press inwards on this spot.

---

[1]   *never use an apricot pit, apricot pits contain toxic chemicals and should never be eaten or taken internally*

If none of these remedies work and you find yourself transcending nausea and going straight to vomiting, try one of the following . . . .

Peach *(Prunus persica)*

In ancient Greece, Esculapius first used peach leaves and bark to relieve vomiting. An infusion of peach leaves and bark, steeped for one hour was the recommended treatment. Take 5 millilitres (1 teaspoon) every ten minutes until the vomiting stops.

Lemon Balm *(Melissa officinalis)*
also known as Sweet Balm and Bee Herb

Throughout southern Europe, an infusion of lemon balm is used to control vomiting. Sip as required during the day.

Bergamot *(Monarda didyma, M. fistulosa, M. citriodora and M. punctata)*

In Spain, drinking an infusion of bergamot leaves and flowers is also used to stop vomiting.

Paprika *(Capsicum teragonum)*

For some people this sounds more like a way to start vomiting than a treatment to stop it—but for centuries Romany folk healers have been swearing by it. Mix a pinch of paprika with 5 millilitres (1 teaspoon) honey and gag it down three times a day.

Neck Pain

If you think it's a coincidence that when something is unbearably irritating we call it a pain in the neck, think again. Few things put a kink in your day like a kink in your neck. It doesn't help your mood to realise that along with being a pain in the neck, a pain in the neck is usually self-inflicted.

A kinky, stiff or sore neck is usually caused by a bad habit (or lots of bad habits). Poor posture and sitting or standing in one position for a long time are common triggers. Sleeping on a soft, lumpy, worn-out mattress and using the wrong pillow have also earned their places in the 'Pain in the Neck Hall of Fame'.

Don't despair, bad habits are made—they can be broken. All you need is a little will power. Mattress and pillow problems are even easier to solve. All they take is a little money. Of course right now the only thing you want to know is how to get rid of the stiff neck you already have. Read on.

Remedies with ☕ are made using an infusion. Those with ☕ are made using a decoction. Instructions for both methods are on pages 4 - 7. Variations and other procedures are contained in the text following the description of that remedy.

White Bryony *(Bryonia alba)*

White bryony became popular with French folk healers during Middle Ages. For neck pain the recommendation was to drink a decoction made from white bryony roots, which according to folk traditions need to be dug up when the plant is in flower to be effective.

Lemon *(Citrus limon or C. medica, var. limonum)*

Native American healers of the Cherokee tribe give this sour recommendation to people suffering with neck pain. Drink the juice of half lemon two times a day. Rub lemon juice on your neck as well.

If you've already read the section on muscle pain, the next two remedies will be familiar. One takes a bit of work the other takes a bit of time—a full cycle of the moon to be exact.

Ginger [1] *(Zingiber officinalis)*

This traditional Japanese folk remedy is still popular in modern day Japan, but it takes a bit of work to prepare.

1. Bring 4 litres (1 gallon) water to the boil in a large enamel pot with lid
2. While the water is coming to the boil wash and grate a large ginger root
3. Do not peel the ginger
4. When grating the ginger turn it clockwise so that the tough inner fibres open up

---

[1]   use sparingly during pregnancy

5. Place the grated ginger on to a piece of muslin, drawing the corners of the fabric up to hold the ginger and secure this 'bag' with a piece of string

6. Turn the heat down under the boiling water

7. Squeeze any ginger juice from the bag into the boiling water then drop the bag into the pot

8. Simmer 7 minutes

9. After 7 minutes use a spoon to press the bundle of ginger against the side of the pot releasing as much ginger as possible into the water

10. Remove the pot from the heat and use the liquid warm as a compress on the sore muscles

11. Use the compress for about 40 minutes and repeat every 4 - 6 hours until the soreness is gone

St John's Wort *(Hypericum perforatum)*

This Romany remedy requires patience and a little foresight, it takes 20 days to prepare. Given their nomadic lifestyle Romany folk healers probably had quite a call for this soothing remedy. A smart folk healer would have had one bottle in use and another brewing all the time. If you're a keen athlete you may want to follow their lead.

1. Fill a 1 litre (1 quart) clear-glass bottle with St John's Wort blossoms

2. Pour olive oil over the blossoms filling the bottle

3. Seal the bottle and place it in full sun for one cycle of the moon (20 days) After 20 days strain and transfer the strained oil to an amber glass container for storage

4. Use a piece of cotton wool to apply the oil to painful muscles

5. Do not expose skin treated with this oil to the sun, it is a photo-sensitiser

Acupuncture

Neck, shoulder and back pain are some of the more common reasons that people in the west try this ancient Chinese therapy. Be sure to consult a registered practitioner if you want to give acupuncture a try.

Reflexology

According to reflexologists you can relieve neck, back, and upper spinal stiffness with foot massage. Be sure to consult a registered practitioner if you want to try reflexology.

Osteopathy

According to osteopaths, postural problems are the key to understanding your body's malfunctions. This includes neck, back and shoulder stiffness. Gentle mobilisation is the method of treatment, be sure to consult a registered practitioner for osteopathic treatment.

Massage

A gentle massage from a friend or partner can help ease pain and stiffness, but for best results consult a registered massage therapist. A professional massage therapist can identify muscle groups responsible for the pain and perform deep tissue massage that often helps relieve not only the pain, but the cause of the pain.

Night Blindness

Before you get the wrong idea, this is not about the sort of blindness you get after a long night at the pub. That kind of night blindness is easy to fix, all you need to do is exercise a little self-control.

But real night blindness, a significant reduction in your ability to see in poor lighting conditions, is something everyone suffers from to some extent. That's because everyone sees better when the scene is well lit. Our eyes are designed to respond to low light so it happens every time you walk into a dark room after being out in bright sunlight. Your iris opens up and your retina adjusts to the lower light conditions. At first your vision is noticeably poorer, then after a few minutes your eyes have adjusted and everything is fine.

The speed with which your eyes adjust to changing lighting conditions and the amount of adjustment they are capable of, are two variables that affect your night vision. Both variables change with age and like so many things they get worse as you get older.

If you have noticed your night vision deteriorating you should discuss it with your doctor. He or she will probably test you

Remedies with 🫖 are made using an infusion. Those with 🍵 are made using a decoction. Instructions for both methods are on pages 4 - 7. Variations and other procedures are contained in the text following the description of that remedy.

for night vision and you may find that your night vision is within normal ranges for your age and overall vision. An examination is important because there are a few, serious eye diseases that can cause progressive deterioration of your vision.

After your doctor gives you the all clear you may want to have a look at one of the following folk remedies.

Dandelion *(Taraxacum officinale*
also known as pu gong ying

An old American folk remedy for night blindness was to drink an infusion of freshly picked dandelion flowers.

Fennel [1] *(Foeniculum officinale)*

The ancient Greeks believed fennel gave them courage. They also used fennel in keyholes to keep away evil spirits and to keep witches quiet. A more down-to-earth use for fennel was as treatment for night blindness. Drinking a little fennel juice, sometimes mixed with carrot juice was the recommended treatment.

---

[1]   *avoid during pregnancy*

Obesity

Here's a secret that everyone knows and no one believes (or wants to believe). There is only one way to lose weight. Eat fewer kilojoules (calories) than is required to maintain your body at its current weight. There are no magical potions in folk traditions or in modern, western medicine.

Food is your body's fuel. If you want to store some fuel for the winter, put it in your kitchen cupboard or pantry—not your mouth. Because if you store it in your pantry it will be there for you to eat come winter. Of course if you do put it in your mouth, it will be stored, on your thighs, your bum and around your waist—you get the picture. If you eat more than is required to maintain your body at it's present weight, you will get fatter. Because your body stores the extra food as fat. The stored fat will hang around until you eat less. That is the truth, despite what any number of advertisements at the back of magazines for miracle fat burning compounds claim.

There is some good news. Eating less does not have to mean starving. Starvation diets are not healthy, nor are diets that severely restrict your intake to one or two food groups. Most modern research has shown that a balanced diet, high in

---

Remedies with ☕ are made using an infusion. Those with ♨ are made using a decoction. Instructions for both methods are on pages 4 - 7. Variations and other procedures are contained in the text following the description of that remedy.

complex carbohydrates and low in fat, is best for your health and your weight. What's more, these diets are the most effective for satisfying hunger. So, if you want to lose weight you can do it in a way that is healthy and does not leave you ravenous.

An excellent low fat, high carbohydrate diet plan is detailed in Dr Dean Ornish's book Eat More, Weigh Less.[1] This book, which includes 250 heart-healthy gourmet recipes, builds on Dr Ornish's experience as a medical researcher at the Preventive Medicine Research Institute (Sausalito, California USA) where he is president and director, as well as his work as assistant clinical professor of medicine at the School of Medicine, University of California at San Francisco, USA. It also includes information drawn from his earlier books, "Stress Diet and Your Heart" and "Dr Ornish's Program for Reversing Heart Disease". It goes beyond defining a weight loss regime to show how lifestyle choices—including diet,—can be powerful forces in determining your health and overall well-being.

While there are no magical brews, elixirs or spells to make you lose weight there are folk remedies that claim to help when used as part of a calorie controlled diet. The least foolish of these are listed below.

Dandelion *(Taraxacum officinale)*
also known as pu gong ying

For centuries traditional Chinese medical practitioners have recommended drinking an infusion of dried dandelion roots for weight control.

---

[1]   *Eat More, Weigh Less is available in Australia and New Zealand and is published by Bookman Press, Melbourne, Australia.*

Seaweed

In many Mediterranean countries dried, powdered kelp is sprinkled on food in an effort to control weight.

Psyllium *(Plantago psyllium)*

Dried, powdered psyllium had quite a heyday as a weight loss product some years ago—thanks to its ability to swell, and presumably fool your body into thinking that you were full of food instead of swollen psyllium fibre. Unfortunately to have any effect considerable amounts of psyllium were required and dangerous conditions in which the swollen psyllium completely blocked the stomach and oesophagus were reported.

Psyllium's ability to swell when mixed with water is used effectively in many commercial diarrhoea and constipation medications. It is used to treat diarrhoea because of its ability to absorb water and return normal bulk to watery stools. It is used to treat constipation because of its ability to add bulk to stools and stimulate the colon to expel the stool. Recent research indicates that psyllium may also have the ability to lower cholesterol levels.

However, psyllium should only be used medicinally in consultation with your doctor. Psyllium must only be taken in controlled amounts and never without sufficient water, otherwise you may find yourself with a potentially life threatening intestinal, abdominal or oesophageal blockage. Inhaling the dust from the seeds can also cause allergic reactions— sometimes severe—in sensitive people.

Oily Hair

With hair it's a case of the grass being greener on the other side of the fence . . . or should that be the hair is better on the other person's head? If you have dry hair you find yourself wishing for a little oil, and if yours is oily you wish it was dry. But if you're a brunette you'll be glad to know that there is some justice in the world—those blondes that are always having more fun are also more likely to have oily hair. Men also have more problems with oily hair than women do, thanks to the male hormone androgen.

Because it's actually your scalp that is oily some people have oily hair near their scalp while the rest of their hair is dry. That's why you need to take care when shampooing and concentrate on your scalp rather than on the length of your hair. This is good advice for everyone, especially people with long hair so that you don't over-dry your hair shaft.

Finally if you have oily hair save a few minutes and a few cents each time you wash your hair—skip the conditioner. Oily hair tends to go limp and lank, flattening through the day as the hair shaft gets coated with oil. Why add insult to injury and coat your hair with more oil—in the form of

Remedies with ☕ are made using an infusion. Those with ♨ are made using a decoction. Instructions for both methods are on pages 4 - 7. Variations and other procedures are contained in the text following the description of that remedy.

conditioner. If you have long hair and the ends are dry use conditioner on the dry ends only.

Ylang-Ylang *(Cananga odorata)*
also called Canangium odoratum

In aromatherapy circles ylang-ylang oil has a reputation for balancing the oil output of the body's oil producing glands. That's why you'll find ylang-ylang oil recommended for oily or dry hair. Use it as a tonic, massaging a small amount into your scalp. Be sure to dilute 1 - 2 drops of the ylang-ylang oil with 10 millilitres of good quality vegetable or nut oil before applying to your scalp.

Patchouli *(Pogostemon cabin-labiatae)*

This oil—once the darling of the hippie set—is making a comeback in the west. It is, and always has been popular in Asia, especially in Japan, China, India, and Malaysia. Its medicinal properties are said to include the ability to contract tissue and stop oil discharge from oil producing glands. It's this ability that has earned patchouli oil a reputation for conditioning oily hair. Massaging the oil into the scalp is claimed to give you lush, oil-free hair. Use patchouli sparingly, its fragrance can be overpowering. Be sure to dilute patchouli oil with 10 millilitres of good quality vegetable or nut oil before applying to your skin.

Oily Skin

If your best friend entertains every one you meet with riotous tales of your pimple-packed puberty, breathe deeply, bide your time. Her time will come. Resist the urge to tell equally embarrassing stories about her first boyfriend. In a few years it will all come back to haunt her.

You see, oily skin may have tortured you during your teenage years, but she is going to start looking her age—or older—long before you do.

Now that you have something to look forward to, what can you do today to avoid blinding oncoming traffic with the reflection off your shining oily skin?

Treat yourself to a mud-pack. Don't use the gooey stuff in your back garden. Most salons offer mud or earth based face-packs in their facial treatments. Or go shopping at the beauty counter of your favourite shop. Retailers like 'The Body Shop' and Australia's own 'Red Earth' and 'Jurlique' make a point of stocking natural beauty products that have not been tested on animals. Use a mudpack while you lounge in a nice warm bath. It's a little luxury that makes you feel like a squillion dollars without spending a packet.

Remedies with 🫖 *are made using an infusion. Those with* ♨ *are made using a decoction. Instructions for both methods are on pages 4 - 7. Variations and other procedures are contained in the text following the description of that remedy.*

Anise, Chinese Star Anise
(Illicium verum)

In ancient China drinking a decoction of anise seeds was the preferred treatment for oily skin. Ancient Ayurvedic physicians also recommended drinking this treatment.

Rosemary *(Rosmarinus officinalis)*

Rosemary oil is often used in aromatherapy to make the skin sweat. This characteristic has earned rosemary oil a reputation for helping control oily skin. Dilute 1 - 2 drops of rosemary oil with 10 millilitres of good quality vegetable or nut oil before using on your skin.

Ylang-Ylang *(Cananga odorata)*
also called Canangium odoratum

Ylang-ylang oil is believed to help balance oil producing glands. Aromatherapists often recommend a massage with ylang-ylang oil to help control both oil and dry skin. Be sure to dilute 1 - 2 drops of ylang-ylang oil with 10 millilitres of good quality vegetable or nut oil before using on your skin.

Sandalwood *(Santalum album)*

Sandalwood has a reputation as an antiseptic and soothing oil. For oily skin aromatherapists recommend a 1-2 week regime of whole body massages using diluted sandalwood oil. Have your massage once a day, before a bath. Dilute 1 - 2 drops of sandalwood oil with 10 millilitres of good quality vegetable or nut oil before using on your skin.

Osteoporosis

Osteoporosis is a condition, not a disease. When you 'have osteoporosis' your bones are depleted of calcium, they lose density and eventually become porous and brittle—so brittle they can collapse or fracture with little or no trauma. Most sufferers are women over forty-five years of age, but men can suffer from osteoporosis too. For our grandmothers, and in some cases—our mothers too—osteoporosis was thought to be an unavoidable consequence of old age.

Now we know that it is nothing of the sort and that a life-long program of moderate, regular exercise combined with a balanced diet that includes calcium—as a calcium supplement if required—will increase bone density and reduce the risk of developing osteoporosis.

Most women will achieve 'peak' bone density at thirty-five or forty years of age. After that, calcium loss from your bones reduces the bones' density each year, and the rate you loose bone density increases after menopause. The best way to maximise bone density is to exercise and consume a calcium rich diet through your formative years. Maximum bone density at your 'peak' is the best way to prevent osteoporosis. A

Remedies with 🍵 are made using an infusion. Those with ♨ are made using a decoction. Instructions for both methods are on pages 4 - 7. Variations and other procedures are contained in the text following the description of that remedy.

sedentary lifestyle and eating too little calcium—whether early or late in your life—are the primary causes of osteoporosis.

It's best to learn good habits when you are young and stick with them throughout your life. But you're never to old to benefit from exercise and calcium. Even post-menopausal women who have already started to experience bone loss can slow the rate, simply by increasing the amount of calcium they consume.

The same goes for exercise. A moderate exercise program helps to reduce the risk of disease and injury, no matter what your age. The special message for older women is that many of the 'symptoms' of old age are really symptoms of a sedentary lifestyle. Aches, pains, increased body fat, weak or stiff muscles, brittle and porous bones, low energy, as well as an increased risk of diseases like diabetes and heart disease—these are all more a function of inactivity than a natural process of aging.

Yoga

Yoga comes from the Sanskrit word for 'yoke' or 'union'. It is a system of spiritual, mental and physical training that originated in India, about 4000 years ago. Until recently yoga was only well known in India, but during this century it has spread throughout the world. During yoga's development teachers studied animal postures and movement in an attempt to help people become more relaxed and effective in their movement. Breathing also plays an important role in yoga, and practitioners believe that osteoporosis, and other bone problems, can be combated through more efficient breathing. Diaphragmatic breathing, they believe, can help the body deal with changes in bone structure. If you want to investigate using yoga in your treatment for osteoporosis, consult a qualified yoga therapist.

Naturopathy

Diet and exercise are important in the prevention and treatment of osteoporosis. Naturopaths use diet as an important part of their healing practices and may be able to help you develop a high calcium diet to prevent or control osteoporosis. However naturopathic medicine usually requires careful monitoring, of your diet and the effects of dietary change on your overall health. Only undertake a naturopathic dietary regime in consultation with a registered practitioner.

Tai Chi Chuan

According to Chinese teaching Tai Chi can be traced to the eleventh century Taoist thinker, Chang San-feng. During the fourteenth century a more advanced form of Chuan, called Tai Chi Chuan, developed. The practice was intended to help develop the mastery of the whole self.

Taoist monks adopted the practice and introduced it into their monasteries and temple schools in an attempt to develop an integrated mind, body and spirit.

Tai Chi, which means wholeness, is based on a series of slow-moving, circular, dance-like movements, usually performed in the open air. It aims to get people to focus on their mental and emotional state as well as their body.

Chinese practitioners believe that Tai Chi is both curative and preventive. The graceful movements are believed to help patients adapt to changes in their bodies and to maintain a positive and creative outlook. Practitioners claim that Tai Chi promotes the use of mental, emotional and physical energies, which together can help you function better. Most metropolitan areas and major regional centres through out Australia and New Zealand will have Tai Chi classes taught through local community centres or traditional Chinese health centres.

Poison Ivy

The best way—the only sensible way—to treat poison ivy is with respect, and lots of it. If you're going to be hiking or living in an area where poison ivy occurs, know how to recognise it and stay well clear. Because if you have never experienced the torment of poison ivy you should be more than happy to maintain your blissful state of ignorance.

If you have experienced the painful, intense itching of a poison ivy rash you'll be quite happy to never go down that road again. If by chance you're one of those people that has been exposed to poison ivy without ill effect, don't feel too smug. You can develop a sensitivity to poison ivy at any time. So consider yourself warned.

If you're interested, the chemical responsible for poison ivy's (and poison oak's for that matter) irritating rash is urushiol oil. It's one of the most potent toxins on this planet, or any other for all we know. Potent and persistent, urushiol hangs around for a long, long time. What that means is that if your camping gear has come into contact with poison ivy or oak it could still be contaminated years—yes years—later. Don't dismiss stories of people being hospitalised after breathing

---

Remedies with 🫖 *are made using an infusion. Those with* 🍲 *are made using a decoction. Instructions for both methods are on pages 4 - 7. Variations and other procedures are contained in the text following the description of that remedy.*

the smoke from a fire in which poison ivy or oak has been burnt. They are't tall tales, those stores are absolutely true. Urushiol is not destroyed by fire. When it gets carried—on smoke and particulate matter—into your lungs, it's bad news indeed. The only thing worse than an itchy, poison ivy rash on your arms, legs or face is breathing urushiol and suffering with inflamed tissues in your throat, mouth and lungs.

Once you start itching there's not much you can do, except try one of the following folk remedies, maybe one will relieve the itching and keep you from going crazy.

Gooseberry (Ribes grossularia)

Native Americans from the Rocky Mountain area of the US used a wash made from infused gooseberries as a remedy for many skin conditions.

For poison ivy try this.

1. Infuse a handful of gooseberries in 250 millilitres (1 cup) boiling water.
2. When the berries are soft mash them to release all the juice.
3. Then strain well.
4. Discard the solids and use the strained liquid on any itchy skin condition.

Grindelia (Grindelia squarosa)

For centuries this herb has been used to treat skin irritated by poison ivy. An infusion of dried grindelia is strained and used to soothe any irritated, itching skin condition, like that caused by poison ivy.

Sage [1] *(Salvia officinalis)*

This folk remedy comes from Nassau, the capital of the Caribbean island group called the Bahamas. The remedy is said to be the brain-child of Momma Marshall, a legendary native cook who used a strained infusion of lightly crushed, fresh sage leaves as a wash to end the itching of irritated skin. After the liquid was used to bathe irritated skin she sprinkled whole-meal (whole-wheat) flour over the still damp skin.

---

[1]   *avoid therapeutic doses in pregnancy. Small amounts used in cooking are quite safe*

Premenstrual Syndrome

Let's get a few things straight. There's Premenstrual Syndrome and then there's PREMENSTRUAL SYNDROME. Neither is a picnic, but one's a nuisance the other a natural disaster and there won't be any question in your mind about which one you suffer from. For years—generations even—women suffering with Premenstrual Syndrome (PMS) were told that PMS was all in the mind. PMS was either the subject of jokes or used as evidence of a woman's mental or emotional frailty. Once medical researchers started taking PMS seriously they found that it was indeed real, and that most of the symptoms could be traced to physical or chemical causes.

 PMS is not a single condition but a catch-all phrase under which a host of symptoms are grouped. That's one of the reasons that PMS was—and still is—difficult to study. About the only thing that is common to all sufferers is that PMS usually strikes about 14 days before the onset of menstruation. Symptoms of PMS include physical, emotional and behavioural changes.

Another difficulty for researchers studying PMS, is that some women never experience anything more serious than mild

---

Remedies with 🫖 *are made using an infusion. Those with* 🍵 *are made using a decoction. Instructions for both methods are on pages 4 - 7. Variations and other procedures are contained in the text following the description of that remedy.*

cramping and water retention. Others suffer anxiety, nervous tension, irritability and mood swings. Others are troubled by weight gain, swollen, tender breasts and severe abdominal swelling. While their sisters are doing battle with headaches, food cravings, a racing heart beat, fatigue and dizziness. With such a wide range of symptoms it's easy to see why the mysteries of PMS will take a long time to unravel.

It may be the luck of the draw that determines whether or not you suffer from PMS, but the latest research indicates the severity of your symptoms may be controlled by some simple modifications to your diet. That's good news on its own, but what makes this even better news is that those modifications are right in line with general recommendations for women who want to improve their health.

Increase your consumption of foods high in B vitamins, zinc, iron and manganese. Decrease your consumption of dairy products, salt, sugar, fats and animal products. You may just see an improvement in your overall health and a reduction in the severity of your premenstrual symptoms. While you are at it, give one of the following folk remedies a try.

Cabbage *(Brassica oleracea)*

To relieve premenstrual symptoms Spanish folk healers recommend drinking 5 millilitres (1 teaspoon) of fresh cabbage juice twice a day. Afro-American folk healers also recommend drinking cabbage juice as a natural way to relieve premenstrual symptoms.

Aromatherapy

Aromatherapists recommend adding the essential oils of sage, geranium and lavender to your daily bath during the two weeks prior to the start of your period. A few drops of the same oil mixture can also be placed on a hankie and inhaled during the day. For really stressful times, mix the oils with a good quality vegetable or nut oil and use as an after-bath lotion. Hmmm, makes you wonder if all those women portrayed in Victorian literature as weaklings—prone to an attack of the vapours at the slightest provocation—were really just treating themselves for PMS?

Hot Water Bottle

This was one of the few ways our Mums and Grandmothers had to battle PMS. Luckily for them, it really works! If you are troubled with lower back pain a hotty tucked behind you, in the small of the back does wonders. And if you have painful abdominal cramps, nothing is more soothing than a hot water bottle held against your tummy.

Massage

Ahh, a massage is wonder remedy if there ever was one. There is hardly an ailment that doesn't respond to a good massage. A relaxing full body massage can help release stress. A simple neck and shoulder massage can relieve a headache. A light abdominal massage can ease the pain of premenstrual cramps.

Bach Flower Remedies

Most premenstrual symptoms can be traced to specific physical causes—even emotional distress and nervousness. But if you are looking for a remedy for the emotional strain that can accompany some of the physical changes you experience each month you may want to try one of the following Bach Flower Remedies, they are claimed to address emotional causes rather than physical symptoms.

Try:

Crab Apple   if you feel disgust towards menstrual blood

Cherry Plum if you feel tense or fear being overtaken by emotion and moodiness

Water Violet if your tension is caused by an unfulfilled need for solitude and withdrawal

Aspen   if you feel heightened sensitivity

Holly   if you feel intense, negative emotions

Beech   if you feel intolerant intolerance towards your condition

Rockwater   if you try to deny your feelings

Acupuncture

In this ancient Chinese therapy, needles are used at particular points along invisible energy channels called meridians. The meridians are believed to be linked to internal organs. The needles unblock, increase or decrease the flow of Qi or 'life force'. The important meridians to treat PMS are the kidney, liver, conception and sometimes stomach and governor. Consult a registered practitioner for acupuncture treatment.

Chaste Tree *(Vitex agnus-castus)*

This plant's common name should give you a clue as to its medicinal uses. It was traditionally used to suppress sexual activity. It must have seemed logical to use it to treat any problem that could be associated with a women's sexual organs—or sexual urges for that matter— including her menstrual cycle. If you want to give it a try, drinking an infusion of the leaves and berries is supposed to do the trick. If you are in need of sexual suppression that is.

But before you do, you should know that many modern practitioners recommend sexual activity as a way of relieving premenstrual tension. The choice is yours.

Psoriasis

Psoriasis is a mystery—but unlike some mysteries there's nothing vaguely romantic about psoriasis. What is known about psoriasis is that everyone's experience is unique. About the only thing you are guaranteed to have in common with your fellow sufferers is the characteristic patches of itchy, dry, flaky skin—called plaques—that periodically erupt on your skin.

The advice folk healers give their patients is to experiment with remedies until they find one that works. Then stick with it. None of the following will cure you of psoriasis, but one might help reduce the itching and flaking, and that's a good start.

French Beans (Phaseolus vulgaris) and Chamomile [1]
(Chamaemelum nobile, Roman, or C. recutita, German)

Native American healers used these beans to treat a range of skin afflictions. For psoriasis (and similar skin conditions)

Remedies with 🫖 are made using an infusion. Those with 🍲 are made using a decoction. Instructions for both methods are on pages 4 - 7. Variations and other procedures are contained in the text following the description of that remedy.

---

[1] avoid excessive doses and the oil in any amount during pregnancy

they used a strained infusion made from equal parts chamomile flowers and French beans. They drank the infusion and used it as a wash too, to soothe painful skin conditions.

Fig *(Ficus carica)*

This remedy comes to us from the Middle Ages, when drinking an infusion of figwort was first recommended as a way to ease the discomfort of itchy, dry and painful skin conditions. To follow the traditional method of preparing the remedy you'll have to collect figwort leaves between June and August. Then you have to dry them to use in your infusion.

Oat *(Avena sativa)*

Oats are popular for treating any itchy or scaly skin condition. To make a soothing oatmeal wash, bring 1.5 litres of water (6 cups) to the boil. Add 250 grams (1 cup) rolled oats and simmer for 30 minutes. Strain, discarding solids and use the remaining liquid as a wash for itchy, dry skin.

Some old-fashioned remedies whose origins have been lost in the mists of time

Pot Marigold [1] *(Calendula officinalis)*

Add 2 drops of calendula oil and 1 drop of oregano oil to 250 millilitres (1 cup) olive oil. Rub into dry skin plaques.

---

[1] *do not confuse with French Marigold, Tagetes patula*

Neroli Bigarade *(Citrus aurantium var. bergamia)*
also called Neroli or Bitter Orange

Earlier this century Algerian healers used neroli oil to help remove the dry, flaky raised patches of psoriatic skin called plaques. Dilute 1 - 2 drops of neroli oil with 10 millilitres of good quality vegetable or nut oil. Gently massage into affected skin.

Pineapple *(Ananas comosus)*

Traditional Hawaiian healers have patients suffering from psoriasis eat pineapple—and lots of it! They also say that you should not eat pineapple at the same meal with cereals or starches.

Sage [1] *(Salvia officinalis)*

This Caribbean remedy comes to us from Nassau, the capital of the island group called the Bahamas. It rumoured to have been developed by Momma Marshall, a famous native cook who used the remedy to soothe painful, and itchy skin conditions. Strain an infusion of lightly crushed, fresh sage leaves and use the infusion as a wash. Sprinkle a little whole-meal (whole-wheat) flour over the still damp skin as an extra, soothing step.

Turmeric *(Curcuma longa)*

In Samoa local folk healers use an infusion of powdered turmeric root to relieve the pain and itching of psoriasis. What they use to help heal the acute embarrassment that comes

---

[1]   avoid therapeutic doses in pregnancy, small amounts used in cooking are quite safe.

from having to explain their skin's bright orange hue is unknown. 🫖

Bach Flower Remedies

These remedies are supposed to correct the mental or psychological causes of a disease or symptoms of a disease. While psoriasis is a physical condition, it can be embarrassing and stressful when outbreaks are severe. If that's the case, try:

Crab Apple - if you feel disgusted or shameful about your condition

Willow - if you resent your condition

Rescue Remedy or Impatiens - if you want to try to relieve itching

Bergamot *(Monarda didyma, M. fistulosa, M. citriodora and M. punctata)*
or Lavender [1] *(Lavandula angustifolia)*

Aromatherapists believe adding bergamot and lavender to your bath can help keep psoriasis bay. If your skin is dry and you are troubled with very scaly plaques, mix 1 - 2 drops each oil with 20 millilitres of good quality vegetable or nut oil and massage into your skin. You can also try sandalwood oil in the same way.

---

[1] *avoid high doses during pregnancy*

Restless Leg Syndrome

If—instead of making you the life of the party—your tapping toes and lurching legs are tormenting you in bed at night. If—instead of relaxing in bed your leg muscles seem to be screaming 'Gota dance! Gota dance'!—you're not going crazy. You've got restless leg syndrome, also known as Ekbom syndrome.

Restless leg syndrome is characterised by an irresistible urge to move your legs. Deep creeping or crawling sensations often accompany the jerking muscles. Typically, the lower legs are affected, although the thighs and even the arms can be involved.

No one knows what causes restless legs but it's usually a harmless condition. But you should discuss your symptoms with your doctor if you experience restless legs for the first time. The symptoms can sometimes be a sign of neurological, kidney or lung diseases.

Remedies with 🫖 *are made using an infusion. Those with* 🍲 *are made using a decoction. Instructions for both methods are on pages 4 - 7. Variations and other procedures are contained in the text following the description of that remedy.*

Tired, swollen legs can drain your whole body of energy

This folk remedy may not do anything for restless legs but it is supposed to soothe tired and swollen legs

1. Wash your legs with the water in which potatoes or other vegetables have been boiled.

2. Strain the water into the tub or basin in which you are going to soak your legs

3. Soak for a while then rinse the liquid off your skin

4. Immediately after rinsing the liquid off your skin wrap your legs in a cloth or cotton towel on to which you have liberally sprinkled hot salt

5. Do this every evening, repeat two or three nights in a row

Acupressure

To try this DIY acupressure remedy you'll need to find 'The Spot'. The acupressure point to be treated is on the back of the knee, about four fingers' width below your kneecap. When you find the spot you'll feel a little hollow between the fleshy muscle and the smaller of the two leg bones. When you find the spot, press inwards and against the bone. If you really want to get the full benefit of acupressure, consult a registered practitioner.

Massage

Either a general massage or a lymphatic drainage massage—concentrating on your legs—can improve circulation and may ease restless leg syndrome. Lymphatic drainage massage is a specialised skill. If you want to try it, find a massage therapist trained in the technique.

Rosemary (Rosmarinus officinalis)

In aromatherapy, rosemary is called a nervine oil, which means that it stimulates the nerves and helps to stimulate muscles, prior to or after physical activity. A gentle leg massage with 1 - 2 drops of rosemary oil diluted with 10 millilitres of good quality vegetable or nut oil may help relieve restlessness, pain and weakness. For best results, consult a qualified aromatherapist.

Naturopathy

Naturopaths believe restless leg syndrome is caused by an iron deficiency and the chronic, mild anaemia that accompanies iron poor blood. A diet rich in iron is their usual recommendation, along with vitamin supplements and alternating hot and cold baths to improve the circulation. Consult a registered naturopath for treatment.

Sinusitis

It's a toss-up really, whether the dull, throbbing pain of daytime sinusitis or the relentless drip, drip, drip of post-nasal drainage at night is worse. The thing is, you can't get rid of one without doing something about the other. Instead of trying to figure out which is worse, try one of the following folk remedies. They won't cure sinusitis, but they may do the next best thing—relieve the irritating symptoms that accompany sinusitis.

Cinnamon [1] *(Cinnamomum zeylanicum in the west, C. cassia in China, C Cassia from the bark = rou gui or from twigs gui zhi)*

Twelfth century German abbess and herbalist Hildegard of Bingen used cinnamon to treat sinuses trouble. She recommended a sprinkling of powdered cinnamon on your food at every meal.

Remedies with ☕ are made using an infusion. Those with 🍲 are made using a decoction. Instructions for both methods are on pages 4 - 7. Variations and other procedures are contained in the text following the description of that remedy.

---

[1]   avoid in pregnancy

Thyme *(Thymus vulgaris)*

For sinus trouble Romany folk healers use an infusion of thyme, with a drop or two of bergamot oil added for extra oomph, in steam inhalation therapy.

Onion *(Allium cepa)*

This remedy is supposed to have been popular during the Middle Ages in Europe. It won't make you very popular with your spouse, that's for sure! Finely chop an onion and place it between two pieces of gauze. Bind the gauze to your neck with a piece of cotton towelling or a cotton bandage. Leave it on over night.

Red River Gum *(Eucalyptus camaldulensis)*

For 40,000 years Australian Aborigines have used eucalyptus as a remedy for sinus troubles. Crush a handful of young gum leaves. Drop the leaves into a pot of water and bring to the boil. Simmer 30 minutes, strain and drink.

Honeycomb, Rye Bread and Grape Juice

Vermont folk practitioners tell patients suffering from sinusitis to avoid tobacco and beer. The also recommend chewing honeycomb, eating rye bread and drinking grape juice.

Some oldies-but-goodies . . . .

Scotts Pine *(Pinus sylvestris)*
or Eucalyptus *(Eucalyptus globus)*

This is an old favourite, steam inhalation using water to which either essential oil has been added. Sit in front of a basin half filled with boiling water. Add a few drops of either pine or eucalyptus oil to the water. Cover your head with a large towel (for best results the towel should be large enough so that none of the vapours escape). Inhale the rising vapours.

Frankincense *(Boswelia carterii)*

Frankincense, which is also known as Olibanum or Olium Libanum, has been used medicinally for some 5000 years. It has a reputation for eliminating excess mucus. Aromatherapists recommend a head and neck massage, concentrating on the areas above the nasal sinus cavities.

Eucalyptus *(Eucalyptus globus)*
Peppermint [1] *(Mentha piperita)*
Lavender [2] *(Lavandula angustifolia)*
or Lemon *(Citrus limon or C. medica, var. limonum)*

If you're out and about, this remedy is more practical than the steam inhalation therapy described above. Mix a drop or two of either eucalyptus or peppermint oil with a drop of lavender, bergamot or lemon oil. Put a drop of the mixture of oils onto

---

[1] *avoid during pregnancy and if breast feeding do not give in any form to very young babies*

[2] *avoid high doses during pregnancy*

a handkerchief. Inhale whenever necessary to help clear the blocked sinus cavities.

If you want to try a preventative treatment, add 6 to 8 drops of any of these oils to your daily bath. Each night massage any of the oils (dilute 1 - 2 drops of the essential oil with 10 millilitres of good quality vegetable or nut oil) into the skin above the nasal sinuses.

Reflexology

Reflexologists treat ailments by massaging and manipulating specific regions on the soles of the feet. You'll need to consult a registered practitioner to test the ability of reflexology to relieve your sinus condition.

Acupuncture

The important meridians to treat sinusitis are points on the governor and the large and small intestine meridians. When sinusitis is caused by allergies the spleen meridian is usually the focus of acupuncture treatment. Consult a registered practitioner for acupuncture treatment.

Sprains

Your heel comes down on an uneven surface, you take an awkward step, you slip or loose your balance—you can feel it happening but you can't do anything to stop it. Once you make sure that nothing is broken you are left with a sprained ankle or wrist— and if you happened to take that fall in front of an audience a bruised ego.

Not to worry, everything, including your bruised ego will heal if you take it easy and give yourself some TLC. One of the following folk remedies may help you mend more rapidly.

Cayenne Pepper *(Capsicum frutescens)*

In Taiwan a hot pepper ointment is used to treat sprains. Make your own ointment with one part ground cayenne pepper and five parts petroleum jelly. Add the cayenne pepper to petroleum jelly that you have melted in a double boiler. After you have added the cayenne pepper, mix well and allow the ointment to cool before using. Apply your 'cayenne jelly' once a day, directly to the injured muscles, tendons and around the sore joint.

Remedies with 🫖 *are made using an infusion. Those with* 🫕 *are made using a decoction. Instructions for both methods are on pages 4 - 7. Variations and other procedures are contained in the text following the description of that remedy.*

Elder [1] *(Sambucus nigra)*

In England an ointment made from elder leaves has been used to treat sprains since the eighteenth century. Make your own by mixing 3 parts fresh elder leaves with 6 parts petroleum jelly. Melt the petroleum jelly in a double boiler. Then add the elder leaves. Heat until the leaves become crisp. Strain, then allow to cool. Apply the strained 'elder jelly' to the sore area a couple of times a day.

Ginger [2] *(Zingiber officinalis)*

Ginger water is a traditional Indian treatment for sprains. Finely chop a large ginger root and boil it in 500 millilitres (2 cups) water for about 20 minutes or until the volume of water is reduced by half. Use the strained water as either a wash or compress on the sore area.

Garlic [3] *(Allium sativum)*

This traditional Chinese remedy for sprains is supposed to be very effective. If it doesn't relieve the pain and help your sprained muscles and tendons heal, the smell alone is bound to give you some privacy. Pound a couple of cloves of garlic in olive oil for a minute or two. Rub the garlic-oil paste on the sprain and surrounding tissue. Bandage the area with a cotton cloth and leave the whole smelly mess on for an hour or two.

---

[1]   *do not use during pregnancy*
[2]   *use sparingly during pregnancy*
[3]   *avoid during pregnancy and if breast feeding*

Comfrey [1] *(Symphytum officinale)*
also known as Knitbone
and Rosemary *(Rosmarinus officinalis)*

To make this remedy the traditional way you need to gather comfrey roots during the new moon.

1. Clean the roots you have collected then cut them into small pieces. You'll need about 500 grams (2 cups) of the cut comfrey root for this remedy.
2. Add 750 millilitres (3 cups) olive oil and a handful of fresh rosemary.
3. Place the mixture in a double boiler, over cold water. Heat gently, while stirring constantly. Do not allow the mixture to boil.
4. Simmer about 15 minutes.
5. Cool to body temperature and strain. Use gauze to line the strainer and squeeze the gauze to extract all the liquid.
6. Next, melt a handful of beeswax in a double boiler.
7. While stirring the wax, add the strained comfrey root and rosemary oil, one drop at a time.
8. Use the ointment cool on sprained muscles and tendons.

Mustard *(Brassica nigra)*

Last but not least it's that olde-tyme favourite, the mustard plaster.

1. Grind mustard seeds with a little water
2. Coat the skin of the affected area with petroleum jelly (this prevents the mustard from blistering or irritating the skin)
3. Apply the paste to the sore area, holding it in place with gauze and adhesive tape. This plaster can be kept on for several hours, for best results leave on overnight

---

[1]   restricted her in Australia and New Zealand due to presence of alkaloid, shown to cause liver damage in rats

Stress

If you think being stressed out is normal—you've got a problem. Even though people think that life in the nineties is more stressful than ever before, the truth is that you can control stress, even use it as a positive force in your life.

What you don't want to do is let stress run your life. You need to analyse your life and figure out which stresses you can and should avoid and what kind of stress inspires you. Then you need to eliminate the negative and encourage the positive. Of course that's easier to say than to do. What's more, no matter how well you understand yourself and the stresses in your life, there are always going to be some things you can't control.

That's where the following folk remedies can come to the rescue. None can eliminate stress. But some can help you get through stressful times, others can help you deal with stress in a positive way. So what are you waiting for, get cracking!

Remedies with 🫖 *are made using an infusion. Those with* 🍵 *are made using a decoction. Instructions for both methods are on pages 4 - 7. Variations and other procedures are contained in the text following the description of that remedy.*

Catnip (Nepeta cataria)

Drinking an infusion of catnip has been recommended for almost every ailment ever known. One of its most enduring uses is as a mild sleeping aid or nightcap. Modern researchers have shown that an infusion of catnip may indeed be a mild sedative.

Chicory (Cichorium intybus)

In the southern states of the US chicory is traditionally blended with coffee. The original rationale behind the blend probably had more to do with cost, availability or taste than any belief in its medicinal value. If you are under a lot of stress you probably should lay off the coffee. But if you love your coffee you'd be crazy to add to the stress in your life by forgoing your favourite morning beverage. If you must indulge, you may take heart from the folk healer's belief that chicory rounds out the flavour of coffee and reduces the stimulating effect of caffeine.

Lemon Balm (Melissa officinalis)
also known as Sweet Balm and Bee Herb

How's this for a recommendation? According to our old friend, Nicholas Culpeper drinking an infusion of lemon balm '. . . causeth the mind and heart to be come merry, . . . and driveth away all troublesome cares and thoughts out of the mind, arising from melancholy and black choler . . . .' What more can be said?

Passionflower (*Passiflora incarnata*)

Drinking an infusion of passion flowers is supposed to soothe nervous tension and relieve insomnia.

Valerian (*Valeriana officinalis*)

Valerian is a natural tranquilliser. It's safe to use in small quantities. Drink only 125 millilitres (½ cup) of an infusion of valerian three times a day when you are feeling stressed and can't relax or sleep.

Tai Chi Chuan

Tai-chi is based on a series of gentle, slow, dance-like movements. It's usually performed in the open air. The aim of Tai-chi is to focus on your mental and emotional health as well as on your body. For centuries Tai-chi has been considered both curative and preventive. Tai-chi's graceful, flowing movements are particularly effective against anxiety and stress, because they encourage relaxation. Tai-chi creates inner harmony in an non-competitive, stress-free atmosphere. Tai-chi groups are offered through adult education and community groups in most capital cities and regional centres.

Autogenic Training

Relieving stress is one of the more common uses of autogenic training, a form of guided visualisation. A trained therapist can help you develop a series of phrases that you can use to relieve tension and stress. The practice autogenics can also be used to help you cope better with stressful situations in the future. Consult a trained autogenic practitioner for best results.

Colour Therapy

Most people will have had the experience of feeling better when wearing something in their favourite colour. Colour can affect your mood and according to some, colour can also affect your health and behaviour. According to photo-biologists, who study the effect of light on living organisms, natural light should be thought of as a nutrient, a nutrient necessary for optimal health. Constant exposure to artificial light, which does not contain the same wavelengths of light as natural sunlight, can make people irritable and sluggish. Some natural healers believe that being out of touch with natural light can upset our natural hormones, circadian rhythms, even our ability to fight infections. According to colour therapists, an unhealthy stressful body gives out an unbalanced pattern of vibrations in the visible spectrum. The therapist works to restore the balance. This is a poorly regulated area of practice, but if you want to investigate colour therapy further, you should be able to find out more information through any New Age book store.

Dance Movement Therapy

Who hasn't had the experience of coming home feeling both invigorated and supremely relaxed after dancing the night away. Most tribal communities recognise the healing power of dance. During the 1940s dance—or movement—therapy developed in the US. Unless you are suffering from extreme stress and require medical treatment for a clinical stress-related condition, formal dance therapy is neither necessary nor recommended. That doesn't mean you can't dance your troubles away.

Ten, fifteen or thirty minutes of vigorous dancing—even if what you call dancing others call jumping around like a maniac—to your favourite music is an easy, inexpensive and fun way to relieve stress. Why worry when you can crank up the volume, shake a leg and sashay your way to a stress free day?

Music Therapy

You don't need to see a music therapist to know that listening to music can relax and help revitalise a sagging spirit. It doesn't have to be therapeutic music, it doesn't even have to be soothing music. It just has to be music that you like. Music that makes you feel good. Like dance therapy, formal music therapy is neither necessary nor recommended—unless you are suffering from a stress-related, clinical condition. But a little DIY music therapy is as close as your stereo.

Yoga

Many people associate yoga with relaxation, but that's just part of the picture. Yoga is a system of spiritual, mental and physical training developed over more than 4000 years. Some forms of yoga are more attuned to relaxation and stress release than others, but most practitioners believe that certain postures and breathing patterns can be used to promote relaxation and balance. Most adult education courses and community centres offer yoga courses and many major cities have yoga centres through which the general public can learn yoga.

Hypnotherapy

A hypnotherapist can help you deal with the causes and effects of stress in your life. A hypnotherapist can also teach you the techniques of self-hypnosis so that you can deal with stress when it occurs. Your general practitioner can recommend a qualified therapist.

Massage

What could be more relaxing than a massage performed by an accomplished master of the art? Go ahead, splurge on a proper massage from a trained masseur or masseuse if you can, but don't turn down a massage from a caring partner, it's the next best thing. You'd be crazy to turn a massage down, no matter who's offering because there's no denying it, a gentle, soothing massage is a fine way to chase your troubles away.

Sunburn

You know better than to be silly in the sun. You know that exposure to ultra-violet light is the enemy of healthy skin. So you slipped, you slapped and you slopped, but then you lost track of the time and ended up with a sunburn anyway. You've learnt your lesson and now you want something to take away the sting of sunburn pain.

Relief is on its way, in the form of one of the following folk remedies, and do be more careful next time, there's more than wrinkled, leathery skin at stake.

Sunflower *(Helianthus annuus)*

The Aztec remedy for painful sunburn was to gently massage sunflower oil into the skin.

Garden or Salad Burnet
(Sanguisorba officianalis)

This plant was a must in all the old European herb gardens. It was also an early immigrant to the new world. Young leaves are said to be cooling and have a reputation as a soothing

---

Remedies with ☕ are made using an infusion. Those with ⌣ are made using a decoction. Instructions for both methods are on pages 4 - 7. Variations and other procedures are contained in the text following the description of that remedy.

treatment for sunburnt skin. Make a wash from an infusion from the leaves and use on red, irritated skin. 🫖

Coconut *(Cocos nucifera)*

Traditional Hawaiian healers recommend applying coconut oil to sunburnt skin.

Potato *(Solanum tuberosum)*

For centuries the Romany people, who are sometimes called Gypsies, have used sliced raw potatoes to soothe sunburnt skin. If you want to try this remedy, just slice a potato and apply cut side to the skin.

Bicarbonate of Soda
(also called Sodium Bicarbonate, Baking Soda or Saleratus)

For all-over relief soak in a cool bath to which you have added 40 grams (2 tablespoons) of bicarbonate of soda.

Cider Vinegar

Native Americans in the north east region of the US used to rub cider vinegar on sunburn.

Lavender [1] *(Lavandula angustifolia)*

Or try 150 ml (5 ounces) of either cider vinegar or lavender vinegar added to your bath. Both vinegars have a reputation for easing the prickly feeling of a mild sunburn.

---

[1]   *avoid high doses during pregnancy*

Aloe *(Aloe vera, also known as A. barbadensis)*

Apply the juice from a freshly broken aloe leaf directly on sunburnt skin.

Oldies, but goodies from the kitchen cupboard

Gin, Milk, Cold Indian Tea or Lemon Juice

Any one of these when applied to sun burnt skin is claimed to bring relief. Though no one would blame you if you shied away from applying lemon juice to tender skin. Come to think of it, if you splashed the gin over a couple of ice cubes, garnished it with a slice of lemon and drank it, no one would think you were crazy either.

Strawberry *(Fragaria spp.)* and Buttermilk

Mash the berries and buttermilk together and apply to sore, sunburnt skin. The strawberries alone are said to reduce redness, while the buttermilk is claimed to minimise irritation.

Cucumber *(Cucumis sativa)*

Cool cucumber, sliced or mashed to a pulp and applied to sunburnt skin, is an old-fashioned remedy for sunburn.

Yoghurt and Rosewater

Mix together 150 millilitres (5 ounces) of plain yoghurt and 40 millilitres (2 tablespoons) rosewater and apply to sunburnt skin. Or apply plain yoghurt directly on your sunburnt skin.

Cornflour (also called Cornstarch) *or Arrowroot*

Add enough water to either cornflour or arrowroot to make a paste. Apply to sunburnt skin. The paste will dry and fall off in about 10 - 15 minutes, keep reapplying until the feeling of heat disappears.

Tartar and Plaque

Tartar and plaque send your million dollar smile straight to the bargain bin. Brush and floss after every meal and see your dentist at least twice a year for a thorough cleaning. In between visits to the dentist give one of the following folk remedies a try and smile, smile, smile.

Peppermint [1] *(Mentha piperita)*
and Spearmint [2] *(Mentha spicata)*

During the Renaissance—when people became more conscious of the appearance of their teeth—mint developed a reputation for whitening tooth enamel. Chew on a few fresh mint leaves, even if they don't whiten your teeth, they will freshen your breath.

Remedies with 🫖 *are made using an infusion. Those with* ♨ *are made using a decoction. Instructions for both methods are on pages 4 - 7. Variations and other procedures are contained in the text following the description of that remedy.*

---

[1]   avoid during pregnancy and if breast feeding do not give in any form to very young babies

[2]   avoid during pregnancy and if breast feeding, do not give in any form to very young babies

Sage [1] *(Salvia officinalis)*

During the Middle Ages, on the southern coast of Spain people used sage when they wanted to remove tartar and plaque. The recommended treatment? Mix powdered sage with a little salt and rub it into your teeth.

Citrus Juice

To keep their teeth sparkling white West Indians brush their teeth with equal parts fresh grapefruit, lemon and lime juice two or three times a week.

Agrimony *(Agrimonia eupatoria)*
also known as Church Steeples

Using an infusion of agrimony as a mouth wash is supposed to help remove tartar.

Fig *(Ficus carica)*

In parts of Africa and Central America they use ripe figs to remove tartar and plaque. To try it, cut a fig in half and rub the cut side against your teeth.

Rhubarb *(Rheum rhaponticum)*

According to some folk healers, rhubarb juice coats tooth enamel with a thin protective film. They recommend brushing your teeth with rhubarb juice to remove tartar and add an extra glow to your teeth.

---

[1]   *avoid therapeutic doses in pregnancy. Small amounts used in cooking are quite safe.*

Teething

Face it, if you had to suffer through the pain of teeth forcing their way through tender gum tissue, you'd be cranky too! Now imagine how you'd feel if you were less than a year old and were going through the experience. Most babies have never experienced anything more uncomfortable than a wet nappy, and now this.

A fussy baby is bad enough. When you know that your baby is in pain it's enough to break your heart. Most parents would gladly do anything to take away their babies pain. The problem is that few, if any remedies—folk or otherwise—are suitable for children under two years old.

The following old-favourites can be used with safety. If you want to try the chamomile remedy, be sure to see a trained herbalist for advice concerning the appropriate dose for your baby.

Remedies with ☕ are made using an infusion. Those with ☕ are made using a decoction. Instructions for both methods are on pages 4 - 7. Variations and other procedures are contained in the text following the description of that remedy.

Massage

Massage a teething baby's gums with your clean finger. It's the best, easiest and safest way to soothe a fretting baby's swollen, sore gums.

Honey

Or try rubbing a little honey on the baby's gums, it's supposed to ease the tooth's passage through the gum.

Gripe Water

Gripe water is cooling, calming and safe for littlies. Rub it into swollen, red gums.

Whisky

When Mums and Dads in Ireland consult their local folk practitioner for advice on how to ease a teething baby's pain, the advice is, "pour a small glass of whisky. Rub a drop of the whisky on the baby's gums. Give the child a rubber ring to chew on. Down the rest of the whisky yourself."

Chamomile [1] *(Chamaemelum nobile, Roman, or C. recutita, German)*

During the Middle Ages chamomile became a popular remedy for various ailments. If you want to try chamomile for teething problems, consult a qualified herbalist or a homoeopathic practitioner for a suitable children's dosage.

---

[1] *avoid excessive doses and the oil in any amount during pregnancy*

Tendonitis

Make no mistake, the chronic pain of tendonitis—whether it comes from too much tennis, typing or tap dancing—is a real pain. The most important thing you need to do is to ease up, give it a rest, and let the sore tendon and muscle heal. While you are resting you can try one of the following folk remedies. They are not strenuous to make and they just may be the very thing you need to ease the pain.

Fenugreek [1] *(Trigonella foenum-graecum)*

India's traditional Ayurvedic healers use an infusion of ground fenugreek seeds as a wash to soothe the pain of soft tissue injuries.

Ginger [2] *(Zingiber officinalis)*

This traditional Japanese folk remedy is still popular in modern day Japan, but it takes a bit of work to prepare.

Remedies with ☕ are made using an infusion. Those with 🍲 are made using a decoction. Instructions for both methods are on pages 4 - 7. Variations and other procedures are contained in the text following the description of that remedy.

[1]   avoid during pregnancy
[2]   use sparingly during pregnancy

1. Bring 4 litres (1 gallon) water to the boil in a large enamel pot with lid

2. While the water is coming to the boil wash and grate a large ginger root

3. Do not peel the ginger

4. When grating the ginger turn it clockwise so that the tough inner fibres open up

5. Place the grated ginger on to a piece of muslin, drawing the corners of the fabric up to hold the ginger and secure this 'bag' with a piece of string

6. Turn the heat down under the boiling water
Squeeze any ginger juice from the bag into the boiling water then drop the bag into the pot

7. Simmer 7 minutes

8. After 7 minutes use a spoon to press the bundle of ginger against the side of the pot releasing as much ginger as possible into the water

9. Remove the pot from the heat and use the liquid warm as a compress on the sore muscles

10. Use the compress for about 40 minutes and repeat every 4 - 6 hours until the soreness is gone

Comfrey [1] *(Symphytum officinale)*
also known as Knitbone

Make a decoction of comfrey leaves and mash the softened leaves into a paste. Apply the paste to the affected joint, it's supposed to help reduce inflammation and swelling.

St John's Wort *(Hypericum perforatum)*

This Romany remedy also requires patience and a little foresight, it takes 20 days to prepare. Romany folk healers had a

---

[1]   restricted herb in Australia and New Zealand due to presence of alkaloid, shown to cause liver damage in rats

batch on hand to soothe aches and pains after a day on the open road, and another batch brewing at all times.

1. Fill a 1 litre (1 quart) clear-glass bottle with St John's Wort blossoms
2. Pour olive oil over the blossoms filling the bottle
3. Seal the bottle and place it in full sun for one cycle of the moon (20 days) After 20 days strain and transfer the strained oil to an amber glass container for storage
4. Use a piece of cotton wool to apply the oil to painful muscles
5. Do not expose skin treated with this oil to the sun, it is a photo-sensitiser

Mustard *(Brassica nigra)*

Don't forget Grandma's favourite, the mustard plaster.

1. Grind mustard seeds with a little water
2. Coat the skin of the affected area with petroleum jelly (this prevents the mustard from blistering or irritating the skin
3. Apply the paste to the sore area, holding it in place with gauze and adhesive tape. This plaster can be kept on for several hours, for best results leave on overnight

Toothache

That cartoon character with a toothache—giant bandage and swollen jaw, seeing stars and groaning in pain—doesn't seem so funny when the toothache is real and the swollen jaw is yours. Only a dentist can figure out what is causing your toothache and until you know what is causing the toothache nothing can be done to cure it.

One of the following folk remedies may help you get through the hours you have to wait for your appointment though.

Green Plum *(Buchanaia obvotata)*
also known as Wild Plum

Australian Aborigines used twigs and small shoots of green plums to relieve a toothache. They used the twigs and small shoots from near the base of the tree. They stripped off the leaves and any rough patches and worked the twig down to the size and shape of a toothpick. They warmed and softened the woody tissue in the fire then worked it into the cavity or between rotten teeth to relieve the pain of a toothache.

Remedies with 🫖 *are made using an infusion. Those with* ☕ *are made using a decoction. Instructions for both methods are on pages 4 - 7. Variations and other procedures are contained in the text following the description of that remedy.*

They also used the centre vein of a young leaf in the same way. They tried to keep the tooth warm, replacing the plant material after it had cooled. For additional pain relief they made an infusion from the plant's inner bark and used the warm liquid as a mouthwash.

Pukatea *(Laurelia novae-zelandiae)*

Chewing pukatea leaves is the traditional Maori way to ease toothache pain. It took a while, but modern scientific research has proven what the Maori always knew—pukatea leaves really do help to ease pain. The leaves have been shown to have both local and general pain killing properties.

As well, the pukatea bark produces alkaloids similar in structure to morphine. Now researchers are trying to find out if pukatea's alkaloids can produce the same pain relief—without the negative side effects.

Kawakawa *(Macropiper excelsum)*

The Maori also chewed kawakawa leaves to soothe the pain of toothache.

Metrosideros *(Metrosideros albiflora)*

Drinking an infusion of metrosideros bark is another traditional way for New Zealanders to reduce pain.

Chaparral *(Larrea divaricata L. tridentata)*
also known as Creosote Bush

This plant—a native of North America—was used by the tribes in the southwest of the continent to treat toothaches.

They heated chaparral twigs to release the plant's resin and applied the hot resin to painful teeth.

Clove *(Syzgium aromaticum)*

Nineteenth century American herbalists were the first to extract clove oil from the spice. They used the oil on the gums to relieve toothache. Even today natural healers the world over use clove oil in this way.

Marjoram *(Origanum marjorana)*

The ancient Greeks used fresh marjoram leaves to soothe the pain of a toothache. You can try it their way, or the modern way, a few drops of marjoram oil diluted with 10 millilitres of good quality vegetable or nut oil and applied to the gum around an aching tooth.

Catnip *(Nepeta cataria)*

This recommendation comes from folk healers from the US state of Alabama, where a poultice of fresh catnip leaves, mashed and applied to the aching tooth, is a traditional treatment for toothaches. If you don't have fresh catnip you can use dried, powdered catnip moistened with a few drops of water to make your poultice.

Lime *(Citrus aurantifolia)*

This remedy comes from the West Indies, where they apply a wad of cotton wool soaked in lime juice directly to a sore tooth.

Blue Flag *(Iris vesicolor)*
also known as Wild Iris and Iris Flag

Many Native American tribes drank—and gargled with—a decoction of blue flag to soothe toothache pain.

Don't try it unless you want to trade your toothache for a giant headache!

Marijuana *(Cannabis sativa)*

In ancient Rome they applied the juice extracted from a fresh cannabis plant directly to an aching tooth! No one remembered whether or not it worked. By the time they were finished no one cared whether or not it worked, but they enjoyed it just the same.

Purple Coneflower [1] *(Echinacea augustifolia)*

Native Americans in the plains area of the US gargled with a decoction of purple coneflower to relieve toothache pain.

Peppermint [2] *(Mentha piperita)* *or Spearmint* [3] *(Mentha spicata)*

Keep a small bottle of either of these mint oils in your medicine cupboard. When a toothache strikes, dilute a drop or two

---

[1]   *restricted herb in Australia and New Zealand due to presence of alkaloid, shown to cause liver damage in rats*

[2]   *avoid during pregnancy and if breast feeding do not give in any form to very young babies*

[3]   *avoid during pregnancy and if breast feeding, do not give in any form to very young babies*

of mint oil with 10 millilitres of good quality vegetable or nut oil and apply to the gums around the painful tooth.

Tulip (Tulipa gesneriana)

An old Chinese remedy for toothache was to apply a bit of fresh, crushed tulip bulb to the gum around the sore tooth.

Garlic [1] (Allium sativum)

Peel and crush a clove of garlic and place it on the tooth. It may not help with your toothache, but it's sure to keep people from bothering you.

'eres a toothache remedy from those wacky Poms

In Britain they dug a fresh plantain root, washed and scraped it then put it into the sufferer's ear!

Not to be out done, those crazy Swiss were at it too!

In Switzerland plantain leaf fibres were rubbed vigorously then put into the toothache sufferer's ear. They believed that if the treatment relieved the pain, the leaf fibres would turn black. If the remedy didn't work, the leaf fibres would stay green. Of course the still aching tooth would probably be an even better indication that the remedy was ineffective.

---

[1] *avoid during pregnancy and if breast feeding*

Ulcers

All right, get ready, this is ugly. Skin ulcers are the result of a small wound that refuses to heal. Poor circulation and poor hygiene are common causes. But a sore that doesn't heal can also be a warning sign of skin cancer. So don't fool around with any suspisious sore. Have your doctor examine any sore that doesn't heal in a reasonable amount of time. If your doctor tells you it's a skin ulcer, be thankful and follow his or her instructions to the letter. Once the wound starts to heal you can give one of the following folk remedies a go. But don't use anything other than what your doctor recommends when the wound is open, that's the way to make it worse rather than better.

Alfalfa (Medicago sativa) also known as Lucerne

For centuries the Chinese physicians have told people suffering from skin ulcers to eat lots of alfalfa sprouts. Ancient India's traditional Ayurvedic physicians also use alfalfa to treat skin ulcers. But don't just chomp them down like a horse in a paddock. You need to eat the sprouts slowly, chewing well before swallowing. While eating the sprouts you should con-

---

Remedies with ☕ are made using an infusion. Those with ☕ are made using a decoction. Instructions for both methods are on pages 4 - 7. Variations and other procedures are contained in the text following the description of that remedy.

centrate on a happy state of mind and savour the sprouts, it's supposed to speed your recovery.

Dandelion *(Taraxacum officinale also known as pu gong ying)*

In ancient China they used a poultice made from decocted dandelion leaves to help skin ulcers heal. Make your decoction, then strain, saving the softened leaves. Allow to cool then apply the softened leaves directly to skin ulcers.

Archangel *(Lamium album, also known as Blind Nettle, White Dead Nettle)*

In the mid seventeenth century the English physician and herbalist, Nicholas Culpeper popularised drinking an infusion of archangel as a treatment for difficult to heal ulcers.

Bugle *(Ajuga reptans)*

Culpeper also recommended an infusion of bugle to help skin ulcers heal quickly.

Chickweed *(Stellaria media)*

Another recommendation from Culpeper, was to use a poultice made from decocted chickweed leaves. Cool the softened leaves, then apply to skin ulcers.

Banana *(Musa[1])*

According to folk healers on the West Indian island of Curaçao, green banana peels— dried then burnt to ash and applied to skin ulcers—are the perfect way to hasten healing.

---

[1] *because all cultivated bananas are sterile hybrid forms they do not have exact species names*

Kûmarahou *(Pomaderris kumeraho)*
also known as gum digger's soap

This native New Zealand plant has at various times been claimed to cure virtually every ailment known to humans. A decoction of the leaves of P. elliptica, a relative of kûmarahou is a traditional remedy for chest and kidney complaints, indigestion, and skin sores.

Kûmarahou has been the star in many patent medicines, like those of the Reverend Edgar Ward, a qualified pharmacist who became the Anglican vicar of Kaitaia. While at Kaitaia he became concerned about the number of Maori children suffering from tuberculosis and treated them with a mixture of herbs, including kômarahou. He called his concoction Kuranui, a word that sounds vaguely Maori, but in fact is not. Rev. Ward eventually left the ministry to become an Auckland herbalist.

Rev Ward wasn't the only herbalist of the cloth either. Mother Mary Aubert, a French Roman Catholic nun was a popular herbalist, both in New Zealand and through out the Catholic Church community. Mother Mary served New Zealand for more than fifty years and her newsletter often contained testimonials about her herbal products from representatives of the church hierarchy.

Mother Mary followed one of Rev Ward's practices, using 'Maori sounding' names for her products. As well she was involved in both religious and social work, serving the New Zealand catholic church for more than

continued over the page

Kûmarahou *(Pomaderris kumeraho)*

also known as gum digger's soap

continued from previous page

fifty years, operating the mission station at Jerusalem, on the Wanganui River during much of this time.

Like Rev Ward, Mother Mary used Maori sounding names for her herbal products, Natanata (for stomach ailments) and Marupa (for throat and bronchial ailments) are two of her better known products.

Sales of her herbal concoctions were used to support novices. She even tried a commercial arrangement for selling her products so that she could better support her religious and humanitarian work. When this didn't work out as she had hoped she took back production of her remedies and until 1913 the products were made by Mother Mary and the Sisters of her order, and sold through Sharland and Company (in New Zealand and Australia).

When, in 1913, Mother Mary returned to Rome she destroyed her recipes but samples of her products remain preserved at the Home of Compassion, Island Bay, Wellington.

Balsam *(Myroxylon balsamum var. pereira)*

To help skin ulcers heal quickly, Peruvian folk healers apply the juice extracted from balsam plants directly to the sore.

Pukatea *(Laurelia novae-zelandiae)*

The Maori infused pukatea leaves to make a soothing wash to help ulcers heal.

Boneset *(Eupatorium perfoliatum) also know as feverwort*

Nearly 2000 years ago the Greek physician, Discorides, used a poultice made from infused boneset to help skin ulcers heal.

Geranium *(Pelargonium odorantissimum)*

On Reunion Island (in the Indian Ocean) where the geranium is a native species, folk healers apply a geranium leaf directly to skin ulcers to help the ulcer heal. When colonists took the plant back to France the folk healers there started using a decoction of geranium leaves as wash to help mouth ulcers heal.

Centaury *(Centaurium erythraea)*
also known as Feverwort, European or Common Centaury

The ancient Greeks applied pink centaury flowers directly to ulcers to help the ulcer heal.

Pot Marigold[1] *(Calendula officinalis)*

Last century German folk healers used a calendula ointment, called 'Dio Gemeine Ringelblume' to help skin ulcers heal. The ointment was made from marigold stems, leaves and blossoms, butter and charcoal.

---

[1]   *do not confuse with French Marigold, Tagetes patula*

Comfrey [1] *(Symphytum officinale)*
also known as Knitbone

In ancient Rome healers used comfrey juice help skin ulcers heal.

Woundwort *(Stachys palustris)*

In the Middle Ages woundwort was used as a dressing for sores and ulcers. A poultice made from decocted woundwort leaves was the recommended treatment. Allow the softened leaves to cool then apply directly to skin ulcers.

Golden rod *(Solidago virga aurea)*

The European herbalist Arnoldus de Villa Nova experimented with this herb and recommended his patients drink a decoction of golden rod and save a little to daub onto skin ulcers.

Persimmon *(Diospyros kaki)*
also known as Chinese Date Plum

For centuries Native Americans healers have applied persimmon juice directly to skin ulcers to help them heal.

Naturopathy

You may want to consult a naturopath if you are regularly troubled with skin ulcers. A naturopath will most likely prescribe a special diet, specific breathing and relaxation exercises and vitamin supplements.

---

[1] restricted herb in Australia and New Zealand due to presence of alkaloid, shown to cause liver damage in rats

Some old-fashioned remedies—from here there and who knows where . . . .

Potato *(Solanum tuberosum)*

Drink the juice extracted from a small raw potato, three times a day, before each meal. If you don't like the taste—and who would blame you if you didn't—blend it with tomato juice, apple juice or cooled soup.

Cabbage *(Brassica oleracea)* and Carrot *(Daucus carota)*

Cabbage and/or carrot juice has also been recommended to help skin ulcers heal. Carrot juice is sweet and tasty all on its own. Cabbage juice on its own is an acquired taste that few have willingly acquired. You'll have to decide for yourself whether the pain of skin ulcers is worse than the taste of the cabbage juice, or blend the cabbage juice with carrot juice, tomato juice or mixed vegetable juice. Then it will go down a treat!

Blueberry *(Vaccinium corymbosum)*

Tasty and tangy, but a bit pricey. So for the most enjoyment and coincidentally the most effect, do not gulp it. Sip it slowly, very slowly and savour the sweet indulgence of it all.

Warts

In children's stories, warts and witches go hand in hand. But if witches were as common as warts we'd all be riding around on broomsticks! Warts are common as muck. They are all caused by one of the papilloma viruses. Unless you have one on the tip of your nose or the bottom of your foot, ignore the wart. Most will disappear without any treatment whatsoever while many treatments designed to remove the wart just gets the virus all riled up and encourages it to spread. Instead of getting rid of the wart you end up with lots of little wartlets!

If, knowing that, you still want to try to remove a wart, the first thing you need to do is make sure it's a wart you are trying to remove. Corns, calluses, moles and pre-cancerous lesions are often mistaken for warts. Stay clear of moles and have your doctor examine any suspicious growth. If you try one of the following on a corn or callus it won't do much harm, many folk remedies for warts are similar to those for corns and calluses.

Groundsel (Senecio vulgaris)

This remedy, a poultice of groundsel leaves and heads, dates from the seventeenth century. Infused groundsel leaves,

---

Remedies with 🫖 *are made using an infusion. Those with* 🍲 *are made using a decoction. Instructions for both methods are on pages 4 - 7. Variations and other procedures are contained in the text following the description of that remedy.*

green heads and flowers were used to make the poultice. After softening the solid material was mashed to a paste and applied to the wart.

Banana *(Musa [1])*

In the Middle East folk healers use a piece of skin from a ripe banana to remove warts. Apply the banana skin, inside white against the wart, tape in place and change once a week.

Milkweed *(Asclepias syriaca)*

This native plant from North America releases a milk juice when cut. Native Americans believed this milky substance could remove warts.

Dandelion *(Taraxacum officinale)*
also known as pu gong ying

Broken dandelion stems also release a milky juice and some folk healers believe that this juice can remove warts.

Potato *(Solanum tuberosum)*

This wacky remedy can—supposedly—be traced to white witches of the Middle Ages. The method—which makes the rounds of every schoolyard at least once a year—is simple. You rub the wart with a freshly cut potato. Then you bury the potato telling the sufferer that as the potato rots away so will the wart fade and disappear. Some people swear by this remedy and it's not surprising that they do. Remember most warts go away whether you do anything or not. So, you try the remedy. A couple of years later the wart is gone and lo and

---

[1]   because all cultivated bananas are sterile hybrids, they do not have exact species names

behold . . . .when you go back to the spot where you buried the potato, the potato is gone too!

Houseleek *(Sempervivum tectorum, also called hen and chickens or singreen)*

According to some folk healers houseleek juice—applied through a hole the size of the wart, cut in cardboard—will remove a wart.

Onion *(Allium cepa)* and Sea Salt

Other folk healers favour this remedy. Cut an onion in half, scoop out the centre of one half and fill the cavity with coarse sea salt. Allow the salt to dissolve and use the resulting liquid on the wart as often as possible.

Garlic [1] *(Allium sativum)*

Romany folk healers swear by wart removing technique. Apply fresh, wild garlic juiceä to the wart at midnight, during a full moon. Apply the juice three times each time exposing the wart to the direct moonlight for 3 minutes.

All warts are contagious, and that includes genital warts. You get genital warts by coming into contact with the wart virus. That means that genital warts can be classified as a sexually transmitted disease. Never treat genital warts yourself. They must be treated by your doctor.

[1] avoid during pregnancy and if breast feeding

Wrinkles

It's unfair and unreasonable, but it's also true, wrinkles give a man's face character but they just make a woman look older. There's nothing wrong with looking mature, but why would you want to look older than you are?

Stay out of the sun and moisturise your skin to prevent it from drying out. Always wear sunblock. If you treat your skin well, wrinkles will be a long time coming, and you may never need one of the following folk remedies. But if you've already done a lot of living and it all shows on your face . . . read on.

Cleopatra's Secret

Cucumber, honey, olive oil and a little ox blood go into this 2000 year old remedy that Cleopatra is supposed to have used.

1. Finely chop 2 cucumbers
2. Mix with 125 millilitres (½ cup) ox blood
3. Grind into a paste
4. Add 20 millilitres (1 tablespoon) each olive oil and honey
5. 60 - 80 grams (3 - 4 tablespoons) fine clay
6. Mix the lot and put it in a jar or container, in a cool place

---

Remedies with ☕ are made using an infusion. Those with 🍲 are made using a decoction. Instructions for both methods are on pages 4 - 7. Variations and other procedures are contained in the text following the description of that remedy.

7. Scrub your face, forehead and neck with the cut face of a lemon
8. Before the lemon juice dries on your skin apply 'Cleopatra's Secret'
9. Leave on for one hour
10. Wash off with warm water and allow your skin to air dry, do not use a towel

Honey

In the US folk healers often recommend splashing your face with warm water to open the pores then applying a thin film of honey. The honey is supposed to soften and smooth wrinkles. After 20 minutes or so, rinse with warm water to remove all the honey then splash with cold water to close your pores.

Patchouli *(Pogostemon cabin-labiatae)*

This oil is very popular in India, Japan, China and Malaysia, where it has been used as a medicinal and beauty aid for many generations. Use it in combination with a facial massage.

Sweet Almond *(Prunus dulcis var. dulcis)* and Coconut *(Cocos nucifera)*

Hawaiian folk healers mix 30 grams (1 ounce) coconut oil with 5 grams (1 teaspoon) almond oil, and apply the mixture to dry skin, massaging upwards.

Yeast Infection

If you need proof that natural is not always nice, *Candida albicans* is it. This fungus is a naturally occurring yeast. It's a resident of every healthy person's intestines and every healthy woman's vagina but when your body's environment shifts a little to the left or right this normally tame citizen goes feral and a yeast infection takes hold.

If you think you have a yeast infection (either oral thrush or a vaginal infection) see your doctor immediately and follow their instructions to the letter. If you want to try a folk remedy, try it with—not instead of—your doctor's advice,

Blackberry *(Rubus ulmifolius)*

Other folk healers recommend drinking an infusion of blackberry leaves.

Cabbage *(Brassica oleracea)*

Mexican and Afro-American folk healers recommend taking 5 grams (1 teaspoon) fresh cabbage juice to control and prevent yeast infections.

Remedies with 🫖 *are made using an infusion. Those with* 🍲 *are made using a decoction. Instructions for both methods are on pages 4 - 7. Variations and other procedures are contained in the text following the description of that remedy.*

Gentian *(Gentiana lutea) also known as gin jiao*

India's traditional Ayurvedic physicians use gentian to fight yeast infections. They recommend three or four 5 millilitre (1 teaspoon) doses of a gentian infusion every day.

Ginger [1] *(Zingiber officinalis)*

Traditional Chinese medical practitioners tell you to drink an infusion of ginger root to control yeast infections.

Nasturtium *(Tropaeolum majus)*

Some folk healers also recommend that women wash their genitals and douche with an infusion of nasturtium leaves and flowers.

Persimmon *(Diospyros kaki)*
also known as Chinese Date Plum

For centuries, native Americans have used a wash made from persimmon to treat yeast infections. To make your own persimmon wash and cut six near ripe persimmons into sections. Infuse the sections in 750 millilitres (3 cups) boiling water. Steep until cold then strain. Use the strained, cool liquid to wash your genital area.

Thyme *(Thymus vulgaris)*

French folk healers recommend douching with a decoction of thyme. Be sure to strain and cool before using.

---

[1] *use sparingly during pregnancy*

Aromatherapy

For oral thrush, try a mouthwash of three drops of tea tree oil, one drop myrrh oil in 250 millilitres (1 cup) water. Stir vigorously before using, three times a day.

Naturopathy

For a specific diet designed to reduce the frequency of yeast infections consult a registered naturopath.

Further Reading

To further your knowledge of the fascinating and important topic of natural healing methods used in the past and present, the Editors of Bookman Health Books recommend the following reading list:

Bailey, Adrian *The Book of Ingredients,* The Penguin Group London 1980

Barr, Chapman, Smith & Beveridge, *Traditional bush medicines,* Greenhouse Publications Richmond Victoria Australia 1988

Castleman, Michael *The Healing Herbs,* Bookman Press Melbourne 1991

Cooper, R C and Cambie, RC *New Zealand's Economic Native Plants* 1991 Oxford University Press Auckland

Cruise, Richard A Esq *Journal of a Ten Months Residence in New Zealand,* first published by Longman, Hurst, Ress, Orme, Brown and Green London 1824, reprinted by Capper Press Christchurch 1974

Culpepper, Dr. Nicholas *Culpepper's Herbal Remedies,* Wilshire Book Co., Hollywood California USA 1971

Dawson, Adele G *Herbs Partners in Life,* Healing Arts Press Vermont USA 1991

Fulton, Robert MD *Medical Practice in the Early Days,* first published by Otago Daily Times and Witness Newspapers Co Ltd 1922 Dunedin, reprinted by Colonial Associates Wellington 1982

Garland, Sarah *The Complete Book of Herbs and Spices*, Frances Lincoln Limited London 1993

Graedon, Joe and Ferguson, Tom MD *The Aspirin Handbook,* Bookman Press Melbourne 1993

Hamilton, Edward *The Flora Homoeopathic,* reprinted by B. Jain Publishers Pty. Ltd., New Delhi India 1992

Heinerman, John *Encyclopaedia of Fruits, Vegetables and Herbs,* Parker Publishing Co., 1988   A division of Simon & Schuster New York USA

Hoffman, David *The Holistic Herbal,* Element Books Ltd., Dorset UK 1986

Jarvis, DC *Folk Medicine,* first published by Fawcett Crest USA 1962, reprinted by Ballantine Books New York USA 1982

Kordich, Jay *The Power of Juicing,* Bookman Press Melbourne 1992

Kowalchik, Claire and Hylton, William Eds *Rodale's Illustrated Encyclopaedia of Herbs,* Rodale Press Inc., Pennsylvania 1987

Kurzweil, Raymond *The 10% Solution for a Healthy Life,* Bookman Press Melbourne 1993

Lawless, Julia *The Encyclopaedia of Essential Oils,* Element Books London 1993

Neil, James *The New Zealand Family Herb Doctor,* first published by Mills, Dick & Co Dunedin 1889, reprinted by Capper Press Christchurch 1980

Nice, Jill *Herbal Remedies,* Judy Piatkus Publishers Ltd., London 1990

Ody, Penelope *The Complete Medicinal Herbal,* first published as The Herb Society's Complete Medicinal Herbal by Dorling Kindersley Ltd., London 1993

Ornish, Dean MD *Eat More, Weigh Less,* Bookman Press Melbourne 1993

Prevention Magazine Health Books Editorial Staff *The Doctors Book of Home Remedies,* Rodale Press Inc., Pennsylvania 1990

Readers Digest, *The Reader's Digest Family Guide to Alternative Medicine,* Surry Hills NSW Australia 1992

Ryman, Daniele *Aromatherapy, the Encyclopaedia of Plants and Oils and How They Help You,* Judy Piatkus Publishers London 1992

Somer, Elizabeth MA, RD *Nutrition for Women,* Bookman Press Melbourne 1993

Thorsons Editorial Board *The Complete Raw Juice Therapy,* Harper-Collins Publishers London 1989

Trattler, Ross *Better Health Through Natural Healing,* first published by McGraw-Hill Book Co., New York USA 1985, reprinted by Thorsons Publishers Northampton England 1987

Usher, George *A Dictionary of Plants Used By Man,* Constable & Company London 1974

Vogel, Dr HC *The Nature Doctor,* Mainstream Publishing Co., Edinburgh Great Britain 1990 German title first published in 1952

Von Hausen, Wanja *Gypsy Folk Medicine,* English translation by Sterling Publishing Co., New York USA 1992

Weber, Marcea *Natural Health and Healing For Children,* Simon & Schuster NSW Australia 1992

Please Write to Us

If you have your own Folk Remedy you would like to share, The Editors of Bookman Health Books would like to hear from you. Please tell us how you heard about the Remedy, what it cures and how to prepare.

Please also write if you would like to comment on any of the Folk Remedies that appear in this book.

Our Address:

The Editors
Bookman Health Books
4/325 Flinders Lane
MELBOURNE VIC. 3000
AUSTRALIA

Index

N